Judas Priest

Decade of Domination

Martin Popoff

First published in Canada, 2018
Wymer Publishing
Bedford, England www.wymerpublishing.co.uk
Tel: 01234 326691
Wymer Publishing is a trading name of Wymer (UK) Ltd

ISBN: 978-1-912782-63-5

Printed and bound by
CMP, Dorset, England

A catalogue record for this book is available from the British Library.

Typesetting, layout and design by Eduardo Rodriguez.

Contents

Introduction

Despite my mixed feelings about some things they might have done later in their career, Priest will always be metal gods to me. Their situation, their legacy… man, it's like winning the Super Bowl or being the President of the United States. In both cases, you have joined a club. Super Bowl… it's kind of cool. It's less important that you've formed a dynasty, or what a player's personal stats were, but it's of utmost importance that you were there and won, even once—you are in the club, a winner forever, your franchise successful. President? Well, the cool thing there is that they call you President forever, i.e. long after you've left the job.

What's this got to do with Halford, Tipton, Downing, Hill and… Binks? Well, like I say, they can forever exhibit any number of shortcomings, and I'll bow to the gods. And this is precisely for one reason: Priest is responsible, in my opinion, for the unassailably greatest run—or vein, or dynasty—of metal classics ever, namely 1976's *Sad Wings of Destiny* through 1979's *Hell Bent for Leather*.

And we're not just talking really damn good albums here. *British Steel* is a damn good album, so is *Back in Black*, so is *Reign in Blood*. No, what we're talking about here is material that kicked metal up a notch or 12, not as much as a lone record like *In Rock* from 1970 did, or even say… oh, let's pick a duo like *Paranoid* and *Master of Reality*.

Sure, it gets a little fuzzy. Yes, one can't diminish the importance of all those subsequent Sabbath albums, or Rainbow's *Rising*, or on more micro levels, the songs "Virgin Killer," "Breadfan," "Fireball" or a couple dozen others. As for full bands, the only rival run of catalogue crushers I see is that of Queen, although I suppose we can set them aside because we're trying to talk metal here. And so for some reason I've always had it in my head, this gulf between 1970 and 1976, and that gulf ending at an immense wall of closely riveted chromium steel in 1976, when a speck of an unknown band in satin shirts delivered something called *Sad Wings of Destiny*, in the power chord process, changing metal forever.

And it didn't stop there. That's the beauty of it. That record rewrote the metal books, raising the bar for riffage, vocal prowess, injecting a slight prog element or at least vibe (Purple and Sabbath, I suppose, match the album for prog elements per se), but then *Sin After Sin*… well, bring in Simon Phillips and metal had just incredibly compacted, intensified and gotten smarter yet again, a mere year after *Sad Wings* and its resulting blank stares but for the perceptive.

Stained Class offered—at this point, superhumanly—another increase in note density, drama and precision, matching its predecessor for unsafe speeds (made safe by this great band). Finally (and lamentably, as you will see argued later in this book), *Killing Machine* (re-titled *Hell Bent for Leather* in America), found the band creating the perfect marriage between their mensa metal magic and a certain carnal metal commercialism. This is the band's crux album—like *Roots*, like *Reign in Blood*, like *Ride the Lightning*—a convergence of two worlds with explosive synergistic results. Yea and verily, despite the pioneering, brave, and immense music-creating of the previous three records, this one is the favourite in my heart because it is the work of a Priest no longer prim.

I've long since started to rankle at telling anybody what is best for them—a best album, this one is bad etc.—so yes, I'm telling you now the contours of my particular interaction with Priest and Priest's records, which, for the scope of this book, focuses only on the first tidy ten. Suffice to say that there are thousands upon thousands of metalheads that have been forever changed by one of these first ten Priest albums, and among them, many famed rockers who were influenced to achieve and change metal in the next decade.

Sure, many an old schooler will tell you *Sad Wings* is the best, but if you took an aggregate of all 'bangers of all ages, *British Steel* often polls highest, second place sometimes going to *Screaming for Vengeance*. But the beauty of Priest's career is that it's been long and varied. If you are a young and raging metalhead, for example, well, tons of you out there think *Painkiller* is the band's best album. In fact, this is the record that won the poll among Priest albums in my book *The Top 500 Heavy Metal Albums of All Time*. It also won the poll we generated for the *Lock Horns* special Sam Dunn and myself commandeered on the Priest catalogue, viewable on YouTube.

Less so than any of the above but still strongly felt, shameless children of the hair band era love *Turbo* for its happy friendliness. I'm sure looking back in ten years, there will be those who were 17 at the time who swear by *Angel of Retribution* or *Firepower* or even those of a rebellious naysayer disposition who clang most convincingly to the memory of the Ripper Owens-era albums (although I ain't met one of those yet).

In any event—and this is me talking again—I personally think desperation and a desire to make a bloody career out of this insufferable life so far, caused the band to dumb down all over *British Steel*. This marked a slide in my relationship with the band. Sure, I've been mostly a very loyal fan since 1980 for almost all of the years after, but in my eyes, Priest were no longer innovators, no longer supermen. They were, on and off, making good to great records that contributed to the metal community but would no longer be held up as examples of the best we had to offer.

Martin Popoff

Metallica would take over with *Ride the Lightning* in '84, making that godly record and then repeating themselves positively on *Master of Puppets*, sliding after that but thankfully, making records that were different from each other. Pantera would cause the next pronounced and prominent Richter blip with 1990's *Cowboys from Hell*, and I don't know if we've ever had a too, too obvious metal stormbringer that has unarguably really raised the ante since.

So, back to that original premise. I literally see 1970 as the first cardio spike: *Black Sabbath, Paranoid, In Rock*. I see 1984 as another, 1990 as another. But in-between, man, there is Priest arriving from utter obscurity (and then incredibly, tragically, unjustly staying there for a long, long time), bringing *Sad Wings of Destiny* in '76, *Sin After Sin* in '77, *Stained Class* in '78 and *Hell Bent for Leather* in '79. Do you see what I'm getting at? Priest had four goddamn blips, and for that—forever, like a Super Bowl champion and a President—they are winners forever, despite missteps, despite, well, never leading in earnest ever again.

And here's their story, or at least as it pertains to the first ten albums, which also nicely corresponds to the first ten years of released recordings: 1974 to 1984. As a point of process, what I've done here is quite extensively expanded upon the early chapters of my original Priest book *Heavy Metal Painkillers*. The word count constraint of dealing with a big publisher tends to clip the aspirations toward the scholarly, and I do believe Priest's incredible run of ten records to begin their career, deserves the red carpet treatment. As for the title, *Decade of Domination*, "decade" doesn't necessarily have to signify the '70s or the '80s; it's a word that can be used to mark any ten-year period. I kinda wanted to check that out first before using, and then became satisfied that I could call '74 to '84, roughly speaking, a decade, so there you go. As well, like all of my bios, what follows is more like a look at the band's albums, song by song, comments where obtainable, using my many interviews with the guys over the years plus some outside press.

Let me tell you though, Priest can be a frustrating band to interview. Without exception, every single (longstanding) member of the band—Rob, Glenn, K.K., Ian and Scott—are exceedingly cautious and decorous about what they say. Even the most innocuous question can scare them into a long-winded response of very little substance. I'm not sure how I want you to take that, for the guys are unfailingly polite, good-natured, but…

Let me give you two examples. I asked K.K. about what would be more of a K.K. song writing-wise versus a Glenn song. You know, the credits are pretty democratic so you can't really tell. The fans would like to know. No big whoop… it might be idle fun to try spot each of their personalities in a few Priest classics. He wouldn't answer, saying, "It wouldn't be fair" or something like that. Second example, Rob says, "It would be unethical" to talk about Halford in a Priest interview or vice versa. First guy I ever talked to who ever told me something like that. Not very loose. Not very rock 'n' roll.

I have many, many examples of questions I thought were pretty soft, that prompted dodged responses or generalities, or most aggravatingly, stacks and stacks of metal clichés, unfortunately, many of which will show up in the following pages, in part because we want you to get a sense of the guys, especially Rob, who can amuse with his pomp and circus pants, can charm you, but then fill up a sentence with far too much fluff!

Which brings up another point—and the guys admit this—they really don't remember. Some of what I think is dodging, is simply an honest "I don't recall" to a geeky fan-boy question that could be eight layers away from them possibly dredging a cogent response. I constantly found myself reminding myself of this and over the years, have tried to ask things differently, or ask questions that I figure might lead them into remembering. Still, I've all too often put the phone down after a Priest chat thinking… there was absolutely nothing of use there.

Urgh. In any event, that's my Priest interview rant. I love the guys, always will, but I wish they'd loosen up a bit. Rob's a gay heavy metal rocker covered in studs and leather for Christ's sake. You'd think he could be a bit more adventuresome in what he says. I mean, he's lived an interesting life. Anyway, enough. Read on, celebrate this band's first decade—a decade of domination—with me, a ten-year running of the bulls that can be neatly cracked into two five-year chunks, the first representing creative domination and the second, a dominance in the record shops and in arenas all around the heavy metal world.

Martin Popoff
martinp@inforamp.net

Prologue
"Victorian times and centuries gone by"

Like Sabbath, like Trapeze and like half of Led Zeppelin, Judas Priest struggled to life under the grey, metal-clanked skies of Birmingham—the Black Country—smack in the middle of the UK, just far enough from easier rock 'n' rolling London to cause a loud lack of hope.

It has often been said—eloquently and often by both all of Priest and all of Sabbath—that Birmingham, by its very nature, breeds heavy metal. Steel, car parts, burning rubber, metal stamping, tool-and-die and early death from blackened lungs... it's all wrapped up like a fist and a cyst smack at the heart of industrial Britain, and it was often the prime motivator to come up with something—anything—to get a handsome young man out from under the yoke that cursed his kinfolk. Often that "anything" was heavy metal, a musical form forged to compete with the factory rhythms pounding upon already throbbing heads, always in the background, always a reminder of a life of toil and doom.

"People talk about it all the time," muses Judas Priest guitarist K.K. Downing, on the Birmingham vibe. "It definitely was a very industrial place and wasn't the most pleasant place to grow up. Personally, I came from a real broken home situation so I guess you become a bit of a rebel. You either become a heavy metal guitar player or you end up jail! (laughs). Obviously, you want to express your aggression and I think subconsciously, I kind of perceive the guitar as an instrument, but not necessarily a musical instrument. It's like a gun substitute. When you look at it, it can be a weapon of sorts. Personally, I get as much enjoyment out of looking at a guitar and holding it as I would actually playing it. Is that weird? Is that perverse, or what?! It definitely is weird."

Incredibly, the original lineup of one band striving to escape such toil, Judas Priest, back in 1969, not only included no one who is in the band now, but in fact, no one that would record the first Judas Priest album, *Rocka Rolla*, five years later in 1974. The band that Alan Eade of Ace Management had on his hands consisted of Ernest Chataway on guitar, Brian "Bruno" Stapenhill on bass, John "Fezza" Partridge on drums, and one Alan John Atkins on vocals, Atkins being the prime vestige of Priest history to leave his mark on the band as we know it, having written songs that would show up on both *Rocka Rolla* and 1976's *Sad Wings of Destiny*.

"You don't see many guys sitting on the foundries playing acoustic guitar here," reflects Al, asked about heavy metal and the Midlands. "It was rough. It's not so bad now, but in those days it was a lot of industry, steel mills and everything around the place. There were a lot of bands coming out of here, first out of the blues boom in England, like Zeppelin. There was a lot of bands who wanted to do a bit more of what Cream and Hendrix spearheaded with the heavier blues feel to everything, like Sabbath. They came out about '68, called Earth. They were spotted up in Henry's Blues House in town, a lovely old crowd pub, which was a great place for everybody to meet. Plant, everybody. Judas Priest played there, I think it was '71 or '72 with Trapeze. But it was Black Sabbath trying to do something a little bit heavier, a little bit different, and they made the way for a lot of bands like Judas Priest. Robert had teamed up with Jimmy Page. I remember seeing them live in a place called Mother's in Birmingham, and they were still doing a bit of the blues thing there but gradually got out of that. Everything went much louder, much heavier, almost pre-shock tactics before punk came out. With the names, upside-down crosses, Judas Priest, Black Sabbath, everybody's trying to shock the world with a heavier sort of music. Brilliant time."

"But foundries were scattered everywhere," continues Al. "Steel foundries and factories were just scattered everywhere. There was Round Oak Steel, a big one towards Wolverhampton way, that made the chains for the anchor for the Titanic. That was a big place. One got called Hell Hole, so these places already had names like that, and you didn't want to work for them. Let's start a band, let's get out of here, let's go to America."

It was in fact Atkins and Stapenhill that had formed the band in West Bromwich, on the outskirts of Birmingham. Chataway got the guitar post after the guys searched out a replacement for John Perry who had been killed in an automobile accident—Chataway had won the job over one Kenneth Downing Jr., who later claimed to have been a little overly ambitious at the time, having only played through an actual amplifier five or six times at that point. K.K. would recall seeing the band's old van tearing down the road with Judas Priest emblazoned on the side, thinking, "What a cool name; I wish I was in that band."

In terms of the early Priest sound, Atkins says he's, "always been in bands which were a progression—whatever was happening, we'd go and see something new, I like this, let's try it. So when Judas Priest formed in '69, Sabbath had already made a name for themselves. Oh, this is great. We need to go down this route. And so we got the name and hit the road and that was it; it was a fantastic time. And we played with Sabbath; Tony Iommi took us under his wing and he managed us for about 12 months and he thought Judas Priest was going to be the next biggest thing. And he was right, but it was going to be a few years later."

"Led Zeppelin was an influence as well," continues Al. "And before that The Yardbirds, Jeff Beck and Jimmy Page and all those guys. Myself, I liked some American bands; we did a couple songs by a band called Quicksilver Messenger Service and we sort of beefed them up a little bit. I saw Deep Purple in '68 and was just blown away; I thought they were a brilliant band. But I think the actual metal started in Birmingham with Sabbath and then Priest coming a couple years later."

Ernest Chataway was a mere 17 years old, but could play guitar, keyboards and harmonica, having sat in with Black Sabbath on the latter, early on when they were known as Earth. Atkins and Stapenhill had been around the block, having played with The Bitta Sweet, Sugar

Stack (also featuring Partridge), Blue Condition (Al calls this "the real Priest predecessor") and The Jug Blues Band. In 1969, Atkins was asked to join Evolution, but was dismayed when a three-month tour of Morocco was proposed, for which Atkins was also to drive the tour bus. He balked, and then tried to get back with the Jugs, but that was not to be. Ergo, the Priest beckoned.

With regard to picking Judas Priest as a name, Al says that, "Bruno, the bass guitarist in Judas Priest No.1 came up with the idea when looking for something similar to the Black Sabbath name which we liked at the time. He got it from a Bob Dylan album called *John Wesley Harding*. The song was "The Ballad of Frankie Lee and Judas Priest." The curious moniker can be looked upon as a mild exclamation, or the duality of good and evil, Judas being a betrayer of Christ, and a priest being a proponent thereof. Just on its own, the religious tone of the name carried a sort of ominous weight. And moreover, nods to Black Sabbath in its choosing are multiple and profound.

Judas Priest at this point was going for a bluesy yet progressive rock sound, covering the likes of the aforementioned Quicksilver as well as Spirit. Eade had prompted the band to record a demo, consisting of Atkins' "Good Time Woman" and "We'll Stay Together," which garnered some interest from Immediate (the much-lauded label run by Rolling Stones manager Andrew Loog Oldham) and Harvest, the latter of which, along with Vertigo, was to figure prominently in British art rock history. A showcase band wars-type gig in Walsall (November 25th, 1969, the band's very first show, attended by Robert Plant!) resulted in a three-year record deal with Immediate. However, it was not to be, as the label ended up closing shop two months later.

The band toured into 1970 but then split, all but Alan moving out of town. Late in that year, Alan had discovered a young band rehearsing a form of louder and faster rock, something he'd wanted to explore, inspired in the main, by Black Sabbath's *Paranoid*. In the band were Downing, drummer John Ellis, and bassist Ian Frank Hill (otherwise known as Skull), but no singer. The rehearsal complex was called Holy Joe's or by some, Joe's Place (run by one Father Husband), and it was in a converted Church of England school, frequented by many local Midlands bands, due, recalls K.K., to its five-shilling price and the fact that you could turn up as loud as you wanted. Rockers using the facility included Slade, Trapeze and Robert Plant. Downing remembered his own audition for Atkins' old band, plus he knew Atkins as a locally famous musician, as well as a talented singer, drummer, guitarist and writer—all told, he was more than glad to have Atkins as part of the group.

"It was literally run by a vicar," explains K.K.. "There was a church over the road, and like in England, a lot of those things were kind of combined. You would have your school, sometimes with the church attached to the school, if not just in close proximity. Which is a really important part in, certainly, Victorian times and centuries gone by, where children would actually go to church to say Mass in the morning and have assembly in the church and events at Christmas time, Easter, harvest times… very important. So it was that type of setup."

"But it was really run-down, deserted, but the vicar was still there in the vicar's house, or the vicarage. So he would try to make some money for the upkeep of the building, even though the rooms were deserted. So he thought, I know what I'll do. I'll rent these school rooms out to bands so they can rehearse. He probably didn't think about that straightaway, but maybe a band knocked on his door one day and said, 'Could we rehearse here?' But we would just go down there every night, five or six bands rehearsing. A racket it must've been as well, with the acoustics of school rooms in those days, all that glass. But the vicar would come around to collect his money, while we were playing. Often he would go straight to the pub which was just down the corner. But yes, Slade were one of the bands, a pop band that huge here in the '70s. And they used to actually pull up with an articulated wagon with their gear in it."

"K.K. was very influenced by Jimi Hendrix," notes Al. "He was a massive influence to K.K. when he first started, and when he died it was a big thing for him. He didn't take it too good. Hendrix was the main, main influence for K.K. when he started out. I don't think K.K. was a great guitarist, I'll be honest, but he looked the part and he could pull the birds and that made all the difference, you know? I've played with better guitarists than him, but he looked the part and his stage presence was very good. He could slide across the stage in his jeans, but he'd rip them all up by sliding across on his knees. He was like… he was a poser before the word poser was invented. He looked good, he played well. Sometimes it doesn't matter if you're the best guitarist in the world as long as the audience is enjoying themselves. Entertainment is number one. That's the main thing, when you're entertaining the crowd. But I think when they got Glenn in, Kenny was the second best out of the two and I think Kenny learned a lot from Glenn, a hell of a lot. But early on he wasn't writing much stuff. I was the main writer."

"I remember when I started to get into music quite seriously," recalls K.K., speaking with Sam Dunn. "There was a DJ in the UK called John Peel who had a late-night radio show, and he would play a lot of the obscure stuff, a very eclectic mix of bands, but amongst them there was lots of blues, in particular, bands like John Mayall's Bluesbreakers, and all of the black blues artists. That really sort of got my interest, was the blues thing, really. It was such a big movement in the UK. In Birmingham, in particular, it just seemed to be a fantastic place to be growing up, with the music that was evolving at the time. Bands started to come on the scene like The Cream, and then of course when the great Jimi Hendrix came over, well, it all took off big time. The man took things to another level."

Further on Jimi, Downing asserts that, "everything he did was totally important. It was totally fresh, it was energy, there was a rebelliousness, it was certainly, at the time, totally insane. But the thing is, the way that he improvised was really such a magical experience. He was so obviously well-connected mentally with his instrument, and being able to just relay his feelings and his energy through the instrument. I saw Hendrix quite a few times, and the charisma that he had on stage, he could literally turn the audience… he could control them. I'm sure that he could, because I've never seen audiences react to a performer, even to this day, as they actually did when the very first time I saw Hendrix, at a place called Coventry Theatre. Literally, he came on and did 'Foxey Lady' and just everybody went absolutely crazy, stormed the stage, like they were totally in a frenzy. And I was one of them. A couple years later, when he played the Royal Albert Hall, people were literally jumping from the balconies. I was there; I saw people jumping from the balconies, you know, just wanting to get closer. Me as well, I just wanted to get more of the sound and the energy and get closer to the guy, because he had such a magical persona."

As for the drawing power of his first love, the blues, K.K figures, "Well, like I say, we hailed from Birmingham and the surrounding suburbs, which is called the Black Country for obvious reasons; it's very industrial. The blues was just something that us as youngsters, young rebels, the young blood, basically on the streets, could latch onto. While other things were going on, like obviously the big pop movement and the soul movement, there didn't really seem to be anything for us guys, you know, that we would really take to. And obviously from the blues came so many great bands in England, like Blodwyn Pig, Ten Years After, Taste. There were just millions, seemed to be millions. You could see a band every night. You could go not too far from where you lived and there would be a pub or club, and you could either see a local band or a band quite well known. It would be nothing to see bands like Thin Lizzy come to a pub, in West Bromwich, or little towns. So it was great, fantastic for us, to get this really good close-up of all these megastars, you know, in our eyes. Like I say, they were wonderful times."

K.K.'s young band quickly dropped their Freight moniker and went with Al's Judas Priest. Al had checked with his ex-bandmates first, and had no problem convincing Ken of the name's merit, Downing still quite enamoured with the important vibe of the name, in fact going so far as to call it the best thing that happened to the band. A few months later Priest began playing around the area, opening for the likes of Slade, Budgie and Gary Moore, covering Hendrix' "Spanish Castle Magic" and

Quatermass' "Black Sheep of the Family," oddly, the song that got Ritchie Blackmore and Ronnie James Dio together and on their way toward forming Rainbow. K.K. recalls that his and Ian's very first gig with the band, March 6th 1971, was in front of 60 to 70 people and that their take on the night was £6. Four months later the band played their first show in London, which K.K. says turned out to be a major let-down, giving its location as "a shed at the back of a pub."

"Obviously it was life-changing," laughs K.K., asked what his discovery of the guitar meant to him. "I lost the existing job that I had, you know. Just because I became totally engrossed in the music world. And really, it was all about whatever you have to do to see your favourite bands, wherever you had to go and travel, whatever you had to do. Like Hendrix was playing at the Woburn Music Festival and I just felt that I should be there, and not to miss it. And I'm glad that I didn't. It's just one of those things; you're young and you are out there, and you're looking for something to latch onto, some kind of guidance."

"I mean, not being brought up with any kind of religious background or nothing, I was kind of a free spirit, really. But the music was something inside you, inside certain people. Glenn and myself must've thought well, maybe I can do this. I mean, I'm enchanted by it and in love with it, and maybe if I get an instrument myself, maybe I can be a part of it? And I think some people... and if you really want it, and are prepared to work pretty hard and dedicate yourself, you can achieve it, which I think is a good message to a lot of youngsters, really, who might be looking in. If you really want something, really that bad, and you feel there's a bit of guidance there coming from somewhere, don't know where, just go for it."

"I think everything—absolutely everything," responds Downing, asked if there was something he was rebelling against. "It seemed like growing up, I mean, you are always oppressed by somebody, whether it was your parents or schoolteachers or people in the workplace. There was always, for some reason, you feel oppressed because you're not a fully grown adult member of society, for starters. And then when you start doing that, and you wear what people think are funny clothes and start to grow your hair, you literally become... life, back then, could be quite difficult, obviously. But it didn't stop you growing and evolving as the person that you really want to be."

The roll-call of bands local to the area that could inspire the likes of a young K.K. Downing was indeed impressive. Says Al Atkins with regard to Slade, another fast favourite, "Absolutely brilliant—what a band. Maybe they were a pop rock band, but they sort of broke down barriers. I know Noddy Holder quite well and we played with Slade three or four times when I was in Judas Priest. We topped the bill over them just once—the rest we had to open up for them. But great band. Really, really loud band, they were, for the time as well. I remember playing with Judas Priest with them one night and they had this wall of sound; it was incredible, the volume they played at, really. Considering Judas Priest is supposed to be more of a hard rock band, they sort of blew us off. But they would also be considered a local band, yes; they come from Wolverhampton, which is the next city across."

Atkins figures another early heavy band, Budgie, from Cardiff, first came to Birmingham sometime in 1970. "Budgie, yeah, a great band they were, and very much like Judas Priest. Hard working lads, great band. We played with them a good five, six times. And I think when I left Priest, they went on tour with them in Europe. Played in Wales on the home ground and then they'd come and play with us at the Birmingham College of Food and Domestic Arts, and in the audience that night was Rob Halford."

Birmingham also gave us "the voice of rock," Glenn Hughes. "Yes, incredible. Trapeze was soon to come on the scene and they were a really good band. They started out being a five-piece and they ended up being a three-piece band. We played with them as well at Henry's Blues House. Great band. Through Glenn I met Dave Holland, as well, so that's another connection there."

Calling their brand of music "goodanloud," Judas Priest ended up cutting a demo in July '71 at the suggestion of their new manager David Corke. "Holy is the Man" and "Mind Conception" were recorded at Zella Records, home also of Black Sabbath's first demos. Atkins recalls the session as a bit of a cock-up, claiming to have had a sore throat and being stoned, also lamenting the live-with-no-overdubs rawness of the recording. Both of these songs can be heard in re-recorded form on Atkins' fourth solo album, 1998's *Victim of Changes*, with "Mind Conception" transformed into a modern heavy metal rocker—like hard hair metal, even power metal—and "Holy is the Man" pulsing with some of the original's funk, but still unrecognizably heavy-handed.

Explains Al, "Zella was the main Birmingham studio. A lot of bands were in there, great studio. There were two studios. The other one was called Outlaw, on the other side of Birmingham. And the main one in town was called Zella. Great studio. But Outlaw was used too. Black Sabbath were there a little while. Judas Priest was doing a lot of demo stuff. Later on, I was going in one day when they were coming out. And I pushed Kenny back in. I said, "Go back in, you've got another session." And he said, "I'm contracted; I can't do it now!" Oh go piss off. Times have changed."

By the close of the year, drummer John Ellis would be replaced by Alan "Skip" Moore—John's last gig would turn out to be October 6th 1971, with Moore picking up the sticks for a show the following week. "I had a job and John had a job," recalls Ian Hill, remembering John quitting the band, telling his version of the band's murky early rumblings. "There was actually a band called Judas Priest before us. They were together for about 18 months before us but then they split up. Their vocalist was walking past the rehearsal room one day and asked us if we wanted a vocalist. None of us could really hold a tune so we took him on. We couldn't think of a name and to make a long story short we just called ourselves Judas Priest. We got well known in our local area in the Midlands. Suddenly people were wanting to see us 200 miles away. I had a job so I could only do it on weekends. The big jump was asking ourselves, 'Do we quit our jobs or do we keep it as a hobby?' That was the crucial point. Ken and I quit our jobs and John unfortunately didn't."

"We have known each other since we were about five," remarks Hill with respect to K.K. Downing. "We were brought up in the same housing estate just outside of Birmingham. We weren't really friends until we were about 15 or 16 and first started to get into music. We were into progressive rock, which in those days was Cream, Jimi Hendrix, John Mayall & the Bluesbreakers and Fleetwood Mac. We had very, very similar tastes in music. It brought us together and we formed a band with John Ellis, another friend from school. But yes, we didn't have a vocalist in those days. We were just quite happy to go to rehearsal rooms and thrash out a few of our favourite songs."

That same year, 1972, also marked the composition of three tracks that would two years hence feature on *Rocka Rolla*, namely "Never Satisfied," "Winter" and "Caviar and Meths," the band's set closer at that time, and originally longer than the version that would show up on the album, sporting some additional impressive modern metal riffing. Atkins has proposed that a standard set list of the day might have run "Spanish Castle Magic," "Winter," "Holy is the Man," "Voodoo Rag," "Black Sheep of the Family," "Never Satisfied," "Whiskey Woman," "Joey," "Mind Conception" and finally "Caviar and Meths." Bands Priest had shared stages with up to this point included White Rabbit, Graphite, Supertramp, Bronco, the aforementioned Trapeze, Slade and Budgie, and on one occasion, Black Sabbath.

As regards "Winter," Al says, "I was looking at Tony doing the big riff stuff and I wanted something like that, but of course singing over top of the riff. 'Never Satisfied' was just experimenting, really. 'Caviar and Meths,' that was a good song, about ten minutes long, although we could drag it out to 15 minutes, which a lot of songs were at the time. You had about six songs in the list, I think, in a one-hour set list."

Moore would shortly leave Priest for a local recording act called Sundance, before returning for *Sad Wings of Destiny*. With new drummer Christopher Louis "Congo" Campbell in tow (black, with a huge afro!), the band opened for the likes of Status Quo, Thin Lizzy and Family. The band was working extensively, having hooked up with early Sabbath manager Jim Simpson, Tony Iommi, Norman Hood, and their Iommi Management Agency, or I.M.A., who also had on their roster The Flying Hat Band, featuring Glenn Tipton. In January of '73, the company was now called Tramp Entertainment, but management stayed essentially the same, with Priest being handled by David Corke and Norman Hood.

At this juncture, Al Atkins would leave the band, citing the poor financial situation of playing gigs for £10 a night (later £25). "My third year with them became a money struggle," says Al. "I was the only one married, with a baby daughter, Sharon, to feed. The bigger we became, the more overheads we got so we always ended up with little to no money at all."

Al was also reticent to tour without an album to promote. He had been writing all the songs, and indeed asked by management to keep cranking them out. But an album deal never materialised, even though there was interest from Gull Records, who would eventually hook up with the band for their first and second albums. Ian Hill says that finances were so dire at times that they would send one of the gals in to charm a drink out of some pub patron, and then bring the drink out to the thirsty rockers. Ken would shake his head and say that after you'd paid off the van rental and the P.A. company, you'd be lucky enough to have enough for fish and chips that night. The guys would also pull into town and announce themselves as artists signed to Atlantic, landing the odd gig that way, including one at a Greek restaurant for £15 and a bunch of food.

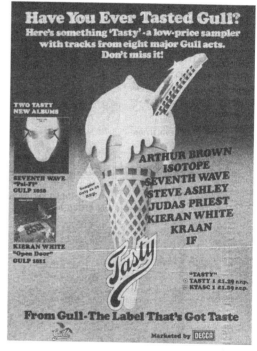

Atkins' last tour with the band was to be called the Heavy Thoughts tour, named after one of the new songs he had written, in and about the time he wrote "Whiskey Woman," which would morph into Priest epic "Victim of Changes." "Heavy Thoughts" exists in unfinished demo form, and a version of it can be heard on Al's 2003 solo album of the same name.

It is of note that Al admits to a certain amount of drug-taking—no big deal in the '70s—but otherwise tried to keep the band in tip-top shape, not even allowing girlfriends at rehearsals. "K.K. and Ian were with me for about three years and were hard-working lads with one thing in mind— they are going to the top of the tree, no matter what. But still, I had to try to keep K.K., Ian and John, the drummer, focused on the band only, but John kept bringing his girlfriend everywhere with us so I told him, 'You don't take your woman to work so don't bring her again with us' and it didn't go down too well with him and he started mouthing off to me so I threatened to beat him up. None of their girlfriends liked me because of this but I didn't give a shit. To me the main thing was the band—that's all."

Musing over the direction of the band, Atkins ventures that, "At the beginning we played covers of bands like Quatermass and it all sounded very blues rock, but in Judas Priest No.2, with K.K. and Ian, it started to get an edge to the sound although we still played covers— even by Hendrix, would you believe?—then gradually added my songs to the list, like 'Mind Conception,' 'Never Satisfied,' 'Winter,' 'Caviar and Meths,' 'Whiskey Woman,' 'Joey,' 'Voodoo Rag' and 'Holy Is the Man.' It was at this time K.K. wrote his first ever song, 'Run of the Mill.' A lot of these songs featured on their debut album *Rocka Rolla*. Direction-wise, I myself wasn't aware of us being a metal band at the time. 'Heavy Thoughts' was one I only half finished."

Atkins would close out touring late into December of '72, with the reconfiguration of the band coming in the winter/summer of '73, one Rob Halford's first gigs with the band commencing in April of that year. By the end of the Atkins era, Priest had added as stage mates, Freedom, Ace, Wild Angels, Burnt Oak, Dr. Ross, Gary Moore, Curved Air, Elf, Mahatma Kane Jeeves, Danta, Strife and Thin Lizzy. "Yes we opened up for loads of top bands," recalls Atkins, "including Family, whom… Roger Chapman was one of my heroes, plus Status Quo and Gary Moore, who was and still is my favourite guitar player."

"I didn't know him," says Al of Rob. "Apparently he was watching us that night I mentioned; I heard the story. I didn't know him at the time. I knew his sister, because Ian Hill was going out with his sister, courting his sister. But I didn't know Rob, not at all. Never saw him live, never even heard of him until apparently our management or Dave Cook, who was looking after the band, had booked his band Hiroshima into a couple of pubs. But I assured Rob when he took my place the first time… it had been a few months down the line that I went to see him play. It was very strange listening to him sing all my old songs. I actually didn't like Rob's voice very much at the beginning. It sounded like he was trying to do a sort of Robert Plant imitation. But he was young and he probably turned out to be the best singer on the planet, I think."

So yes, Atkins would be replaced by the indomitable metal god Rob Halford, but a mere mortal back in 1973. Campbell would also leave the band (as would roadie Keith Evans, who moved on to a job with AC/DC), with Ian and K.K. deciding to soldier on. Rob came from a band called Hiroshima, bringing with him his drummer John Hinch. Al eventually left his office job and returned to rock 'n' roll, touring until 1978 with a band called Lion, featuring his Priest cohort Brian Stapenhill along with Budgie drummer Pete Boot. Adds Al, "I almost joined Trapeze when Glenn Hughes left to go with Deep Purple. They were looking for a bass player and vocalist to replace him but I turned it down. And with regard to the Priest guys these days, we did a reunion meeting about five years ago for one of our old roadies to raise money for a charity he organised at the bar he had bought. I still phone Ian when he's in town and I met up with them backstage at a gig last year."

K.K. is wont to tell the story of visiting the Halford household with Ian Hill (Ian is married to Rob's sister, Sue; Ken was dating her friend Carol Hiles), and hearing Rob (at that point Bob, and later Robert) do harmonies to Doris Day on the telly, Downing quite impressed with his trilling. Rob affirms the gist of the story, but won't cop to the idea that it was Doris Day, noting that K.K. is known to exaggerate. Later, Ken phoned Rob (once described as "stage lighting designer and would-be actor from Walsall") to come out for an audition. Here's where it gets confusing, as some reports have it that Rob was singing along to the radio, not the television, and that it was at K.K.'s and Ian's apartment, having already been called up for an audition.

Back into younger days, Rob was always superlative in the high school choir, forming his first band—with one of his teachers on guitar—called Thark, in 1966 at the age of 15. Rob also featured in a band called Abraxis and then prog rockers Athens Wood, and he did indeed work the lights, for the Grand Theatre in Wolverhampton, earning good money and causing consternation with his parents when he left to rock out. Also in an act called Lord Lucifer, Rob had a Francis Barnett motorcycle with that name painted on the gas tank—Rob later recalled that parents would shuck their children away when he would drive by. But it was immediate Priest predecessor Hiroshima—on plate for about a year—that was closest to Halford's future esteemed directive. Of note, and in fact somewhat analogous to the story of another metal god Ronnie James Dio, Rob briefly played bass in the band, when their erstwhile bassist Ian Charles was put on waivers.

Fondly remembering the first time he had been bitten by the rock 'n' roll bug, Rob says that, "My aunt Pat gave me an old Dansette record player when I was about 12-ish, maybe? And I opened the lid, and there were three or four 45 singles. It was Bill Haley and the

Comets, Little Richard, Elvis and Chuck Berry. And I put them all on, and I was just mesmerised by the whole vibe of it all. Just really wow, what is this? The energy and the excitement, and the determination of the performance. I always recount that as being the catalyst, the spark and the start of the adventure."

As for his desire to front a band, says Rob, "I was always fascinated by live performers that you can get all those people to just focus on what you're trying to be, what you're trying to do, what you're trying to say. Before I became a professional singer I worked in a theatre, and I would stand on the side of the stage and watch opera, I would watch repertory theatre with lead characters, famous actors, I'd watch famous classical performances, and I'd look at the audiences and at the performer and back and forth, and it was intriguing to see how all of that could be part of the performance. How the collective conscious of 30,000 people could all unite because it was all focusing on that one thing that was happening there. It's just incredible. It's magic. So it's just a combination of people. But no doubt in the history of rock 'n' roll there are people who stand out, including who we now know as the king that was Elvis. He leads the pack for a lot of people still."

"I wish I could say I was like a freak at school, but I don't suppose I was," reflects Halford, asked if he was rebelling against anything as a young man. "I was a gay freak, but I was a hidden gay freak. I just went through the motions. I quite enjoyed… as a person I've always been interested in a lot of things in life in general. I was interested in English language literature, interested in history, interested in all those things that were being put into my head as a kid growing up. I enjoyed the whole experience, but then at the same point you go through the, 'I fucking hate everybody, everything sucks. I don't want to do this anymore, the school stuff.' It's come to a point where I'm looking for something and I can't find what it is, but I'm getting some solace, some release or relief with the music I'm listening to. At a certain point in your life, as a teenager, the only friend you've got is your music. You listen to a message in a song and it's exactly what you feel right now. For the most part I enjoyed that experience. I wasn't really the rebel, but there was a kind of disconnect that was going on, that I was piecing together through the music that I was listening to."

"I was just this long-haired freak," continues Rob, on his fashion sense back then. "God, I wish I had hair again. Particularly through those transitional times, late '60s and early '70s, it was a really exciting time, musically. I couldn't figure out how I wanted to look or dress. It was that kind of Hendrix hippie mixture of looking like some… I don't know, homeless waif on the street. 'You're not going out looking like that, are you?' 'Yeah.'"

Concerning Birmingham, "It was bleak and it was rough and just grime and industry and a dead end. There was this drudgery. I'm painting a bleak picture of what maybe it wasn't genuinely like, but that's how it was for all of us. It was, 'I gotta get out of here, and if I'm in a band, maybe that will be part of the dream.' Just to get in a van and go up the motorway and see what the next town is like, the next city is like. And once you start doing that you don't want to stop."

Back in Priest world, a jam session took place at Holy Joe's, and Rob, having been previously impressed to the point of mesmerised, with, in particular, K.K. Downing, was promptly hired on. K.K. in turn had been impressed with Rob's harmonizing to radio—or TV— broadcasts, as well as his reputation on harmonica. John Hinch was also part of the deal, and after hours of discussing music and playing it, both were offered the job.

Drummer Hinch, in relating the story of joining Priest, recalls Rob as, "a young chap, screaming and wailing for all he was worth. I felt that this guy was the man. He could do the business for us. So back in those days, there was always this sort of heavy political situation, backstabbing the other band, secret talks and all very cloak and dagger. So anyway, that was when Rob joined our band. And that band was called Hiroshima. And off we went, did quite a number of gigs up and down the country, and it wasn't too successful. We weren't terribly happy with this band. It all fizzled out, and Rob and myself thought we would carry it on, and we would try to find other guys to join our band and go from there, still under the name Hiroshima. So we went to the Birmingham College of Food, and on the bill was a band called Judas Priest, and they were horrible. I mean, they were bad, hated them. There was this strutting lead guitarist, long blond hair, as I remember it, this sort of very thin bass guitarist standing stock still, and a black drummer, and I didn't really take any other notice of them other than that they were bad."

"And as chance would have it," continues Hinch, "Ian Hill came from the same area as Rob Halford, and dated Rob's sister, and one day me and Rob were over there, just tinkering around, and in walked Ian Hill, or Skull as he was affectionately known. And he mentioned to us that the singer, Al Atkins, and the drummer, a guy called Congo, had left the band and they wanted replacements, and would we be interested in going to audition for Judas Priest? Rob and I discussed the matter, and felt that we really didn't want to be associated with this band, and if we did, we would certainly change the name. And anyway, we ended up at the rehearsal, went through all their songs; Rob could sort of sing a song he'd never heard before and just throw words in that happened to suit. And because the band had gotten a tour already lined up, as support to a band called Budgie, Rob and I thought, well, what have we got to lose, if it's going to put us out there? In time we'll take this band over and they'll become our band. Or, if it doesn't suit, we will carry on. So off we went on tour, after a few bitty sort of rehearsals. And by the end of the tour, which was three to four weeks long, we sort of moulded into the Judas Priest situation very nicely. Rob had successfully changed it, and from there, Dave Corke, if I'm right, was already in contact via Budgie with Gull Records, and got David Howells to come see us at a gig."

Recalls K.K. about Priest's friendship with Cardiff's finest, namely Budgie, "They were my big, big favourite band; I was a real big fan—great band. We used to do 30-odd date tours with those boys. And even when we weren't on tour with them… I can remember one night, because we used to live together, me, and Ian, the bass player, this other school friend we had who used to get us some gigs, and two girls, living in a one-bedroom flat. So there were five of us. That's where I perfected the art of silent sex. Or, did I ever perfect it? One of the girls was my girlfriend. And occasionally, you would get a knock on the door at the middle of the night, and it would be Budgie, because they were from Cardiff which was quite a way south. So when they would be playing up north, Newcastle or something, often they would be too knackered to drive the rest of the way home. Knock on the door, pouring rain, there would be Burke Shelley standing there, 'Guys, can we crash on the floor for the night?' And of course, we would do the same when we were down south. So they would often be there, and in the morning we would get up to get the guitars out of the van and jam a bit."

K.K. Downing's first song of record would be a beauty, "Run of the Mill" establishing a levity that would carry the band beyond *Rocka Rolla*, through to their classic *Sad Wings of Destiny* album. "Run of the Mill" would be recorded as a demo, along with Halford singing old Al Atkins chestnut "Whiskey Woman." Halford's "Red Light Ladies" would be added as a slow second movement coda, turning the paste-up job into "Victim of Changes," one of the all-time Priest classics. The demoing of "Run of the Mill" with "Whiskey Woman" would turn into the Gull Records deal, now and possibly forever a poisoned thorn in the leathered hides of all of Priest. Sealing the deal in principle was a showcase at The Marquee, February 11, 1974, with Priest in support of Budgie. Although K.K. figures the label and its leader David Howells didn't like the band's music, they saw potential due to the manic crowd reaction on display that night.

Leaving the UK for the first time, the band logged a few dates in Germany and The Netherlands (sleeping in their Mercedes van, despite it being winter), then back home, then over to Norway and Denmark (more sleeping in the van, now a Ford transit), where, a girl couldn't pronounce Downing's first name, coming up with K.K. instead, which has been his rock 'n' roll-ish moniker ever since. Earlier in the Halford era, Priest notched their first extended support slot, accompanying Budgie on that band's *Never Turn Your Back on a Friend* tour through the summer of '73 and into early '74.

Priest arrived home from their Scandinavian sojourn to sign on the dotted line with Gull on April 16th. "We opted to pursue the deal," recalls Hinch. "We came down to London, to South Malton St., and went into the burger bar across the road, and eventually signed the deal. And grabbed the money (laughs). Which, wasn't a huge amount of money at that time, but from my business point of view, it was a lot of money. I mean, it enabled us to get a better P.A., all sorts of things."

The band learned that Howells would prefer they fill out their sound a bit with another band member, something the guys were a bit wary of, simply due to the idea of splitting their slim pickings five ways instead of four. Howells figured that there were too many bands out there operating as a power trio with vocalist, and a keyboard player or even a sax player was suggested. Rehearsing one of the band's songs, it became apparent that a second guitarist would fit the bill best, with drummer John Hinch figuring that the idea came from Howells and producer Rodger Bain. Downing was also quickly on board, liking what Wishbone Ash had pioneered with their twin guitar solo sound, as well as pointing out that live, it sounded better if during a solo, there could be a rhythm guitar bed beneath it. Comments Hinch, "I have to say, it did work. Glenn joined the band, and as soon as Kenny became comfortable with him, it improved the music a great deal; it did fill the sound out. They managed to work out a lot of dual guitar runs, lead runs, I think, very, very effectively."

"We were familiar with Glenn from his band The Flying Hat Band," recalls Ian Hill, with respect to Glenn Tipton's fateful arrival. "We had been on the same circuit in Germany. Rob was with the band by then. It was the nucleus of the first recording band. We already had our deal with Gull Records. We were at a place called What's Music in Birmingham and Glenn walked in, and out of the blue Ken went and asked him if he wanted to join the band. We were just standing there agog. After meeting us and having a couple of pints he said yes. He brought in another dimension to the band and as the cliché goes, we have never looked back since. The only other twin lead at the time was Wishbone Ash. They were very lightweight compared to us. It was chalk and cheese really. We were one of the first bands to have two lead guitars in a heavy rock format."

Notes departed vocalist Al Atkins on The Flying Hat Band, "They were sort of in the same agency. Tony Iommi had this agency he'd formed with Norman Hood, and it was called International Management Agency. It was based in Hirsch Street, right in the middle of Birmingham. And he wanted to show off a lot of the young talent to the rest of the country and the world, and one of the bands he signed up was Judas Priest. He looked after us. We played with Sabbath and he put us on the Hippodrome with a band called Family. And also we played one at the Plaza, big gig—we played there quite a few times in the '60s. He put us on there once with Flying Hat Band from the same agency, and that's when we first met Glenn. Glenn was doing okay. The Flying Hat Band was an awful name, but you know, I think he'd already been touring Europe. So Glenn was a great asset for Judas Priest when he came in because he could write, he could sing, he could play great guitar, and I think that was the missing piece of the jigsaw when Glenn came in. And that's when they started really writing some heavier stuff. But they were a three-piece rock band, and quite heavy, certainly not pop."

"In my early days, because I'm getting on a bit, there was a lot of soul music," laughs Tipton, concerning his own pathway toward rock 'n' roll as a career. "I was also into blues. I got into blues and rhythm and blues and it just progressed from there. This is in my teens, really. And then one of the first live bands I ever saw was at Birmingham Town Hall—we used to go to all-nighters there—Spencer Davis Group, Stevie Winwood. But as music progressed right around that era, Birmingham in particular was great. They had some great clubs. I've never seen The Cream—I didn't really know who they were at the time—but there were lots of bands I did see, early Fleetwood Mac, Mott The Hoople, things like that. Great acts, great songs, people expressing themselves, moving away from the blues, progressing."

"And there were lots of little clubs, particularly in Birmingham, and Birmingham is renowned for having a lot of important musicians and successful musicians, and I think that had a lot to do with it. There was quite a large amount of outlets out there for bands to play, small venues—it was great to see them really close up. It was a great era, because everybody was taking the blues and doing whatever they wanted to do with it. You had Hendrix doing what he wanted, Cream doing what they wanted. There were a vast array of bands, open house, really."

Specifically on guitar influences, Glenn offers that "the two guitarists who influenced me were Rory Gallagher from Taste—the energy that he put out on stage was just unbelievable—and the other guy, initially, was Hendrix. And where did he come from? Okay, Seattle, but he just emerged from nowhere. A black guy playing the guitar like no one else ever had, and with an attitude that no one else ever had, you know, interpreting, the way his music came through. He was just a very innovative guy, and a genius, really. I don't think there is a guitar player, really, that isn't a fan of Hendrix, at least in some little way; even if they don't realise it, they were influenced by him."

"And being an industrial area," continues Tipton, on choosing music, "I think that—and I've often said this—how did it affect you? It gave me, personally, a lot of determination to find a better life, really, which is music. And I'm not putting the Midlands down or even Birmingham. I still live not too far away and I'm proud of where I come from, proud of being British. But you see these guys... I used to work for British Steel in the steel works, and it was a labyrinth of old derelict canals, and really, you sit there for a bit and say, 'Yeah, there's a better life out there somewhere.' And I found music. So I think it gives you a lot of determination. And then in the early days, it was quite difficult for a Birmingham band to be accepted, for instance, in London. And then we had to cross the Atlantic to the States. So it was all true grit in the beginning. It gives you a lot of stamina and strength and willpower, you know what I mean?"

Glenn also received some early lessons in hopes dashed. The Flying Hat Band was a power trio all set to record for Vertigo, however the label figured the band was too much like Black Sabbath— considerably heavy and doomy—and put the

project on ice, even though the guys were well on their way, having toured with Deep Purple. The Flying Hat Band's previous incarnations were Shave 'em Dry and then Merlin. Tipton's early training was actually on piano (his mother's instrument), not guitar (that was the domain of his brother Gary, who had a band called The Atlantics), so some keyboards were supplied to his early bands, as well as lead vocals.

As mentioned, Tipton had actually logged five hard years of work in one of Birmingham's notorious factory jobs, seemingly a rite of passage for a metal man, and had actually not picked up the guitar until he was 18 years old (he was 26 when he joined Priest). He says that as an "energetic bloke," the piano had been a bit too confining. Early influences such as B.B. King and Freddie King led to Jimi Hendrix and at that point, his life had changed forever. The Flying Hat Band included Steve Palmer on drums (brother of another pretty good drummer, Carl!) and notably Mars Cowling on bass, who would move on to critical acclaim and considerable fame with Pat Travers—Cowling passed away March 20th 2018.

And so Priest was re-born (Tipton's first gig with the band was May 9th 1974), somewhat crucially with the help of producer Rodger Bain, who was house guy at Vertigo, and now helping out with Priest, now that the Flying Hat Band record he was to work on was stopped, with its lead guitarist and vocalist off to this new set of guys. Thus far, Rodger's big claim to fame was that he had produced the first three Black Sabbath albums, despite rude and crude tooling, coming up with three productions very different from each other but each bulldozing in its own brutish manner.

Heavy metal synergy reared its head once again where an unknown chap by the name of Rod Smallwood, later Iron Maiden's manager, had been thus far an 18-month employee of London's MAM Agency, where he wound up signing to the booking group, Be Bop Deluxe, Cockney Rebel, Golden Earring and Judas Priest.

"We were of course picking up fans, but we didn't know it at the time," muses John Hinch, in the enviable position of getting to watch Priest grow from his perch on the drum riser. "A few people here or there that liked us, to a point, preferred us to Budgie. We came out at the end of that first tour, which was only a short tour, but it was successful. So after we had completed the initial tour, David Howells went about getting all sorts of work for us. We did pick up gigs ourselves, local gigs, as it were, but we really got into a very nice situation of working virtually every night; I would say on average we used to work 20 to 25 nights a month. There was no planning as such, as to where the gigs were, the routes and that. Literally one night we could be down in Penzance, and then up to Cromer, and Links Pavilion the next. And then we might be up to Inverness. And I'm not just saying this as a windup; I mean literally up to Inverness, which was usually a two-day hike, up through the Highlands and what not. And say, come back down for The Marquee the next night. It went on month in, month out."

"And though you didn't really realise it at the time, night in, night out, you are getting tighter and tighter. The band really began to gel. All along, you are picking up fans. We had some pretty dreadful nights with Priest, from the point of view of audiences. We would sort of come off stage and say, 'Let's just pack it in. It's a complete waste of time. It's not the music of today.' The whole band thought, we are never going to make it. Sabbath had already been and done the heavy metal bit, although it wasn't known as heavy metal in those days."

"Having not, at that stage, released an album, we had no way of gauging how many people really liked the band. Later we managed to get on the Reading Festival, which was the big festival of its day. The first band went on stage to total abuse. I mean, they were literally bottled offstage. Things are being thrown… again, because it's the early days. There wasn't any restriction on taking glass bottles into gigs, so they were literally thrown onstage (laughs). And they had to come off. So we were all sitting in our caravan, our dressing room, and dreading, I mean, very, very nervous about going on stage. And everyone would try to put a brave face on, and we went on, and the place exploded, rapturous applause, thought we were wonderful, couldn't go wrong, and we did, I think a pretty good set. It went down, and I really think that that was one of the major starting points for Judas Priest."

Chapter 1:
Rocka Rolla – "People would kill to get some of those sounds now."

Not exactly telegraphing the heavy metal pageantry to come, Judas Priest's first album, *Rocka Rolla* nonetheless is the work of a band operating smartly within a heavy rock realm that wasn't exactly brimming with talent, especially at the baby band end of the spectrum. Nor does the record hint at the grand religious overtones the band would adopt one shocking step up the ladder later with *Sad Wings of Destiny*.

First with the wrapper, Gull Records artist John Pasche would spin a pun with Coca Cola into a cover concept, and then top it with a logo that would turn out to be used once and then discarded like a bottle top. It was then photographed by Bryce Attwell, with Alan Johnson handling the live performance photography on the back.

Although the cover would be admired as an artistic piece, the band were none too pleased with it (Mel Grant would later supply a rote and forgettable heavy metal illustration called "The Steel Tsar," straight from a Michael Moorcock novel, for a reissue of the record in 1984). The idea was that with this vague imagery, Priest would not be stigmatised as a hard rock act. Flip over to the back—the Judas Priest bassist looks very much like the Black Sabbath drummer, "Bob" Halford is sporting long, blond hair, and Glenn Tipton is looking sartorial behind a moustache.

Onto the music, and one found a band willing to be proggy, heavy, riffy, all sorts of things, even doomy, but not so concerned with the logic that makes commercial songs comfortable and thus saleable.

"Ken and Glenn did the lion's share of the music," says Ian, trying to grapple with the issue of the band's early influences. "But I don't think there were very many outside influences. I try not to, because it will show in my bass lines, and I'm sure it's the same for K.K. and Glenn. But we all liked Cream and Ken was a Hendrix freak—you always keep those. But it was almost a conscious effort not to sound like anybody else, and it used to baffle people because they couldn't put a tag on us and say, 'Yeah they sound just like Sabbath or Zeppelin.' Sure, we'd go out and buy other heavy records and listen to them because we were interested, but it was always separately; it wasn't like, 'We better go get this one.' You wouldn't let it influence you."

K.K. gets a bit more specific on the origin of the band's sound. "When people set the precedent, like, I have to agree with you, Deep Purple - *In Rock* is one of the greatest albums of all time. But growing up in England, there had to have been another 150, 200 bands who were equally as influential, from John Mayall's Bluesbreakers to bands like Cream, Hendrix, The Who, Rory Gallagher, Free, Blodwyn Pig; you've got Jethro Tull, Chicken Shack, a lot of blues bands, Savoy Brown, Foghat, Fleetwood Mac, great bands like Budgie who are pretty much unknown now but whatever—they did some great stuff. They were all great influences, so if you were going to compete with the likes of Sabbath or whatever, you damn well better come up with something pretty good and unique. Otherwise you're not going to go anywhere. And even if you were good, it was hard to make any headway. So we decided to come up with stuff we thought was top quality, to have quality control over what we put out, and that's stayed with us to this day."

The operative phrase in there is "compete with the likes of Sabbath," for *Rocka Rolla* distinctly bears the characteristics of a band balancing prog, heaviness, short songs, long songs and extreme dynamic range, much like the Black Sabbath of, certainly, *Sabbath Bloody Sabbath*, somewhat *Master of Reality*, and most closely, *Sabotage*, which of course wasn't out at the time.

Priest at this point were managed by David Corke and MAM. John Hinch was the band's drummer, with, curiously, Tipton providing some synth work as well as backing vocals on the album. *Rocka Rolla* was recorded late June, into July of 1974 and issued September 6th, on Gull Records. The production on the album was handled by Rodger Bain, with Vic Smith mixing. The guys in the band have always

thought the production job on the record wasn't the greatest, with Ian calling it "lame," noting that various remasters and reissues have spruced up the sound a bit. In this writer's opinion, there's very little wrong with the production, other than a touch too much intimacy and twee-ness. It is indeed warm and woody, but other than that, the bass and the treble and the placement of the instruments are all more than acceptable for 1974—it really wouldn't be until *Hell Bent for Leather* that the band would get a production where no complaints whatsoever could be levelled against it. Still, the tinkering with *Rocka Rolla* would start as early as 1981, with the exploitative *Hero, Hero* compilation receiving remixing and remastering by original producer Rodger Bain.

Back to 1974, and into the studio (Sparks and Paul Rodgers were also working there), Priest found themselves intimidated by working with the man who produced Black Sabbath. What's more, poverty had them sleeping in the van outside the studio and recording at night when the rates were down. John Hinch complained about being rushed through his percussion parts, and the rest of the band were instantly disappointed with the transfer of their aggressive, loud performances to the relative tepidness of the final product. In fact, K.K. has said that Rodger Bain had fallen asleep on the couch after having worked 36 hours straight. He then had to pop up and put the album straight to vinyl, with most of his faculties still fogged.

"Rob would come up with his ideas on a cassette," explains Hinch, looking at the songwriting process, "and we would listen to them in the van. Or we would listen to them down at Holy Joe's, the rehearsal room we used to go to. And an attempt would be made to do something with the song. Things would change, of course; words would change, the music in fact would change. The beat would be created to it. So we all had a big contribution, to actually construct a song—I wouldn't say 'write' the song—in our own way, including Ian on the bass and myself on drums. We could each totally turn a song, as we felt. We could direct its pace, its force, its whatever. We would then put it into the set, maybe have to drop one of the earlier songs, or shorten them, and then find out what the reaction was."

"Rob had free license to change the words as and when he felt, even at the gig. I mean, he would just go rambling off into a complete verse we had never, ever heard before. He was very good at ad-libbing. If we liked—or if he liked—what had changed, it would tend to stick. Although Al wasn't with the band, the songs he wrote for Mark I or Mark II Judas Priest, are there on the first album, *Rocka Rolla*, and they were good songs—they didn't get dropped because he wasn't with the band. Which is usually the case. If that would have been the situation, Al Atkins would've disappeared into obscurity. From what I can gather, he is still writing songs, and pretty good songs at that. And good luck to you."

"So off we went into the studio," continues Hinch. "And I think we recorded the album over a three-week period. We went to Island Studios, Trident Studios, and Olympic Studios. We met the Stones at Olympic Studios, I think it was, and Supertramp in Trident Studios. So yes, we were really excited; we were happening. Rodger, who had been to many rehearsals up in Birmingham, to format the songs, was there to guide us. We were totally into Rodger, because Rodger had had a history of successes with bands such as Black Sabbath. So we felt that he was the right guy to produce the album. I wouldn't say that Priest were trying to go down the line of Black Sabbath. The songs were more sensitive, I would say, and a lot quieter, in parts. Or put it this way, the set was interspersed with pleasant songs—'Run of the Mill,' 'Dreamer Deceiver,' that sort of thing."

As it would turn out, *Rocka Rolla* opens with "One for the Road," Rob penning a lyric about all of us appreciating music together, band and fan in communion with "fascinating" melody lines and "divine" rhythm. To a man, as we've learned, music was a near necessity of an escape for the boys in Priest, and this spare set of missives at least underscores the band's collective desire to make a life in music. Rob's well-meaning invitation floats atop a complex but contemplative riff that would have held its own on *Sad Wings of Destiny*, lyrics of this world and not mythical others, notwithstanding. The chorus possesses its own upper crust integrity on this fitting opener to the recorded canon of the Priest, establishing a charted course toward the relentless spirit of invention Priest would possess through the rest of the decade.

The title track is next, and it's a hard working, hard rocking charmer, easily the album's singalong anthem. Lyrically, the song is a colourful, humorous, light-hearted look at a man-eater of a woman. Stuffed with rough 'n' tumble imagery, Rob's character sketch resembles the one Bon Scott draws up for "Whole Lotta Rosie." Halford is ever the thespian, shaping his lines (even adding a bit of harmonica that is scrubbed off on select future remixes) while K.K. and Glenn give us their first highly tuneful twin lead duel, along with a Celtic melody straight out of early Thin Lizzy.

Putting the concept of the twin lead in context, Halford explains that, "You have to go back to Wishbone Ash, because K.K. was a huge fan of Wishbone Ash. As you know for the longest time Priest was guitar, bass, vocals, drums. So when the decision was made to have two guitar players, everything changed. Everything changed. I think again to some extent it set a new template for bands to go, you know when you have two guitar players in a live setting and the one plays lead, that rhythm is still roaring. It's not like this hole that suddenly appears sometimes."

"And also if you've got two distinctive lead stylistic players, thinking and playing totally different to one another, this is great because look at again at the potential. It's always great to be able to share the load in what you do no matter what it is in life. So if you've got two guitar players that are looking at each other and playing, not against each other but with each other, and checking each other out: 'I've got this great riff and if you play it this way,' you know, it's all that wonderful sense of potential and growth, that optimism that can be there by having two guitars instead of one. There are a load of great… I mean look at what Dimebag did. God! Look at what Eddie Van Halen did. Tony Iommi. But this was very important. Suddenly Priest, to the best of my knowledge, surely we were the first heavy metal band with two guitar players. And that's very important in the make-up of the music we made in Priest."

"We're always trying to make music that is interesting that you can't really second guess," continues Rob. "When you've got two lead guitar players as well, not just one rhythm and one lead, it just makes things way more interesting to listen to, from my point of view. I love it when I hear Glenn do his bit and K.K., man this is great, you know? It takes it to another level of interest and curiosity; that's the joy of having that. Sometimes it works and sometimes it doesn't. You really have to know where you are going and what you are doing when you have two guitar players in the band. You really have to have a balance to make that work. I've always had tremendous respect for Glenn and K.K. that they have been able to work that out. They've always been able to keep it even, balanced and respectful. Nobody is dominating; they are both doing very important things. Nobody's being pushed out to one side or whatever. You can only make it work through years of dedication, patience, practice, loving each other, loving the music that you make. It's a deeper story than the music or the music as the dominating thing."

"Rocka Rolla" was issued as a single in August 1974, b/w "Never Satisfied," in France, housed in a nifty picture sleeve on which the band suggest for themselves an even funkier logo than the idea fleetingly used on the jacket of the LP. Into 1975, the taut rocker was trotted out for the band's inaugural appearance on The Old Grey Whistle Test, along with "Dreamer Deceiver" from the next album. One can hear horns honking along inside of the band's performance of "Rocka Rolla;" another band working on the day had horn players, who decided to play along to Priest as a lark, the result of which indirectly got picked up by the mics.

Then Priest get progressive on us, turning in a four-parter later dubbed the Winter Suite, or less circulated, the Judas Priest opus. This collection of movements would cause no end of distress to CD reissuers who would variously leave the songs as one block, or assign partitions correctly or incorrectly. In any event, the songs proper are "Winter," "Deep Freeze," "Winter Retreat" and "Cheater," with only the latter leaping out as a semi-classic. "Cheater"'s gallop and old school Sabbath marriage of doom and hard blues positions this technical rocker as, again, a *Rocka Rolla* track that could have easily fit the trundling bluster of the band's sophomore album.

Comments Al Atkins, unsurprisingly credited with some of the songwriting on the album, "I wrote the lyrics to 'Winter' in 1969 on a tour of Scotland when the first Judas Priest got stuck up a mountain in the snow in the middle of winter. God it was cold, and we were all penniless."

"Cheater" doesn't have much to do with Atkins' contemplative reflections on winter's chill of the soul (distressed and exposed to the elements, our protagonist doesn't die, saved in the nick of time by the arrival of spring), but nonetheless, it kind of breaks the listener out of his or her reverie. In essence, the fairly uneventful preceding bits serve as a dramatic introduction to this modern metal classic. Hinch in fact grooves forcefully on this one (aided percussively by cowbell), with Glenn handling the solo and Halford providing spirited harmonica work with a jamming blues band vibe. To go with its heavy post-blues boom riffing, the song is essentially a "murder ballad," with the protagonist discovering his lover in bed with another and shooting them both dead with a "cold black metal '44. All told, for myriad reasons, the grouping of "Cheater" with the suite is now considered by the band to be an error.

Still, the Winter Suite is an admirable piece of work, with the opening track "Winter" capturing very much a Sabbath vibe, huge mournful guitars oozing all over simple but effective fills from Hinch. "Deep Freeze" recalls Sabbath's "FX" and Rush's "Didacts and Narpets," which it precedes by a year. In fact the whole 9:40 stride of the piece predicts the epic constructs Rush would adopt, with "Winter Retreat" sounding uncannily close melodically to passages from both sides of Rush's *2112*. Another touchstone perhaps is Uriah Heep's "The Magician's Birthday" given a shared sense of foreboding doom as passages ebb and flow and guitars howl in the night.

Onto side two and another leaden interlocutor on par with "Cheater" and "One for the Road" emerges. "Never Satisfied," credited to Al and K.K., feels in fact like a cross between the two. It is a track self-sufficient and powerful yet obtuse and bluesy, laced with intelligent riffs warmly recorded and modulating, atop full-bodied bass and a square-ish but not unpleasant drum sound. Other features include spare twin leads, Ian following the riff, and then a complete switch for the solo break into what is practically a new song. Over this new sinister riff and time signature is a solo heavily treated and then buried.

Says Atkins, "I wrote this song about greed and changes in life and will we ever be satisfied at all? K.K. wrote some extra lyrics at the end: 'There's nowhere left to go/This could be our last show.' I don't know what he meant by that, but he was credited for it for what it was worth." The bubbly, volcanic, iconic riffing of Glenn and K.K. can be heard in its impressive infancy here, again, this being a track befitting the brooding, medieval totality of *Sad Wings* with nary a dust-off needed, save perhaps for flashier lyrics. As alluded to, the song's closing sequence features an unwinding slow down along with deflating Sabbath-like melodic trademarks, punctuated finally with a Halford wail that predicts the much better "Victim of Changes" crescendo to come on the band's next ground-breaking record.

Come "Run of the Mill," Rob finds something to enthuse about after all these years, claiming that the "You can't go on, can't go on bit" is of a range he hasn't been able to hit for heavy metal ages. Still, the track, written by Rob, Ken and Glenn, is all but forgotten today, serving to remind us of a much more naïve and in fact adventurous time in rock 'n' roll history. The song is a dark, despondent ballad with huge Sabbath chords breaking the contemplation before a return to the bluesy stealth of the pre-Rush progressive mid-rock tip-toeing through the verse. Much of the middle of this 8:30 meander is dedicated to deft and jazzy jamming by the guitarists over a classy groove from Hill and Hinch. Toward the end, the song breaks open for an impassioned melodic close with Rob, as mentioned, singing high but back in the mix. The clean, laid-back guitar soloing is straight out of the British blues boom handbook.

"Dying to Meet You," credited to Rob and Ken, is often paired with "Run of the Mill" as a track also largely forgotten but crucial to the psychological effect of *Rocka Rolla* as somewhat uneasy and malevolent, yet progressive and almost esoteric and outside of discernible influence.

The track in fact contains the most ambitious lyric of the album, only challenged by the hugely epic "Mother Sun," partially worked up but never recorded proper for this album or any other. And not only are the proceedings violent and action-packed, they are rendered timeless and oblique, a perfect match to the tone set on subsequent album *Sad Wings of Destiny*.

Once again, the band shoot directly for a Sabbath vibe on the heavy bits, but then strum electric and stormy yet folky for the softer passages. Rob's vocal is restrained and low of register. A pleasant surprise is tucked into the back half of the track. Amusingly, like the Winter Suite on side one, a classy, modern rocker, seemingly self-contained, explodes from nowhere. This time however, it is simply the second half of "Dying to Meet You"—no extra naming required—with the band rocking like Nazareth or again, Thin Lizzy, capturing the metal potential of both the hard rock gallop and certain strains of Celtic. As well, Rob's metal god voice is back, most of this section sung high of register and high of energy. Embedded in this passage is the "Hero, hero" lyric that gives name to a Priest reissue from Gull once the band was famous enough to warrant repacks.

"'Caviar and Meths' is about two people of the same age growing up into two different directions, one wealthy, one not," says Atkins concerning *Rocka Rolla*'s closing track. The track was however rendered for the record in instrumental form. Atkins' fairly extensive original lyrics were not used, only emerging in 1988 on his *Heavy Thoughts* solo album and then on his *Victim of Changes* record in 1994.

One must again bring up Tony Iommi, for this two-minute bit of fluff could very easily have fit on *Master of Reality* instead of that record's "Orchid" or "Embryo" or even as an intro to "Solitude"—it is dead Sabbath-like in every imaginable way. "My record's a documentation of the early years of Priest, '69 to '73," said Al about working up the full-blown "Caviar and Meths" plus others, adding a little reminiscing of his Priest days. "It was strange for me to record songs I wrote over 20 years ago, but people often asked me about that material and I enjoyed doing it. It sounds like a '70s metal album! I don't think the band were aware of how good those songs were. I think I've proven that the early songs can be recorded now and they still sound great."

"Priest were all great rock 'n' roll guys," sums up Atkins, "no different than anybody else at the time. I was the oldest member of the band, and if anyone stepped out of line, I would just threaten to beat them up, which I only had to do once. So we all got on very well. They were all pretty good players early on. I know Ian Hill comes from good stock. His dad was a bass player in a jazz band, unfortunately dying young. In '69, the band had none of the members who are there now, but in '70 the lineup solidified, although we went through three drummers from John Ellis and Chris Campbell to Alan Moore, who played on *Sad Wings*. Last I heard from him, he was driving a tour truck around America for the Rolling Stones. Drummers are a breed of their own. The reason I ultimately left Priest was simply because I was the only one married with a child to support and found it hard to survive in those early days, especially without that elusive record deal."

Evaluating years later, the assembly of *Rocka Rolla*, Rob figures, "When you are making your first record, you go into the studio with the gear that you've been using on the road forever—the old amps, the old pedal boards, all the old stuff that you've got—which is great because it's vintage. People would kill to get some of those sounds now. And then of course the big dilemma when you are in the studio is how do we get that sound? How do we get the live representation of the sound in the studio?"

"We've always felt a little bit unsettled about the overall production and feel of *Rocka Rolla* for lots of different reasons. In hindsight it's a great thing isn't it? But I think in terms of the songs, it's all about the songs to a great extent. The songs will always be great, but the development of production, engineering, mixing, mastering; we learnt a lot in the studio. We've always been a band that's been very inquisitive: how does this work?, and what happens if you turn the knob over there?, and learning, learning, learning. That's an important part of being in a band in a studio. You're hoping you are working with a producer that can get you all the things that you want. Sometimes that works and sometimes that doesn't, but we learned very, very quickly."

Of note, some reissues of *Rocka Rolla* include a powerful version of Joan Baez's "Diamonds and Rust" recorded in December of 1975 at Morgan Studios, where *Sad Wings of Destiny* was being mixed, following recording sessions at Rockfield. The band would of course revisit the track two years later, placing an updated version on the *Sin After Sin* album. Still, as we peer toward the classic that is *Sad Wings*, this rendition graphically illustrates a palpable growth of confidence and skill that was being exercised by the band as they moved past the sessions that produced *Rocka Rolla*.

And so Priest—with a certain metal god replacing Al Atkins—hit the road in late '74 in support of their proud first baby. Unsurprisingly, the *Rocka Rolla* tour would be little more than a cold and rainy pub crawl around England, the band staying on the road for most of September and October, while logging a couple of dates in November and December.

Shockingly, barely a year-and-a-half down the trail, this long-suffering bar band was about to issue one of the greatest heavy metal albums of all time. But for the time being, life for Priest before and after issuing their first album was pretty much the same: a hard sell. Reviewing a September date at the Marquee, the NME's Steve Clarke demonstrated what Priest were up against, trying to push a form of music played "in a style that dates back six years—at least."

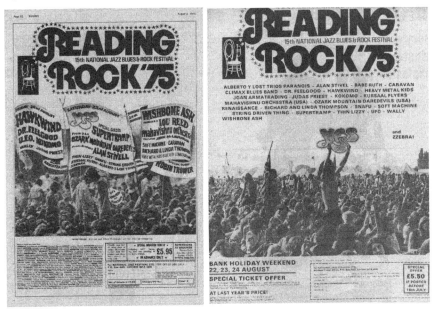

Clarke further writes, "Guitarist Glenn Tipton, a man who bears some resemblance to a younger Jon Lord, and K.K. Downing, who in cowboy hat and long, straight, blond hair could pass for an Allman Brother provided he kept his mouth shut and his fingers still, display a complete lack of originality, and their guitar hero posturing is all a bit laughable when you consider that Eric the Cee just stands still and plays. Their singer Bob Halford has that horrendous Uriah Heep-type high-pitched scream off to a tee. The rhythm section could be tighter. Oh, so tighter. Drummer John Hinch is no newcomer to professional rock 'n' roll as he used to play with that nifty blues band, Bakerloo, from whom sprang Dave Clemson. And he really ought to be playing a lot better. Still, however much reviewers hate bands of the Judas Priest mould, they usually end up figuring high on record sales. I mean, look at Budgie who, despite the fact that they hardly ever got a favourable mention in the press, managed to have a hit album. Maybe Judas Priest'll do the same."

Chapter 2:
Sad Wings of Destiny – "How many producers does it take to change a light bulb?"

Sad Wings of Destiny

It's funny, but slap a dramatic cover drenched in weighty allegory on the front of *Rocka Rolla*, and the leap between that derided album and the magnificence that is *Sad Wings of Destiny* shrinks by a third or maybe even half. Still, with history getting the final say, and only after a long look back through the wilderness of the band's tenacious poverty years, in 1976, Priest had a towering classic on their hands.

Sad Wings of Destiny was an incredible leap forward for the ill-reputed world of heavy metal, quite possibly the first record to make a real creative difference since Deep Purple's *In Rock* from six years earlier.

"Rodger Bain did the first one and obviously we didn't use him again," explains Ian Hill. "We went with Max West and Jeffrey Calvert. They were riding high at the time on the pop charts in England. They had done a pop song pretending to be Jamaicans. The song was called 'I Want to Go to Barbados' and the band was called Typically Tropical. Everybody thought they were black soul artists and of course they are not. One is Welsh and the other is a London Jewish guy (laughs). They were great in the studio and we used them as the production team. The difference is noticeable to say the least."

Sad Wings of Destiny was recorded in November and December of 1975 at the venerable Rockfield Studio in Wales, home of mates Budgie, and then mixed at Morgan, in London before the year was out. A future production star by the name of Chris Tsangarides was one of the engineers on the session. Simultaneously at Morgan, UFO was working on *No Heavy Petting*, with. K.K. also revealing that progster Dave Greenslade had asked him by to play on his album. Sabbath were working close by as well, on writing sessions for what was to be *Technical Ecstasy*.

"I wasn't in awe of them; it was just what they did," says Chris, who began the session as tape operator and rose to engineer through chance. "I'd seen them at gigs and I was really pleased to be working with them. Like I said, there I was working at the studio, and I was really pleased because I loved their sound. Basically they were rather large fans of Queen at the time, and Queen had huge productions at the time and what have you. Of course, we had nowhere near the budget to do what Queen could achieve, nor the type of studio. Nonetheless, that was the goalpost and that's what we tried to do. But it was them, really. It was their vision."

Asked about Calvert, credited as producer along with West, Chris explains that, "Basically, Jeffrey had to leave the session because he became really ill, and that's how I sort of managed to be promoted (laughs) into engineer. And Jeffrey was a pop guy. He had a hit single at the time with that 'Typically Tropical' song, this funny, sort of reggae pop song. It was a massive hit for the company, and so there was a huge budget for him and his partner Max West to produce Judas Priest, because they were on the same label. I mean, they were good technical people. They knew how things should be recorded, but weren't into rock or metal by any stretch of the imagination, so it was a very odd pairing, if you think about it. But whatever they had, whatever input they might have had collectively, we all managed to somehow piece together what has become a bit of a classic, I suppose."

Most fans and critics, as well as the band themselves, consider this to be the record on which Judas Priest discovered their sound, located their special purpose in life, came into their own. "I think we all did," agrees Hill. "The band became more prolific; it was a learning curve. We were all getting more professional. It shows to a huge degree on the second album. It wasn't just the production, it was the performances themselves."

The *Sad Wings* album cover depicts, in a glorious illustration topped with religious-fonted text, a fallen angel, "Fallen Angel" in fact being the title of the piece. "That was done by a guy named Patrick

Woodroffe," says Hill. "It was commissioned for that album. The head of Gull Records actually has the painting on the wall of his office. It is a classic album cover, one of the all-time classics."

Woodroffe (b. 1940 in West Yorkshire, England; living in Cornwall since 1964) cut his teeth doing approximately 90 book covers in the '70s. His other notable rock 'n' roll clients include Pallas, in 1983, with covers for Ross, Strawbs and Greenslade preceding his Priest work, issued in '74, '74 and '75 respectively. Woodroffe's ebullient *Sad Wings* cover would be reinforced and supported by a back cover shot of Rob Halford (they're still trying to get his name right on this one—he's calling himself Robert) in a sort of Jesus Christ pose. The album's song titles would be rendered in the same substantial gothic font to complete the gravitas of the visual presentation. John Pasche at Gull Graphics was art director on the cover (the facelift of the band's 1972 logo came from him as well), with much of the concepting coming from agent Neil French, who understood that the band wanted to present themselves as dramatic. Running contrary to Ian's comment above, it's elsewhere been said that the commissioning of Woodroffe was at the behest of label head David Howells, who, Patrick recalls, was the first person he had ever seen use a mobile phone.

On the cover, around the angel's neck, is a symbol adopted by the band, referred to by the guys as "the devil's pitchfork," or more politically correct, "the devil's cross," as if the milder descriptor would turn away sanctimonious detractors.

"We can't pat ourselves on the back and say we knew what we were doing," says Tipton, amused at the accolades heaped upon the band far too many years after the creation of *Sad Wings*. "We just sat down... there's a natural formula in the band and it just works, you know? And it just turns classic stuff out. And I don't mean that in an immodest way. Classic Priest... let me put it that way: it's the way we write and perform as five individuals. And we're just fortunate that that occurs. Rob obviously dealt with most of the lyrics. I think if you go back through our songs, you'll see that the titles are actually heavier than the lyrical content. It's a different sentiment in there than people think. But you tend to get tarred with the same brush. We used to get people outside the gigs with placards, saying, 'God will crucify you! Don't see this band! Don't go in!' And it's like, well, what have we done? Our lyrics have never been about bad things—it's just a turn of phrase."

"Musically, we've always been very versatile," adds Ian, in response to comments from Rob that he had considered Queen an inspiration. "We've covered a lot of ground in 25 years. We've done ballads that will make you weep and we've done stuff that would make you crap yourself and everything in between. So there have been no boundaries from a musical point of view."

Specifically looking at the growth of the band from *Rocka Rolla* to the second record, Halford mused that, "Like most bands, your first one or two releases are always very, very interesting because you don't really have to stride to do anything. I mean when you become successful, when you start to get a foothold in the work that you do, then all the kind of pressure things start creeping in. The suggestions, 'Oh can you do a record like this?' or 'Can you make a song like that?' So generally you can get a really good idea what a band's potential is going to be over the first two or three releases."

"That's how it was for Priest. When we made *Rocka Rolla*, sleeping in the van outside—you probably heard Glenn or K.K. talk about that because we had the night shift—we went into Island Studios at eight, nine o'clock at night 'cause that was the cheapest time we could record. We'd work all night and finish about 12 hours later and then get back in the van and sleep until it was, you know..."

"I liked that first record that Priest did because you get a little bit of a feeling of the potential of what's going to happen next. I mean even from day one, Priest was a band that would go into many, many different possibilities and many different areas. I think it's a great legacy that Priest has left as a metal band. So those first early metal songs from *Rocka Rolla* and *Sad Wings*, they've got a lot of elements of blues in them, which is where all the roots of rock 'n' roll come from. So there was a general feeling of exploration seeing what the potential was, because as it was with Priest, Glenn joined the band just before we went into *Rocka Rolla*. So we were still in a kind of new state of flux if you want to call it that."

"So I think the difference between *Rocka Rolla* and *Sad Wings of Destiny*, the band grew up very, very quickly because we'd never been into that kind of level of, okay now we're a professional band. Right up into *Rocka Rolla* we'd all got second jobs. We were doing that, like a lot of other bands do to make ends meet. So suddenly by the time we were into *Sad Wings of Destiny*, we knew that we were off and running. And the writing changed, as well as the combination of writers. Some of those *Rocka Rolla* songs were already established in the band's repertoire. So by the time we got to *Sad Wings*, there was definite growth going on."

As Ian mentioned, lack of boundaries was important to Judas Priest right from the start, but by the time they had finished this monumental second album, they had realised that too many compromises had been made on *Rocka Rolla*, and that the band's influences had been worn too prominently on their sleeves. The guys also gained confidence and piped up more with respect to production differences. Over the years, few complaints from the guys have been levelled at *Sad Wings* on the production front, with Hill going so far as to say that the sound here versus that of *Rocka Rolla* was "a hundred times" better. In this writer's opinion, the sound is marginally better, with both being quite good, if not at the high end of high fidelity for the age—*Dark Side of the Moon* and *Wish You Were Here* had been out, to name a couple, and in the hard rock realm, Aerosmith's *Rocks* is a 1976 album and it sounds fantastic. Still, the band absolutely slags *Rocka Rolla*, with Halford, as far back as 1976, joking about starting a campaign to have fans burn their copy of the album—definitely a career-limiting move when you've only got two albums to your name and no money!

"I think we really had our own sound by then, and we just got on and did it," continues Ian, along the same train of thought. "The first album, we had a tiny budget and the second album we did as well. I mean, we were on the night shift. We would work from dusk 'til dawn because that's where the cheapest hours in the studio were (laughs). We would sleep outside in the van during the day and that was the scene that was going on with those two albums."

"But the major difference on the second album is that the production was much, much better. *Rocka Rolla*, the material was fine, there was nothing wrong with that, it was just poorly put down. It was funny because Rodger Bain, he had just come off… he was just producing Black Sabbath and we thought, 'Oh god, we're onto a winner here!' But it just didn't sound good. It just didn't come across at all—no dynamics, nothing."

"That's another one that is ripe for remastering I suppose, but we don't get along that well with Gull. Maybe they've done it already; we never get to know. We've washed our hands of each other. They were looking upon us as their meal ticket. I think they were hoping that we were going to make the record company big rather than the other way around. And they did try hard. You can't knock the effort that they did put in but they just didn't have the financial clout to make it happen. When you have to record overnight (laughs)… I mean, you're young and you just do it because you want your album up there on the shelf. But when you think back with what you put up with, I don't think people would do it today (laughs)."

"I don't believe there are any musicians who weren't playing other people's stuff when they were just starting out," said Glenn Tipton just after the release of *Sad Wings*, on the subject of advancing through the stages of being a rock band. "On one hand, you need lots of exercise, I mean both musical and onstage, and on the other hand you also have to make a living. That, at that time was nothing but reproducing and if you can do both of them well enough, to a certain extent, you can both accumulate touring experience and work on your abilities. This drags on for a while, until you suddenly realise, 'Now I've made it far enough to be able to purely express what I want and think.'"

"I mean, that's also the actual turning point in the life of a rock musician," continues Glenn. "Suddenly you're not content with what you're doing anymore. You want to do your own thing but you aren't famous enough to make a living out of it. Even with our LPs you can see the exact same problem. Our first LP, *Rocka Rolla*, still shows our indecision very clearly. But the results, not very well-seen according to sales, were positive, and gave us the strength and will to do it exactly the way we wanted, now on our second LP. This is our own individual music, it carries our stamp and there are no more compromises. People may like us or not—it doesn't matter to us anymore!"

Sad Wings of Destiny, issued March 23, 1976, opens eerily with mysterious, classical-shackled twin leads that soon crash into a torrent of malevolent power chords. What emerges is an instant Priest classic. "'Victim of Changes' started life as 'Whiskey Woman,'" explains Ian. "It was written by Ken and Alan Atkins originally. It was sort of put on the backburner for the first album and it ended up being put on *Sad Wings* in a very, very revamped way. Robert put some new lyrics to it, and Glenn got involved and worked closely with Ken and changed the rhythm and the format of the song. And that one is evergreen; that is a song we could not drop (laughs). It's one of those songs that we would get lynched if we dropped it. It's one of the all-time classic songs. It's got everything, the rock, the melody, it's got two great lead breaks. It's what Priest were and are known for really, the light and shade, the heaviness, the aggression and it's all summed up in that one song, really."

Adds original vocalist Atkins, "'Whiskey Woman' was about another down-and-out alcoholic who lost her man to another woman because of her drinking habit. I got the idea for the music when listening to Led Zep's 'Black Dog' song with Robert Plant singing a passage on his own without music and then a big riff coming in. Rob Halford then put one of his slow songs on the end called 'Red Light Lady' and the band re-titled it 'Victim of Changes.' What a track! As I've often said, I was the main writer in the band in the beginning but things get kicked around over the years and lyrics are added, but as long as everyone's happy with the outcome, that's all that matters."

"Victim of Changes" indeed contains everything Hill alludes to. Priest is still somewhat Sabbath-steeped in their menacing riff-writing, but with the shifts in mood, the "Black Dog" stop/start structure, and the addition of Rob's "song" to the back section (actually a vestige from his pre-Priest band Hiroshima), this is an involved stormer of a track.

"The earlier song 'Whiskey Woman,' we'd been playing from day one," recalls John Hinch, drummer on *Rocka Rolla*, replaced for *Sad Wings* by a returning Alan Moore. "I mean, that was the demo that they'd heard, and several other companies. 'Whiskey Woman' and 'Run of the

Mill.' And 'Whiskey Woman' is a powerful, powerful song. I've still got the demos, very strong. But it wasn't recorded on the *Rocka Rolla* album; it was sort of held back. It was, of course, changed and joined onto 'Victim of Changes.' Because it was the first number of the set, it was the key song to our whole being, almost, with the dual guitars. Ken and Glenn would start off (sings it), and then it would come in really, really powerful and off we would go. It would always go down; a really good opener for us."

Reflects Halford upon "Victim of Changes" as well as his king-making vocal performance, "I think the great special feeling about 'Victim of Changes,' it's become almost the archetypal metal song. It seems to have so many ingredients of what great metal music is about. You've got incredible dual harmony lead break that brings the song in. Then you've got the crushing riff you know, and it's a very unusual rhythm and time sequence if you break the song down. It's kind of sparse as well. It doesn't have a lot going on musically if you really break it down again, but it's got all those great elements of metal."

"It's very primitive to some extent, and from a singing aspect, you are doing everything. You're doing the vocal gymnastics; you are doing the nice kind of breakdown slow passages. So it's like a metal combo of all the things that we love in that one track. And it has to be in the repertoire. It's a great title isn't it? 'Victim of Changes.' It's got the whiskey woman and all of this business, and it's about a breakup and all the classic type of attitudes about relationships put into a metal song. I mean, it still does the business all those years later—it still connects."

"Even now when I'm putting vocals down for Priest," continues Rob, "it's an instrument and you want to get the most out of the song that you are working with. So you look at all the possibilities and 'Victim of Changes' definitely put me into a different way of singing. I've never really approached a vocal that way before. To get to all of those extreme places, all the high stuff, was a first for me on that particular track. You don't really think that much about, you know... is it time to show off? Is it time to say, 'Hey guys, check what I can do?' I don't think it's about that, but about doing the best that you can do for that song. As a singer I was still learning my craft. I was still a new singer to a great extent. I was learning as much as any new band is when you are making those first releases, exploring. What is the potential? What can you do? Okay this is a different song, this is a different level of intensity, let's see how far we can push it. That's where I was going as a singer particularly on 'Victim of Changes.'"

As for the album's prevalence of twin leads, introduced in fine fashion on the record's very first track, Tsangarides compares the work of Priest versus Thin Lizzy, a band Chris would work with a few years later, a band developing their own twin lead trademark on *Jailbreak*, also a classic from the spirit of '76.

"Thin Lizzy would probably go more into harmony lines, and it would be sort of written for everything that they did, whereas Ken and Glenn, it would be occasional. It wouldn't be, 'We have to put a guitar harmony in there.' It was just, if you needed it, call us do that—that would be good. Whereas Thin Lizzy would be conscientiously writing like that. Lizzy were a rock band and Priest were a metal band. But you listen to the stuff back now, the guitar sounds are a lot clearer than they are nowadays. Now you can get loads more distortion than you could do then. But that's all you could do then—that was it. So that's as heavy as it got back then. But I'd almost call Priest a progressive band, because the tunes we were working on had that progressive element to them. They would be quite long and they would go through changes, tempo changes, key changes, moods, everything; everything would go, and it would be part of it as opposed to writing a three-minute tune balls-out from start to end. Like, 'Victim of Changes' is booming on for years, and it's got the slow part to it and it's got this solo and that part and definitely, yeah, progressive metal—there you go."

With 'Victim of Changes,' not to mention the record as a whole, being such a production tour de force, I wondered who really deserves the credit for its sonic crafting. "I think the production credit should go to the engineers and the band, together," figures Chris. "It was, you know, them having ideas sometimes and engineers having ideas. And that's really… and Max!—he was there all the way through. He did have ideas also, and he's also the castanets sound on 'Victim of Changes.' He did that with his mouth; we didn't have a castanet (laughs)."

Dave Charles too? "Dave did some backing tracks at Rockfield and that was it. A few backing tracks out there and then we moved back down to Morgan. They're all good people and they know what they're doing. But it would've been a different thing, as you would imagine, if somebody would have done it alone. And that's it. You know, how many producers does it take to change a light bulb? One, of course, and then well, it's 16, and the other 15 are to say how they would've done it."

Next up on *Sad Wings* is "The Ripper," which opens Queen-like in the extreme, fantastic with the vocal acrobatics, the twin lead, the machine gun riffing. Once the song progresses, the band settle into a grinding groove, punctuated by fastback bits laced with elegant twin leads of a classical nature. Returned drummer Alan Moore is a big part of this song's thrust and parry. Moore had come back to the band in October of '75 after a spell away with Sundance, with which he managed to record an album for Decca, 1973's *Rain Steam Speed*.

Comments Tipton on the drummer muddle, "Well, John… when I joined the band, John was the first drummer in the band, and I think both John and Alan Moore, really, had bad luck in this instance. We got management interested in the band, or record companies, and they got voted out. And I think, particularly in Alan Moore's case, (note: between *Sad Wings* and its follow-up, *Sin After Sin*), it was unfair, but we had no choice at the time. If we were going to get signed, we had to get a new drummer or we weren't going to get signed. And we were living, really, in the face of poverty at the time, where we couldn't even really afford petrol to go in the van. And some of these decisions are made for you, and it's unfair on individuals, but that's life. It could've been me, it could have been anyone. You're forced to go with it. With John, there were some personality problems. He didn't really see eye-to-eye with certain people in the band; I'm not going to say who. So it stemmed from that, unfortunately. But I'm not criticizing anybody, you understand."

For his part, Hinch claims he left the band after he had had his thumb bitten in a bar fight between he and Glenn on one side, and a number of the patrons on the other. K.K. had claimed they only kept Hinch around because he had a van and Glenn was known to disparage Hinch's drumming skills. Hinch went on to a career in artist management, dealing with the likes of Uli Jon Roth, Uli's brother Zeno Roth, and NWOBHM upstarts Jameson Raid.

Of note, Tipton collars "The Ripper" when asked about Priest tracks he is most proud of among those which he had a bigger than usual hand in creating. "It's a very Priest-like song, that I put pen to paper with. Yes, I would declare that one. Which is a bit odd though, because I never got any royalties for that, because Gull Records own it (laughs)."

But it is rare that Glenn will cop to being chief songsmith on anything. "It's very difficult to say. I mean, I wouldn't ever state and claim the responsibility for a Priest classic, because even if it's only a small part of the song that you have, that you contribute, the magic is in myself and K.K. and Rob getting together. And that can spark up a simple idea and make it into a great song. So I would never claim any of the magic for any particular song, because everybody contributes. And when we walk into a room, we never know quite the way it's going to go. It's that magic formula, really, that spark, the energy working off each other, the room suddenly lighting up, that makes Priest hit as a songwriting team."

"God! Ooh crikey, to do those effects that are on 'The Ripper' was just insane," laughs Tsangarides, asked about this compact masterpiece, Judas Priest's version of Sweet's "Action," as it were. "Just to get vocal delays to spin out of this speaker, 'You're in for a surprise, you're in for a shock, shock, shock.' That was left, right, left, right. There was no digital shit then. We had to use a separate multi-track feeding back on each track, panning it… there were like eight tracks used just to get the vocal effect. Ridiculous. But you did it, slowing down the cymbals to make them sound like gongs, because we didn't have a gong (laughs). All sorts of stuff. We would put bits of what we had, to try to make something that was, you know, 'I've got an idea, I want to do this; okay, how do we do it?' Get the paper and the glue and start doing it."

Emphasizing the Queen flourishes to the album that are very much found on "The Ripper," Chris explains that, "Rob liked Freddie because Freddie would do loads of vocal overdubs and harmonies and things. He was very into that. But I think Freddie was very classically trained, classical intervals and everything. Rob used to discover his own intervals, where you would not necessarily choose that one if you were going to do a harmony. But he did it; like, it was his style. He generated his own technique, his own sort of intervals between melody and harmony lines, that most people wouldn't use. Because he had the range to be able to do it, and also because it might not have been the exact correct one to use, because of his lack of classical training. Well, if you play this, then the harmonies are the third, but he would find a fourth or sixth or something weird, but it sounded amazing. So, naïveté definitely helped his style."

"The Ripper" opens with what is arguably the best and most graphic twin lead from the band to date, arguably trumping "Rocka Rolla" and the opening salvo to "Victim of Changes," barely cold before "The Ripper" heats up. The twin-guitar attack, generally speaking, will of course forever be a Priest trademark, even if Iron Maiden's relentless commitment to the twin-lead harmony would cause that specific idea to be associated more so with Maiden than with Priest.

"Obviously a four-piece band with the standard lineup, there literally were a lot of bands like that," notes K.K., explaining how Priest came to be a band with two lead guitarists. "So musically and visually and performance-wise, it was always a case of trying to stand out a bit, to be a bit different. When certain circumstances, a certain time came, it was decision time to consider, you know, what the lineup should be. I must add there, I wasn't really a big fan of West Coast rock, you know, when you have bands like The Doobie Brothers and James Gang or whatever. So many of those bands had two, sometimes three guitar players. So that was no big influence."

"But there were a couple of bands in the UK," continues Ken. "One band in particular was Wishbone Ash; they had a couple of guitar players and they did a few kind of harmonies, but they were less heavy. It just seemed to be a good idea at the time, to want to be like a heavier band, but with the advantage of having two guitar players with similar capabilities, both able to play lead and rhythm. That wasn't around in any abundance. I knew Glenn and I had seen them play, and I'm sure they were aware of us. And when the opportunity came around, it was just a great opportunity; it was obviously an experiment I suppose, to see if it would work. But immediately, we got together and started to rehearse some songs, and it was great, because the sound was just fuller and almost like a stereo effect on stage. We were very excited about it."

"Everything fell into place," seconds Glenn. "Priest were looking for either a guitar player or a keyboard player. And we were the same agency, which was Jim Simpson. The Flying Hat Band had almost ground to a halt, management and other problems, and we were familiar with each other, and so I think that's when the band decided, we'll approach another guitar player. And Ken... I actually remember the meeting. I was living at somebody else's house, I think, up at a place called Acocks Green in Birmingham (laughs). And Rob, Ken and Ian came around and we talked it through and I joined the band. And it was from that point onward that we were all surprised by what happened. We immediately recognised the writing capabilities, first and foremost. We just got a massive influx of ideas; when we pooled our ideas, we said many times, it was like a magical quality there."

Further on the effect that the two-guitar approach had, Glenn says, "First of all there was the writing. We're both writers and we write well together, particularly as a trio, with Rob. So that was the first thing that really gelled—suddenly we'd ignited in that area. But you've also got a lot of power, because you've got two rhythm guitars playing in stereo, if you like. If Ken takes the lead, I can play rhythm, so you don't get anything falling out. If I play lead, Ken can play rhythm, exactly the same. Then we can do harmonies, and we can do fast harmonies together, which is heavy metal harmony guitar playing, as opposed to the Wishbone Ash thing that Ken mentioned. And trade-offs are exciting as well, especially on something fast like 'Freewheel Burning' or whatever; it all adds excitement to the metal moment."

"But with me and Ken there are no rules. We just did what we wanted to do. When we have writing sessions, a lovely melodic song like 'Last Rose of Summer' might happen right next to something like 'Painkiller.' We love heavy metal, but we also love melody, and we always believed that you can do whatever you want to do. You shouldn't be restricted by the so-called code of heavy metal. You can do what you want, and I think that gave the band a lot of inner strength, really."

"Personally, I think it's very exciting when I see two guitar players in a band," adds Downing. "And when the guys are just pounding at a riff, just headbanging together, or just like trading off solos, as we did, it's an exciting thing to look at. There's a lot more energy there, seeing two guitar players thrashing at it."

"The Ripper" was launched as a single in March '76, backed with "Island of Domination," contemporary with the launch of the full album. Much happens within the track's short timeframe, its Queen-like surges making for a smart, event-rich track that indeed captures the sense and sensibility of the Victorian era in which the actual Jack the Ripper performed his dastardly deeds.

Moving on, "'Deceiver' is the title part to 'Dreamer Deceiver,'" clarifies Hill, of the two-fer that comprises the second half of the album's first side. "'Dreamer' is a ballad, and the latter part of it, where Ken does a lead guitar solo, is very much up-tempo. So we just called it 'Deceiver.' I just got on my bass parts and music bits, and the lyrics were by Rob."

"Dreamer Deceiver" features Rob singing mostly in a low croon, with a few high bits as a sort of break. Backward cymbal swishes recall Sabbath, while a bit of acoustic soloing spruces up the track. Again, the band's Queen influence can be heard in Rob's singing at the intro, as well as in the fact that when Priest played lightly, there was almost always a renaissance or medieval tone to the affair. "This is not one of mine," clarifies Atkins, who is sometimes included in the writing credits. "I think there was a riff of mine in there somewhere which I am credited to, again, for what it's worth. I love this song though and have just recorded it on my new album."

"Deceiver" might be considered the band's first recorded instance of truly modern technical proto-speed metal. Sure, the tempo is only perhaps brisk, but there's an insistent "no compromise" chug to the riff, as well as a gorgeous, recurring coda to it. The soloing is also wild, as is the hugely heavy and sinister break, over which Rob hits a pile of super-high notes. The track ends with a shudder and a lurch, after which Iommi-like acoustic wake music sends the song off on a boat down the river.

Drummer Hinch knows quality when he hears it. "I could always get very emotionally involved with 'Dreamer Deceiver.' Glenn did what I consider to be this phenomenal lead break. I used to love that song. I mean, some nights it would choke me up. It was that good."

"Halford wrote songs for Halford," continues Hinch. "He believed in the songs that he wrote. As can be seen on the first two albums, those songs, by and large, are quite meaningful, if you listen to the words. And you know, they do come from a sensitive person. Is this the difference between a star and just another performer? Despite his screaming, wailing voice, he had a powerful voice and he did have a presence on stage—he had star quality; that is undoubtable. He could

Martin Popoff

write songs, and he had this ability to adlib in the song and just come out with words that actually did make sense. I mean, from the soul, from the heart."

As mentioned earlier, in April 1975, nearly a year previous to the release of *Sad Wings*, Priest had gotten themselves on The Old Grey Whistle Test, playing "Rocka Rolla" and the then-unreleased "Dreamer Deceiver"/"Deceiver" package. This appearance featured John Hinch still as the drummer for the band, as well as a battle with the producers over how loud the band was allowed to go. Tipton can be heard prominently, if not all that accurately, on back-up vocals, K.K. is wearing his big floppy white hat and an exploded abomination of a shirt, and Rob looks thin and frail in a pink satin top and long, blond hair as he looks the camera straight in the eye and makes heavy metal history.

More history would be in the offing as the band got themselves a slot at the Reading Festival four months later. Recalled K.K., speaking to Harry Doherty in June '77, "It's the kids in the audience that count. Say for instance, two years ago, we did the Reading Festival and that to us was a major success. We were the second band on, with no lights or anything, and a lot of kids in the audience got something from watching the band. But the press was totally negative. Not a mention, when we at least deserved a mention for what we did. That's where we build the confidence up in ourselves, not just at Reading, but at gigs throughout the country. We can see their reaction."

Priest were in fact scared out of their wits in advance of taking the Reading stage given that the first band on the day, Stella, were ruthlessly bottled off the stage, posting a hasty retreat before their set was over. But in a win for quality, Priest managed to get over. The fact that they played with authority and were not rejected by the tough crowd settling in to three days in the elements just might mark as both a flag-planting for Priest as the first great baby band of a second metal wave, as well as—if projection is allowed—the birth of the New Wave of British Heavy Metal. One look at the crowd, and you could spot here, over there, everywhere, converts to a new kind of metal army essentially being handed their conscription papers. Those who weren't losing it and headbanging were clearly drinking it in, processing it, with the smartest among them realizing that the giants of metal from the first half of the decade had essentially been toppled creatively, if not yet commercially.

"Oh, it's got to be the early Old Grey Whistle Test things from the '70s," laughs Ian, asked to name the funniest of the band's video experiences over the years. "The dress alone is hysterical. We went through many, shall we say, contemporary images (laughs). The leather and studs really came about *British Steel* time, about 1980. Before then, it was a whole catalogue of different looks and styles, satins, all the... it was cool at the time, believe me. I know it doesn't look like it, but it was cool at the time, high-heeled boots and all the rest of it. We were individuals. There wasn't any real coherent plan. We didn't sit down and say, this is the image we have to portray. We just got on with our own images. It wasn't until the leather came along, when it sort of fit perfectly with what we were trying to do. The leather and studs and heavy metal were really made for one another. But we were shocked when we saw the earlier tapes recently again, what people were wearing."

"Top of the Pops everyone used to mime on there," answers Ian, asked to distinguish between the two venerable British music shows. "Basically because there were so many acts on it, it would have been logistically impossible to have everyone playing live. You'd spend a week trying to record it. But Old Grey Whistle Test was live. You would set up in the afternoon, do sound checks. And I think there were only a couple of bands on. It wasn't too much of a nightmare getting in there with changeovers. But for Top of the Pops and miming, there are pads put on the drums and you use plastic cymbals. And then there was a playback, not too loud. We were never really good at miming, I must admit. We were a live band and we hated doing it. It was against our philosophy."

In a situation reminiscent of *Rocka Rolla*'s confused partitioning, on some copies of *Sad Wings*, the second side starts right in with "Tyrant," while on others there's a two-minute baroque-style instrumental piece called "Prelude" opening the record—inconsequential and frankly illogical as an introduction, given that "Tyrant" starts simply with a riff, one unrelated in any way to "Prelude."

"Like 'Victim of Changes,' 'Tyrant,' again, is a very inventive and intense song," muses Hill. "It's a clever song with a lot of parts, a very involved track with different breaks and different tempos." "Tyrant" indeed is the album's second full-bodied epic, twin leads lacing the song with importance, Halford spitting out the song's timeless message with military precision, the whole thing feeling hugely important, again, medieval, given the biblical meter of the lyric phrasing. Says Rob, "I love 'Tyrant' simply because of its class and style and approach in its lyrics. It's an area that I want to re-explore actually. It just talks about the fact that in the world there are these tyrannical figures in life that control and terrorise people. It's a combination of fantasy and reality but I love the musical composition because it's a real rollercoaster. There are twists and turns and a lot of information and a lot of musical directions happening within that one moment."

"I wouldn't say that there's no fantasy at all in our lyrics," said Rob, on the press trail for the record in the fall of 1976. "Our lyrics are firmly bound to the present, but there's still a certain freedom in their organisation which enables the listeners to include their own fantasy, their own experience, their own environment. For example, I wrote a song with the title 'Tyrant.' In this piece I expressed my aversion towards any form of control, that is very concrete, but still the lyrics are chosen in such a way that the listener is able to find his own frustrations of this problem interpreted within this framework."

Continues Rob, in the same interview, "Generally speaking, we don't care what we do to people, I mean, which motivations we release in them. We come on stage to play high energy rock, and if people like it, then I don't give a shit what they do afterwards. Whether they go and buy guitars, or knock each other's heads in on the way home or whatever it is that they do. We've done our music, with all the power and energy we have and that's it! We also don't give a shit whether we become rich and famous through our music. Obviously, you need money in order to survive, but we'll never change our music only because we could earn this or that much more money. What we write and what we play is genuine and authentic, and it pleases us to play rock music."

"Whether we can succeed or not depends on so many factors which don't have anything to do with music at all," explained Rob. "But we try, and if it works—good; if not, then at least I can say to myself that I've tried. But I'm confident that we'll make it! Why do I believe that we'll make it? It's very simple to explain. As long as there are cities like Birmingham, cities without room for an Idol, as long as the children of these cities have to grow up between those large buildings and dirty roads, without any place for real development, it also gives birth to frustrations, which rock—or, in former times, rock 'n' roll—lets out into the open, and represents their discharge."

"We grew up in Birmingham, and our childhood wasn't any different from that, same as any childhood in any other industrial city with an insane population density. And the music we make today is nothing but the expression of these feelings and frustrations. It's like that in any form of personal self-manifestation; whether you're a painter, a musician or a writer, your whole background obviously shines through.

It's obvious that the imprinting you get from your family, your friends, your whole environment, gets a focus in your work. It's an interpretation of what you are—aggressive, gentle, sentimental or whatever. I can explain very well who we are."

"Most importantly, we're not a band like Kiss. We put on a good show, but our music comes first. When we're on stage we physically express who we are. With bands such as Kiss the music is secondary and the show is more important for them; I don't want that—that would be bad. When we're on stage, everything we do is genuine; nothing is rehearsed, apart from the music. The physical tension which comes from standing up there and doing something that the people want and feel is so big that it makes everything else disappear. You're standing there upon the stage and the audience is staring at you; no matter if it's 50 or 10,000 people, the energy, the tension which is released in us is just uncontrollable."

There's a bit of revisionist history going on, particularly with Rob, about the band wanting to be considered a heavy metal band back in 1976. Tipton at the time adamantly came out and said we are much more than that, more about light and shade, which is something Sabbath championed as well.

Ian demurs at any Sabbath comparisons levelled at a track like "Tyrant" or the band as a whole (even if outsiders might see Sabbath as the main source of the Priest sound, if one must be offered). "I don't think so, no. Although I personally admired Sabbath very highly, I don't think I own one of their albums, to be honest. I was more into the progressive side of things like Cream. Sabbath had already made their mark. We just missed that boat. They were the first wave of metal bands and we came on just afterwards. There was never any rivalry. We didn't want to sound like them and they didn't want to sound like us. We didn't want to sound like anybody else. We just wanted to get on with our own thing and do it the best we could."

If you ever wondered why Ian, who does play guitar and composes, hasn't wound up writing for Priest, he says it's because, "I do write, but not really. I have some ideas that, from time to time, I stick down on tape. Who knows? One day I should be doing a solo album, I would imagine, when I get a little time on my hands. There's no reason why not. And singing, no (laughs). It's one of those things. I can stand up there and play bass to thousands and thousands of people but you put me in front of a microphone and I freeze. I'm just one of those people that can't put myself across. Like weddings and things like that, a best man doing a speech, I'm petrified. But I'll stand up there and do a rendition of one of the bass lines if they like, no problem (laughs)."

Back to the track list, if "Tyrant" might be considered the band's sequentially second composition of a sort of metal modernity, follow-up

"Genocide" most definitely fits the bill as well, Priest hitting their stride with a succession of smart, slashing riffs. What's more, the song coughs up the title to the next album, Rob speaking like Moses on the mount, the words "sin after sin." Of note, Halford at this point has turned in a barnstormer of a vocal performance, through six tracks establishing himself as a new form of vocal technician, the prototype for countless power metal practitioners in the years to come. "Genocide" finds him adding to his legacy, playing artfully with phrasing and counter-melody.

Comments Halford, "Once again, 'Genocide' carries for me the same types of feeling as 'Tyrant' in that the language is quite strong and graphic, and I'd like to feel that some of the things that I've done with my lyrics is to be provocative and somewhat controversial and to stimulate people. When they're listening to these things, I want them to see what I'm trying to express. I leave the listener up to their own choice of what they wish to do with them. That's one of the great things I love about the power of music, that you can either take it in and enjoy it or take it to a deeper level.

But again, 'Genocide' has a very strong story to tell. Some of the great unfortunate moments in history have come from genocidal situations. But again, it's great too because of the complexity of the song and the journey that it takes you on."

It's quite interesting the timelessness of the lyrics across *Sad Wings*, save for "The Ripper," which nonetheless is pegged to a time long ago, the Victorian era. Apart from this topical track, along with a few bits of space-age imagery, the lyrics are untethered, universal and grand of theme. In fact, Glenn was onto something as early as the press trail for the album, expressing the idea that the tone is apocalyptic, going so far as to say that if you read enough of the daily news, we might be doomed. In other words, Rob could be talking about myriad points throughout history, but it wasn't lost on the guys that history might be on the verge of repeating itself.

"Well, again, very progressive," reflects Tsangarides, asked to articulate the lyrics of the album. "They're singing about tyrants and genocide and not the typical... no one had actually done that, as it happens, to that extent. There were no love songs as such. You might argue that 'Victim of Changes' was a love song, but I think it's about a crazy woman who changes her mood every five seconds (laughs)."

"But they started writing lyrics that kind of set the way forward for most of metal, doom, gloom, that kind of thing, the odd demon here or there, but it was mainly that. They loved the Sabbath. In fact, they were recording in the next studio to us—another one at Morgan there—and we would talk with them and go in there, listen for a couple hours and whatnot. Definitely Black Sabbath was the band that they liked and loved very much, and from the same area. They were not much older than them, and had gotten big-time before them. We were making *Sad Wings* during that period, '75, into '76, and they were beginning with *Technical Ecstasy*, literally in studio four, and we were in studio two. I think when they did *Technical Ecstasy*, they started there, went to Miami, and then they came back. Robert Black, the engineer for Morgan, went out to do it, and then they came back home and finished it off."

How about any inspiration from *Physical Graffiti*? After all, that's the other epic record from that period (notwithstanding Rainbow's *Rising* from '76, but issued two months after *Sad Wings*).

"Oh, that was me," says Chris. "That was my favourite of all time and I would try and replicate everything I ever heard. If we were going to do some kind of overdub, oh, I wanted to sound like it's from *Physical Graffiti*, and that's why the ambient sounds and heavy duty stuff developed for me, because that was my sort of benchmark. That's what I wanted to do. Clearly, you can't, but you go for it, and then you develop your own nonsense. But definitely major influence to me, that album."

"Purple, Sabbath, Zeppelin, yeah, I was a fans of all those bands," says Tipton, reasserting a list that makes sense as a springboard unto *Sad Wings*. "And I think Purple were a very heavy band. I think the combination of guitar and organ, Jon Lord's organ with Ritchie's guitar, just made for an extremely strong character in Deep Purple, something that had never been done before. You hear tracks like 'Smoke on the Water,' with the organ and the guitar playing the same, it really pounds out, you know? And yes, all the bands from that era all had an indirect effect upon Priest, on our composition as well."

And let's not forget, Glenn had supported Purple as part of his pre-Priest act, The Flying Hat Band. "Yes, I was a singer/guitar player. You hit the nail on the head there, Martin. An actual baptism of fire. I knew Glenn (Hughes) anyway, vaguely, and we obviously came into contact with the band, and Jon Lord in particular, I had a few drinking sessions with. But they were all good, and they looked after us, and it was quite an intimidating, scary tour. You know, before that I think we'd been playing clubs, and to get in front of 15, 20,000 people in Europe was a challenge. Everything seemed easy after that, let me tell you."

Back and immersed in the cathedral of metal that is *Sad Wings*, it seems that Priest's sort of lyrical philosophy was firmly in mind as a bit of an over-arching concept when this landmark album was being put together. Glenn and Rob both spoke at the time about how kids should get out and have themselves a good time, but also realise that the world is about to go through some catastrophic changes. Both Tipton and Halford also seemed proud of the fact that they applied a liberal dose of contrast to the album, with "Epitaph" and "Dreamer Deceiver" there to represent a terrifically quiet and delicate side of the band. In fact second to last track "Epitaph" is another nod at Queen, with Halford singing in a thespian voice over solo piano, plush Queen-like harmonies present for added class. It's a touching track, a reverie on the ravages of age, and a nice foil to the mayhem around it.

Remarked Rob with respect to "Epitaph" back in 1976, betraying a formality that persists in his manner of expressing himself to this day, "As there are no places for children in our modern cities, there's also no place for the old. And it's simply frustrating for me to see how these old human beings are forced to live their lives. From these feelings developed the song 'Epitaph.' Besides, the lyrics and texts still have strong importance for me. The words have to mean something for me; they have to help me articulate my feelings. Just like Glenn can make you happy or sad with his guitar playing, it has to be exactly the same with the lyrics. The sound must express what is stated in their logical content."

A choice bit of mayhem is what closes the album, the band turning in yet another front-edge metal classic with a riff that presents note densities raised beyond those of Priest's now maturing and declining competitors. Jokes K.K., "I think that there are probably a few innuendoes in 'Island of Domination,' obviously with Rob's lyrics and stuff. Probably better to speak to him about that song (laughs)."

Adds Ian, "'Island of Domination' started a bit differently, went through a couple of changes. 'Epitaph'… just piano and kettle drums (laughs). But *Sad Wings* as a whole was comparatively easy, being that the majority of the songs were already written. In latter days, we tended to write in the studio, which tended to extend the recording period. But in the early days, we couldn't afford to do that (laughs). Up and coming band, we had to get in there and do things as quickly as possible. So in that way, it was quite easy, and the production wasn't as elaborate as future albums. The songs were quite new, except for 'Victim of Changes' of course."

Summing up the experience of making the band's second album, Rob figures, "By the time we got into the studio for making *Sad Wings of Destiny*, the band had grown tremendously; it was a wonderful feeling of confidence for the first time. It's like you get one under your belt and that's something you don't get cocky about, but you think, well okay we think we got an idea of what we need to do next. So we went into *Sad Wings of Destiny* with more of a set plan if you want to say that. We knew that *Rocka Rolla* was a good beginning but we felt that this was the record that was going to be a bit more defining, and put a standard that we needed to achieve."

"We basically said to each other, well this is it isn't it?" reflects Rob, on the topic of the band being champions of heavy metal, still a somewhat fresh and sparingly used tag in 1976. "We are very proud to be known as Judas Priest, this heavy metal band, the heavy metal band. I think that right from the beginning we were just sending the message out in the press especially, this is who we are and this is the music that we want to be known to represent: heavy metal music."

"But in terms of press and media, there was a push-back right from the start. Immediately people were going, heavy metal? What is this, you know? If that's what you want to call yourself… K.K. has got this wonderful scrapbook with a clipping from a British music newspaper that talks about… I think they talk about *Sad Wings of Destiny* and something to the effect of, well if this is heavy metal; guys keep your day jobs because you ain't going anywhere. That's the kind of push-back that we were dealing with."

"So when you do that to Priest, you do that to most bands, you go what the hell are you talking about? You know, don't talk about us like that. Don't push us under the carpet. We are who we are. We believe in ourselves. We are strong about what we feel we want to do, and we already got this great fan base of support that is extremely important for any band obviously from day one, if you can get that type of topical connection. So there were already Priest fans going, hey, this is my band, they are a heavy metal band, don't talk about them like that, you know. So yeah, right from the very beginning that's all we wanted to be known as in Judas Priest was, we're heavy metal."

And how does the band's previous man at the microphone assess what Priest had accomplished on *Sad Wings*?

"I think it's an incredible album," figures Atkins. "I didn't like *Rocka Rolla* that much. I'd left the band, and Dave Corke, management came and knocked on my door to put this cassette in the car outside and said, 'Listen to this.' I didn't like it. I said that's not Judas Priest. That's not heavy enough, no balls in there. But the next time, I heard *Sad Wings* I thought yes, that's more like it. I thought Judas Priest had nailed it. I'm pretty sure they would say the same thing. I don't know, but they'd probably say *Rocka Rolla* wasn't the debut album they would have liked to have. Judas Priest were more of a live band. We'd been playing for four, five years, and I think they'd been better off just doing a live album. But everything's more sophisticated. But when they did *Sad Wings* they got that right. They got that spot-on. It'd already set the benchmark for all the albums they were going to do. There was the progressive side of the band and also the heavy metal side of the band. You could see them coming out, and yet still, it was probably not the third album but maybe even the fourth album they did when they finally discovered their true sound and the heavy metal sound they wanted."

Sad Wings of Destiny crept to No. 48 in the UK, but remains uncertified in the US despite many industry-watchers believing that surely the album has surpassed half a million in sales by this point—it is surmised that the patchy label release history in the US has led to a lack of effort in getting a gold certification taken care of. Astonishingly, the esteemed but usually anti-metal Rolling Stone ran a review of the album upon its release, with Kris Nicholson calling the record, "chock full of ear-piercing vocals and the thick, sensuous rhythms of a Fender Stratocaster," adding that the album "recalls the intensity of the Deep Purple of *Machine Head*." The short review closes with "Judas Priest have a fair chance of success through copying Deep Purple, especially since their antecedents are no longer contenders for the throne."

Key point there from Kris. *Sad Wings of Destiny* did indeed represent a changing of the guard due to the fact that the old gods were all busy letting down the side, although, in effect, this was more of a transitory blip, with the bigger more pronounced deluge of fine and purposeful heavy metal records coming soon with the New Wave of British Heavy Metal. Still, representing the mid-'70s, Priest, Rainbow, Scorpions, and maybe Riot, Legs Diamond, Moxy and Teaze (if anybody noticed) but also Kiss, Aerosmith and Ted Nugent... these bands carried us over up to and before metal kicked in for real in 1980, only to thrive for a solid decade, all of the '80s, in a rainbow of colours.

Of note, Kris Nicholson's review would have been predicated by the fact that the album saw US issue, on the small Janus label. There is no "Prelude" to "Tyrant," and Al is not credited on any track. In Canada, the album was issued on fledgling indie Attic Records. Side two indeed opens with "Prelude," at 2:02, credited to Tipton. Al Atkins is credited only on "Victim of Changes." The original UK Gull issue also includes "Prelude," with Al credited on "Victim of Changes." Curiously, on the back cover of the UK Gull issue, side two is listed before side one. On all issues, the back cover shows "The Ripper" as "Ripper."

"Absolutely didn't have a clue, except I really liked it," sums up Chris Tsangarides, asked if he could tell at the time that he was in the midst of what would become one of metal's most iconic albums in history. "I liked the tunes, but like anything you ever do, you just don't know. It's not for me to say that it's iconic or legendary or classic, any more than the rest of the world really. At the time, you're just making the best record you can with what's available to you. And that was basically it with them. But I knew it was special because I really liked it, and I'd had this sort of gut feeling about, oh, I like this, it should do well. And it's about as basic as that, really. That was the barometer I used. I think it's their influences that made their music what it was. You know, Rob was way into Queen. So he wanted to do Freddie Mercury stuff. The others… Glenn really liked the Isley Brothers, so you want to get like on some of the songs, like an Isley Brothers guitar sound, you know, heavily phased, chorus guitar, and play solos with that, and that sounded brilliant too. And we used keyboards as well, the gong effect I told you about, all sorts of stuff that was lying around the place. To make the record what it was."

Back in reality, the band hit the road broke but with a hell of a record on its hands. Recording had been conducted under the harshest of circumstances, the band allowing themselves one meal a day, and eventually getting jobs to support themselves after Gull wouldn't cough up anything for the band to live on. Glenn became a gardener, K.K. worked (and mostly shirked) in a factory and Ian drove a delivery van.

Before the album actually dropped, in early '76, sporadic touring had taken place, Priest supported by the likes of Tuesday, Sounds, and Ray Phillips' new band, Phillips being Budgie's ex-drummer. A trip to the US supported by Motown/Tamla, who was attempting to get into white rock 'n' roll, fell through, with summer being filled in by a jaunt around England, at one point, as the undercard to Stray and Babe Ruth. As mentioned, October saw the return of Alan Moore (recording of the album took place in November and December of '75) as the band ploughed on, sharing stages with Pink Fairies, Reds, Whites & Blues and Consortium, with a memorable gig logged on December 28th at the Roundhouse with Stray and UFO co-headlining, Priest and Strife as support.

After the release of *Sad Wings of Destiny*, a headlining tour began in April 1976, through May, with a single Roundhouse show in June, supported by Isotope and Alcatraz. And that would be it for the band's modest, limited, anticlimactic but character-building *Sad Wings of Destiny* tour. That would also be it for the band's relationship with Gull Records, and good riddance, as far as the guys were concerned.

But still, despite their high quality headbanging, Priest were still banging their heads against the wall as far as the official live notices went. A review in the NME came with the title, "Judas Priest fail to live up to the presentation." Following, writer Chas De Whalley at least found something good to say about the Metal God. "With a crash of firecrackers, Judas Priest take to the stage. Vocalist Robert Halford makes an immediate electric impression, silhouetted against the smoke like a Machiavellian Marat Sade and a rock 'n' roll Iago in assorted satins and leathers. His silk kimono and a long red cane flashed through the air like the Vicomte's horsewhip. There's a very subtle and intensely adult menace in this man's imposing stage presence and his seductive and cajoling croon. His heavy metal falsetto shriek him in a class of his own."

"Unfortunately, the rest of this five-piece Birmingham heavy band failed to measure up to Halford's magenta-lit magnetism. I watched Judas Priest from up front, among the shaking heads, and the vicarious peace signs, as lead guitarists K.K. Downing and Glenn Tipton powered through 'Tyrant,' 'Genocide, and 'Rocka Rolla' from the first two Gull albums. The sheer volume alone was, naturally enough, physically exciting. Sadly, they frequently crossed over into that twilight zone where the already unoriginal riffs and runs broke down into a sort of painful cacophony, the kind of thing I thought was sacrificed long ago at Black Widow's last Sabbat."

Early local newspaper notice for a band "boasting perhaps the largest following of any up-and-coming 'Brummies' at the current time. Left to right: Ian Hill, Ken Downnng, Chris Campbell, Alan Atkins.

French issue picture sleeve for the debut Gull single, "Rocka Rolla"/"Never Satisfied." The home country issue was non-picture sleeve.

JUDAS PRIEST

Judas Priest are a hard-working Birmingham band, boasting perhaps the largest following of any up-and-coming 'Brummies' at the current time. The interest is aroused by their loud, adventurous music and visual stage presence, almost harking back to the freaky, progressive days of a few years ago. A very exciting live band.

The Band consists of :-

KEN DOWNING (lead guitar)
IAN HILL (bass guitar)
CHRIS CAMPBELL (drums)
ALAN ATKINS (vocal)

Watching Black Sabbath leave for America: drummer Christopher Louis "Congo" Campbell, K.K., Ian and Al.

Studded belt and studded wristband. It's a start. Oklahoma, 1978. © Rich Galbraith.

Classic K.K. in black satin and studs. © Rich Galbraith.

Company promo shot. Left to right, K.K. Downing, John Hinch, Rob Halford, Glenn Tipton, Ian Hill.

German picture sleeve version of "Better by You, Better than Me." The b-side is "Invader."

Glenn's trademark would later be a mix of red and black leather. Here he is in a red one-piece, 1978. © Rich Galbraith.

Rob in denim. © Rich Galbraith.

High priest of the fat strings, Ian Hill, 1979. © Rich Galbraith.

A band in transition.
© Rich Galbraith.

Five beers for the band, please!
© Rich Galbraith.

K.K. with Flying V; the other big supporter of this iconic axe in
'70s hard rock was Michael Schenker. © Rich Galbraith.

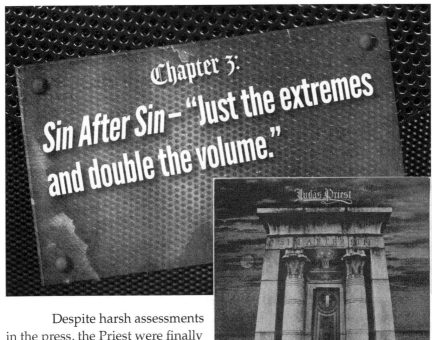

Chapter 3:
Sin After Sin – "Just the extremes and double the volume."

Despite harsh assessments in the press, the Priest were finally garnering some attention, at least in the underground, as something uncommonly heavy and serious, all within a heavy metal time when Sabbath was on the wane, Deep Purple was getting funky (and then breaking up), and the locus of hard music had shifted to sunnier, fun-fuelled American bands such as Kiss, Aerosmith, Boston, Heart and Ted Nugent (notwithstanding the alchemical railings of Blue Öyster Cult and Canuckleheads Rush).

But the band also had to deal with punk rock, more acutely felt because they were stuck in the UK watching it burn brightly. Already irked at press indifference to their band, nonetheless when talking to the press, they could circle the wagons and fly the flag. As Rob Halford told Harry Doherty from Melody Maker back in late '76, "As far as being 'new' is concerned, let's face it, nothing is really new today, but we certainly have the ability to create a particular sound, and we feel the type of sound we create live and on record is a unique sound. Trends are set by the media. People are always looking out for what they think is a new thing. If the media hadn't suddenly taken up on punk rock, it would still be totally in the wilderness and obscure, but because it's there, everybody wants to know about it."

"A lot of people say that rock isn't fashionable, but I disagree entirely," added Tipton. "The punk rock thing is terrible, absolute rubbish.

My theory is that you get your fans who are adaptable and they can like a lot of other things as well. But then you've got this other percentage of music listeners, if you like, continually after something new. They're a separate set of people, and they'll continually absorb new sounds and discard them. They eat them up. These trendy bands are all short-lived. There are a few, such as Roxy Music, who were both trendy and original, with so much ability that they lasted. The rest who haven't particularly got a lot of talent are just used by the management and the press until they get sick of them, and then they just discard them. Then you've got your rock giants, like the Stones who will always be around, because the rock population is still there."

"We suffer a bit because of these trendy bands," groused Rob, "but the thing is that we are going to be around for the next five or ten years, so at this particular stage, we don't really mind. Rock will always be the backbone. You've got rock there, and then you get all these little things spinning off left, right and centre. Rock will keep going on forever."

A year later, also speaking to Harry Doherty, K.K. showed himself to be at least a bit more receptive to the charms of punk rock. "I certainly don't think that rock is dead. To me, punk is rock. There are hard-working rock bands now who will be successful in the future. Every big band has gone through what we have gone through. That's the way it works. I mean, I saw the Sex Pistols, and I got something from the band when I saw them, a lot more than I thought it would. From write-ups and reviews and things, I had the impression that they didn't know how to tune their guitars, let alone play them. But when I got there, I found that not only were they in tune, but they packed a wallop. It was good, raw rock material and it created a reaction. If anything, I would say that with bands like Led Zeppelin and ourselves, our music is like an advancement from their music. Because their rock is basic and so much more direct. In the past, I've written some things that I thought were too direct musically, so I've just forgotten about them. So are they new or are they going back? I like their directness and musical punch. We're not far detached. They haven't left us behind, though, musically, we may have left them behind."

For their gumption and ambition, Judas Priest were rewarded with a new record deal, and applause to the buyer, CBS, for noticing that talent deserves exposure. And so they threw Priest a bone, giving this ambitious band a major label contract, removing the boys from the skinflint machinations of the guys at Gull.

Crucial to this turn of events, the boys had canned their previous management, signing on with David Hemmings of Arnakata Management, who drove the move away from Gull, essentially a breaking of their contract, which resulted in the band losing all rights to that material and any demos that might be found scraping about. It was in fact a Brit transplanted to America, Paul Atkinson, founding member of The Zombies, then 30 years old and in A&R in the States, who would sign the band to CBS, the label shelling out a £60,000 advance with which to forge the band's new collection of pliable, space-age heavy metal anthems. In contrast, Gull's budget for the band's first two albums was £2000 apiece.

And Judas Priest are the ones who are selling it. From Birmingham, England, Judas Priest have been riding high on the charts in their native land. **Now they're bringing their** devilish brand of rock and roll to America—on their first U.S. tour and on their debut Columbia album, "Sin After Sin."

Judas Priest—Summer Tour 1977

17	Civic Center Amarillo, Tex.	22	Memorial Coliseum Corpus Christi, Tex.	2	Fox Theatre Atlanta, Ga.
19	Texas Hall Dallas, Tex.	28	Music Hall Oklahoma City, Okla.	5	Municipal Aud. Charleston, S.C.
20	Music Hall Houston, Tex.	30	Coliseum Jackson, Miss.	6	Freedom Hall Johnson City, Tenn.
21	Municipal Aud. San Antonio, Tex.	**July**		7	Rupp Arena Lexington, Ky.
		1	Civic Center Dothan, Ala.	9	Busch Stadium St. Louis, Mo.

There's no redemption from Judas Priest's "Sin After Sin."
On Columbia Records and Tapes.

"Well again, those were kind of hard times," says K.K., remembering all too clearly that there still wouldn't be much dosh for years to come. "We were going between record companies. Lots of things were happening, changing producers, changing studios. We were still struggling to get the band's sound onto record, onto vinyl, so to speak. Obviously it's much easier now with today's technology. But we were still struggling to do that. And changing drummers, I might add as well. But we were doing well. We were still trying to find our feet, really, with those early recordings. A little bit of frustration that we couldn't get the sound of the energy and the strength of the band on record. Obviously, being able to remaster those recently, it's helped us satisfy ourselves a little bit."

"We've had to do it the hard way," said Tipton at the time, also from the chat with Harry Doherty. Glenn was defending the band's decision to hold back on the shows for a bit, make the band a little rare, and whether it was a factor in the new deal or not, it must have given the band a bit of space for a re-think. "There's a lot of shortcuts and we haven't had any of them. We've just had to keep playing until we've reached the point where it now costs us a phenomenal amount of money to go out. We believe in putting a good show on. It cost us more money to get out now than we're getting. We're at a standstill at the moment in England where we're going to wait until we've got a completely new show together before playing again. We know we can go out now and do, not a 40-date tour, but a good 15-date tour, give the people something new. We feel that we've achieved what we set out to achieve this year."

"Personally, I'm against shortcuts anyway," seconded Rob. "I think bands should serve an apprenticeship in the small clubs, as in any job. You serve an apprenticeship; that's where you get your experience of audiences, how you perform on stage, how you work together, and then you go on. During the last two years, we've gone from literally doing every club in the country on a small level, from pub rock venues to fairly small clubs to

JUDAS PRIEST HAS SIN FOR SALE.

Judas Priest, a new group from the industrial heartland of England, is selling sin on their new album, "Sin After Sin." But don't worry, you'll still be saved. It's pushing, driving, insistent music that dulls the brain but delights the senses.

Produced by ex-Deep Purple bassist Roger Glover, "Sin After Sin" explores a primitive electric energy which bubbles beneath the surface of contemporary English music. It's a diabolically attractive proposition.

"Sin After Sin," fiendishly ingenious sounds from Judas Priest.
On Columbia Records and Tapes.

the stage now where we can fill fairly big town halls in certain areas of the country. We've not taken any shortcuts. We've got set ideas as far as advance is concerned. We could probably go down the Marquee for three nights if we wanted to, but we don't want to do that, you know. We've got set standards, which we want to keep. We really don't want to go out and plug ourselves to death. We want to become successful. We want to make some money out of it. It's a job. It's a profession, right? We feel that everything we've done in the past two years has been one more step higher on the ladder. That's why we're not going to bother in England now until next January. I think the fans will have the intelligence to understand that reasoning."

Asked whether the band was indeed going through a big "re-think," K.K. says, "I guess we probably did, because we were a bit disappointed. *Sad Wings of Destiny* was a very successful album for the band, you know, and we felt very let down and disappointed in the record industry, because Gull Records, really, weren't doing what they should do for the band. They were kinda milking us a little bit. So obviously we moved to what was then CBS, which was great. But we really didn't know what we were supposed to do, I don't think, musically, to try to achieve success. It was a dark period in the band's career, is what I think. And I think it shows with the songs on that album—if you listen to it, it's really very dark (laughs) and quite moody. And I think the title fits: *Sin After Sin*."

Mused Rob about the new deal, in conversation with Sam Dunn, "It's like any band, if you go from those early moments of an independent label it's great because firstly you have an opportunity to make a record and to get your record sent out wherever it might go. But there are certain limits. Gull was a subsidiary of Decca Records, which were a huge label at the time, but I think that label could only do so much because they only had so many resources. Didn't really fully understand the metal sound, the metal experience, the metal journey that we wanted to go on."

"And then the famous stories, we went down to Gull one day and we said, "Can you help us out?" Like we're broke and we're still doing day jobs, so if you can give us like 25 quid each a week, we can stay together and make another record. They went, no. No, can't afford it. So we were just... what's going on? So looming on the horizon on the Arnakata Management, David Hemmings; all those great people were ready to kind of come in and help the band. Help us grow up because they can see the potential, and take us from that small little label onto CBS, Columbia, a worldwide label with America."

"Oh my God, this is just unbelievable, you know? So there was a tremendous amount of excitement there as we moved to a world class label. It was very important because it gave you the... just the inspiration and the energy to keep going, because suddenly you knew. Okay, well, now we're going to go to a lot more places we couldn't do before, and there's this potential for growth. Every band needs the motivation of growth and development. You can't do it all yourself. I think your music is going to go that way to a degree, but if you are surrounded by people that are going, "Come on, lads, let's go, let's all do this together," that's wonderful. That's tremendously inspiring. So that transition onto CBS was vital."

Turns out that the transition to the band's third record represented a bigger re-think than first impressions would warrant. In fact, the band aborted their first sessions, leading the label to call on Deep Purple bassist and up-and-coming producer Roger Glover to bail out the production. "We had started the album ourselves and the record company didn't think it was a good idea," recalls Glenn. "Actually we started with another guy, Jeremy somebody. And in those days, we had to listen to the record company, so they suggested Roger. But we didn't mind that suggestion because Roger had always been involved with production, and had been with Deep Purple. It was the first album we did with CBS as well, so they had a lot of influence on us at the time. You know, I think when you look back on anything, you can be critical about it. At the time we were happy with it."

"As far as I was concerned, it was a career move," muses Glover, on tapping the Priest job. "The band wants me to produce them, so I went okay. They weren't that well-known but they were well-known enough. They had two albums out before that, and it was actually the record company that approached me. 'We want you to produce Judas Priest' and I said fine, and I went along to a rehearsal. It was at Pinewood Studio in London and I went along and said hi, introduced myself. It's very odd meeting five people for the first time. You don't know who's who and who's what."

"Anyway, they set up and I said, 'Play me some of your stuff.' And they played various songs that they were writing and I'd make various suggestions or noises of encouragement, 'That riff sounds good, but you should put it after the punch line.' That sort of thing. And I got the feeling that they weren't really interested in what I had to say. And it was kind of a strange atmosphere. So at the end of the day I said, 'Come on lads; let's go have a drink.' So we went down to the pub, and I laid my cards on the table and I said, 'Look, I get the feeling that you don't want me to produce you.' And they said, 'Well actually, we're glad you brought that up because that's the truth. We don't want you to produce us.' And I said fine. And they said, 'It's the record company. They want you and we don't want anybody. We want to do it ourselves.' So I said, 'Look, I don't really want to produce anybody who doesn't want to be produced, so let's just call it a day.' And they were like fine, okay. And that was the end of it; we parted on good terms."

"And I called up management and said, 'It's not going to work out; they're not interested in having me as a producer.' And that's all there was until a month or two later when they were actually in the studio and I got a call begging for help basically. They'd been in the studio for like two weeks and in the process they had sacked the drummer and they had six studio days left. So I got in the car and went down to the studio and said, 'Well, play me what you've got.' And they played me what they had and it was awful. There was nothing really worth salvaging. And I said, 'Right, what do you want to do?' And they said, 'Well we have six days and we're going to get Simon Phillips,' who I happened to know anyway, and I said, 'Right, well, we're going to start from scratch, and we're going to do it really quick' and boom, we did. So we recorded everything again. But it was done really, really quickly and listening to it now, there are things I would change in an instant, but then again I think that about most of the albums I've been involved in."

"I think they really found their genre after that," continues Roger. "What metal is to me is a kind of… if you take a hard rock band, any hard rock band, doesn't have to be us, but something that came out of the '60s, when you had an eclectic mix of musicians with all sorts of musical influences, and you take the extremes of that, and just the extremes and double the volume, and simplify it all—that's what heavy metal is. It's the extreme end of the screaming part and the loud part and the riff part, and it doesn't take into consideration the jazz, funk, the pop, the folk, the classical. It's one-dimensional music. And sometimes you get strength by being that simple and Judas Priest were that kind of a band. They're obviously good musicians, but good musicians do not great albums make. Great writers make great albums. And they were finding their feet. They found their feet and they became heavy metal with the whips and chains, which eventually overtook them. No question, Judas Priest were a precursor of the heavy metal thing."

"You know, I got the job on the basis of Nazareth's 'This Flight Tonight,' which was basically my arrangement. Nazareth had run out of songs. They were going to do 'This Flight Tonight,' but they were going to do it the way, I don't know, Rod Stewart might have done it on a solo album. And I said no, that's kind of boring, let's do something different. So I came up with this whole chugga concept and the arrangement for it. And it was on the strength of that, I think, that Judas Priest wanted me to do 'Diamonds and Rust,' which, you know, if you listen to it, you see the similarities. So I can't remember particularly what suggestions I had."

Ian Hill simplifies but basically corroborates Roger's version of events. "It was the first album we did for Columbia and the budget was bigger for one thing (laughs) so we could spend more time. We also had Roger, of course. Everything seemed to run quite smoothly. It was a bit strange working with Roger at first but once we got to know him and vice versa, things seemed to go along—easy-going guy, smashing bloke, really. It was also the first album that we ever used a session drummer on. Alan Moore left us for one reason or another, and sort of left us in the lurch—we had an album to record and there was no one to help us put it down (laughs)."

"Roger's a great guy," notes Tipton, "and when we were working with him, he was very tired a lot of the time. He was going through a divorce, one or two things. But he's a legend, and Purple was one of the first bands I supported, as a guitarist and singer as a three-piece, throughout Europe, and I still get hot flushes when I think about it. That was my real baptism of fire. But I've got a lot of respect for Roger, and Purple were always one of my favourite bands in the early days. So we've got a lot of respect for him; he was a good guy to work with."

The drummer shooting sparks and flying high all over what was to become *Sin After Sin* was a young, curly-haired prodigy by the name of Simon Phillips, who would go on to all sorts of high profile gigs after Priest, most notably The Who and Pete Townshend solo. "When Simon Phillips came along and started to play, it was amazing," recalls Ian. "He was only 20 or something, only a kid and only a small bloke anyway, but he was absolute dynamite. He got behind this enormous drum kit, and you can hardly see the bloke and you're giving hand signals to him and everything and he started to play and he blew us away. And of course that set a precedent then. We had to go find somebody who could replace him (laughs). Unfortunately Simon couldn't join the band; he had committed himself to Jack Bruce. No, I got along great with Simon. We wanted him to join the band, but as I said, he had previous commitments so he couldn't even do the tour. So we had to search high and low to find someone as good as Simon. And of course, Les Binks came along, and he was in excellent standing."

Glenn concurs on the subject of Simon. "Simon is fantastic. At the time we were between drummers and we needed somebody to play on an album. I mean, he's magical; really you just can't fall out of time with him; he's so solid and capable of so much. And of course Les came in and filled Simon's shoes, which were big shoes to fill. And Les did it admirably, but Simon is magical. And at the time, we did ask him if he wanted to come out and tour, but he had other commitments, so we just had to leave it at that."

"It was in the days when making music and recording music was really fun," recalls Phillips on his brief collaboration with the band. "There were no machines, no metronomes, no ProTools; there were 24 tracks, but there weren't 24 tracks, if you know what I mean. No digital reverb, and you all just sat in a room together and you played. Roger Glover was producing it, and it was really down to him that he asked me to do it, because I played on his solo album *Elements*, which also had Cozy Powell on it, and also the original Whitesnake album. And we went to a rehearsal room for one day, and we started playing. There wasn't listening to any demos, because there weren't demos. Glenn just had all the songs in his head, and we went through them. In those days, not everybody had demos. With Pete Townshend, he had a finished record and used to play that to the band (laughs). Yes, he made incredible demos. But with Priest, I would play along, and when there was a riff to learn, we would stop, he'd show me the riff a couple of times and we would carry on. And that's how we moved it along."

"We moved into Ramport Studios, and Glenn's guitar rig was loud, and the whole drum kit was resonating because of it, and the bass player was next to me as well—same setup as the one I had with Gary Moore doing *Back in the Streets*... fantastic. They had all their stage gear, and Rob Halford was in a booth, actually, the vocal booth where Roger Daltrey used to sing all those songs. And that's how we made the record. Very straightforward, simple and fun; it was great."

"They did ask me to join the band, but I had actually joined a band with Jack Bruce, and we had just made a record for RSO Records, and I was actually a member of the band, so I couldn't really split after making the record (laughs), you know what I mean? So that was the reason I didn't join them. And it's funny, because I bumped into the tall guy who plays with them now, Scott Travis. I bumped into Scott in S.I.R. in Los Angeles years ago. They were rehearsing next door and I was rehearsing with Joe Walsh and Keith Emerson and John Entwistle (laughs); we were putting a project together. It was funny, because I hadn't seen any of those guys since 1977. And here we are 1990; it was amazing, not actually running into each other for so long."

Further reflects Phillips, "It was the beginning, yeah... really the beginning of heavy metal, I guess. But obviously compositionally, I didn't write any of the songs. But when it came to doing any playing, I had always been given pretty much free rein. And I think that's why people ask me to play on their records—because they know they're going to get something pretty radically different. It's not conscious at all. It's very strange; I hear a song and then I play it, like I say, the way I figure it should be. The only thing that I used to find... I mean, we're going back to the '70s, early '80s, where I used to do a lot of sessions, and a lot of records, and I was pretty—as Pete Townshend used to call me—anarchic. And I think that's why he liked the way I played because I did things that weren't safe; I really pushed the envelope."

"And what I really used to do—because I enjoyed many types of music—if I was playing in a situation that was rock 'n' roll or metal... It wasn't called metal back then, but maybe heavy rock, but I was always trying to make it sound funky. Because I loved Band of Gypsies, and I loved the way Buddy Miles played with Hendrix. To me, it was the funk factor that really made it work. What it does is it grounds and puts groove to heavy rock, which, most people were pretty light on at that time. Ian

Paice with Deep Purple was fantastic, that's what I love about his playing, because it wasn't heavy rock, but he always had a solid groove. John Bonham with Zep, same thing."

"But there were a lot of rock 'n' roll bands where the groove was... it came from a different place, and that's what I wanted to do. So while I was playing heavy metal with Judas Priest, I was thinking Bernard Purdy, Buddy Miles, Sly, you see what I mean? Actually, nobody had any idea that's what I was thinking, but that's what I was thinking: let's place it in a groove that is more funk than metal. Now obviously, you probably can't hear that, but what it does is gives it a really good grounding. And vice versa: when I used to do sort of the funk sessions—I played with Edwin Starr, Olympic Runners and all sorts of things like that—I used to put more of a thrashy rock 'n' roll approach to it, more splashy high-hats, more openness, especially the open sound, which I really like, which is totally wrong for funk. You see what I mean? That's where, I guess, in terms of any influence or any style, that is what I brought to it."

Asked about the extent of his visit with the Priest, compared with his other famous metal session, namely the first Michael Schenker Group album, Simon says, "Oh God, we did one day's rehearsal and we were in Ramport for a week and that was it. And I had my 20th birthday; I do remember that (laughs). It was February '77, and I don't think it was any longer than a week. And with Michael Schenker, we did one rehearsal, one afternoon, and the record, again, was probably about a week. Typically in those days, tracking used to be seven to ten days."

"Oh, they were fine! They were doing great," recalls Simon, asked about Priest's chemistry during his tenure. "This is the other thing; when you get down to it, every band is made up of one or two key people. They are the writers, they know where everything is. And it's no slight to the other guys; they are the backbone of the band, but they tend to be a little quieter, because they know where the music is coming from. The problems you get, usually, are with the main artist, which in this case is Glenn. He's the guy that really drives it. Rob obviously had a hand in all the lyrics and a big part of the writing, and K.K. was actually in the control room most of the time with Roger Glover."

"And Roger... the most friction you will get, will be between the producer and the main guy in the band. Every single album you make, there are differences of opinion and it can get quite heated, quite passionate. There's nothing wrong with that, as long as it doesn't get unproductive. And normally, a good healthy disagreement and a rethink is not bad, because sometimes you're both going down the wrong path. But in terms of that project, everybody was great. I got on very well with the band. I knew Roger as well, so maybe in some ways, it was quite handy because we had one guy, like myself, who was very experienced in making records, and being in that position, joining a band for a week... that was sort of what I was doing quite a lot of, I guess (laughs). In a certain way, I could be the leveller or the catalyst between the producer and the lead guy."

"Yeah, that may be coincidence," reflects Simon, on the idea that his style really propelled the band forward into the technical dexterity and speed demonstrated all over the present record but even more so on *Stained Class* and to a lesser extent, *Killing Machine*. "If what I contributed changed what happened to them, then that's fantastic, that's great. I can't take the credit for that, really. Because Glenn wrote the songs and I just played them from my perspective and from the experience I had playing music."

Judas Priest's third album *Sin After Sin* would hit the racks in April 1977, on CBS in the UK, Columbia in the US and Canada, and Epic in Japan. As mentioned by Roger, rehearsals for the album had been conducted at Pinewood Studios, known for James Bond and *Superman* production work. Accommodations were at a nearby convent, with nuns running a bed and breakfast. Apparently, perhaps taking a liking to the band's religious name, they had asked Priest to play at a garden party they were putting together, a gig that had not come to fruition.

The album would be recorded in January '77 at Ramport Studios (which was owned by The Who) in Battersea, with Mark Dodson as engineer helping out Roger. Mixing would take place at Wessex Studios, Highbury, London. For artwork, CBS art director Roslav Szaybo hired on Irish-born art school grad Bob Carlos Clarke as illustrator—Clarke went on to become a top erotic photographer, working mostly in black and white, and had produced five photography books, before dying in March 2006 at the age of 57. Cause of death was reported as suicide by a leap in front of a London commuter train, although his publicist has deemed the death accidental. Before his worldwide fame, he would also work on cover art for Barclay James Harvest, Band of Joy, Pete Townshend, Ric Ocasek and Bonnie Tyler.

Once inside the record, the listener got to hear the new, gleaming, impressive and finessed Judas Priest through opening track "Sinner," a song one might liken to Deep Purple's "Flight of the Rat," given its hummable, serviceable chug, its immediacy and its melody. Come break time, Rob raises the apocalyptic fire and brimstone tale to new heights of urgency, accompanied by riffing that is elegant then downright elegiac. A gorgeously groovy mellow respite occurs, strafed by bluesy, noisy guitars, before an eventual return to the previous premise and an intelligent heavy metal rise to crescendo.

"Sinner" is ultimately an epic without resorting to epic length, its impressive religiosity positively springing from Rob's vocal performance and arrangements. All in all, it's a fiery yet measured and sophisticated way to open the band's major label debut. Ian is wont to joke that "Sinner" was Ken's "party piece" given the theatrics he would inject into the back section of the song when performing it live to the max, Hill adding, "That's another epic song, a production piece. There are two or three different solo parts in it, intricate rhythm parts. It was a very involved track to put down. And it's another one we played on stage for a long time."

"We always tried to be different," says Hill, further on "Sinner" and those times. "With every album, we always tried to take at least one step forward, make it a little bit better, a bit different from the previous one. But obviously, it always sounded like Priest with the same musicians, same vocalist. We were really conscious of saying, oh yeah, we've got to do this, got to do that, to stay ahead of the game. It was a natural thing that came to us. Obviously, you listen to other people's material but I don't think we looked at it from a competitive point of view at all."

Explained K.K. of his approach to soloing, "Pretty mad and way out, really. I try to go to the areas of the instrument that hopefully no man has ever gone before (laughs). I always try to be as innovative as I possibly can, and try to generate as much energy and excitement as I can. And I must say, the great Jimi Hendrix… I knew how that affected me. Because he literally was going to places no one had been before. So basically, in his footsteps, I try to do something a bit different, but pretty wild and frenzied; I like that sort of stuff. On record, in most cases, I just pick up the guitar and wail away. And the recorders are going. And often I'm thinking yeah, that's cool, and I'm not generally happy to do too much more research. I might go in and refine a couple of parts. I try to keep it as natural as possible. Because I need to do it when I feel like doing it, so whatever naturally comes out, comes out. I like it to be as 'me' as much as possible."

The band's nimble, pop metal version of Joan Baez ballad "Diamonds And Rust" comes next, Joan meeting the band in future years and finding them very nice boys, thanking them for turning the song into a considerable hit, its release as a single (backed with "Dissident Aggressor") helping drive the album to a No.23 placement in the UK charts, and gold status in the US, but not until a certification round-up for the band took place November 10, 1989.

As discussed, the band had already worked up "Diamonds and Rust" during the *Sad Wings of Destiny* sessions (suggested to them by Gull president David Howells) and so due to the behest of CBS trying break the band with a cover, they thought they'd pull out the familiar track again. As Roger alluded to, the polite metal gallop of the song necessarily recalls what Glover was to achieve with "This Flight Tonight" for

Nazareth three years earlier, the second connective tissue being that both songs were by folk-based female singer/songwriters. Projecting out, one could essentially draw a line from Deep Purple's "Hard Lovin' Man" through these two songs, through Iron Maiden to the birth of a whole heavy metal subgenre called power metal, for which the heavy metal gallop is one of a half dozen notable characteristics.

"Starbreaker" comes next, the song being introduced by Simon and his drums, the sound of which… well, Glover's production on this record is decidedly non-heavy metal. There isn't much bottom end. It's pretty much an "intellectual" sound. Nonetheless, the guitars are molten on this one, with Rob spitting out his curious, ambiguous tale with venom, yet from somewhat of a remote area within the mix. Lyrically, Rob mixes an element of earthly seduction (abduction?) with space age imagery, building upon early traces found across the previous record, but then recurring regularly throughout the balance of the catalogue to this day.

"Last Rose of Summer" would be the band's most seriously layered and considered ballad to date. Bluesy of vibe, it's actually not a funeral dirge as was the band's predilection one and two albums back with respect to light music (another habit Priest may well have picked up from Sabbath). Still, lyrically, one can look upon this song as in the same family as Atkins' morose "Winter" sentiment, winter of course being the most heavy metal of months. The last rose of summer is a reminder of love, hopefully inspiring and bringing happiness through the fall and winter, until new roses arise in the spring.

Side two of the original vinyl opens with the manic panic of "Let Us Prey"/"Call for the Priest," one of a handful of songs that can claim serious legacy with respect to the origins of speed metal, Deep Purple's "Fireball" perhaps achieving first accolade status. Priest continue to raise the bar with respect to fireworks, acrobatics, dexterity and sophistication within the heavy metal realm, goaded on by their rented young dynamo behind the kit. Hill keeps pace, K.K. and Glenn riff and resolve like demons, and Rob bestows upon the world the increasingly intense vocal operatics that would earn him the title of Metal God.

There's much confusion over the naming of these tracks. Logic dictates that "Let Us Prey" is essentially the instrumental intro to "Call for the Priest." although it's technically not instrumental, with its languid churchy guitar strains concluding with a multi-tracked Rob singing "Call for the priest, I'm dying..." (generating further confusion) before the dramatic, cascading chords of "Call for the Priest" commence. "Let Us Prey" was never performed live by the band; however the recording of it was used as the band's intro music for the ensuing tour dates. Lyrically, "Call for the Priest" is a curious one, built of two distinct sentiments. Initially there's a quick sketch of a night on the town, presumably to relieve some sexual tension, and then with the last two stanzas, the band mounts an attack on its critics. These two together constitute one cohesive piece at about 6:15 and should be viewed as such.

"Raw Deal" follows, and this is another self-contained song at pretty much six minutes on the nose. Unfortunately, the track list says "Call for the Priest/Raw Deal" which doesn't make sense, causing a situation forever to this day where, quite crucially, it's hard to say what one of the most important songs in the Priest canon—
The super-fast first proper song on side two—is actually called.

In any event, with the "Raw Deal" lyric, one can't help but read Rob's lyric as a sort of paean to gay cruising. Once he came out, he admitted as much, adding that he was quite surprised that few people got it. Some of his best lines are in there (and amusingly, it was the reference to Fire Island that eventually started to raise some eyebrows), plus some innovative phrasing, a necessity due to Glenn's innovative riffing and Phillips' funk end-around. An admirable, lesser celebrated Priest composition, this one's a smart cookie, demonstrating the band's skill and bravery to break rules like their cohorts in Queen or Sabbath or Zeppelin.

"Here Come the Tears" finds the band back in listless, despondent terrain when courting mellow music. Yet really, the song is more like a proto-power ballad, jagging along to heavy, doom-laden chording circa Sabbath, as Rob howls impressively, harrowingly, over a wide groove punctuated by Phillips' precise, tightly tuned and attuned tom patterns.

It all serves as preamble to "Dissident Aggressor," a corker of a heavy metal construct, a furnace blast of brainiac metal, a critical tour de force that also crushes. Arguably, this song, from all the way back in 1977, represents the pinnacle of Priest's front edge writing, even if three decades of records have come to pass since its impressive jag. One wonders if Glenn saw the song becoming what it did, although really, it is Simon Phillips that sends it into the jazzosphere. Phillips essentially plays the song as the Neil Peart of that same year, 1977, might, also introducing the trashed cymbal effect most attributed to Bill Bruford on King Crimson's *Red* album. The song tugs and shoves, just like the lyric, just like Rob's guttural to soaring vocal, just like the violent leads. The band continue to raise their game and press on to the track's all-too-soon close and that's it—*Sin After Sin* ends on a symphony of highs.

K.K. concurs that Simon lends a big boost to "Dissident Aggressor." "Yes he does, and I really think the album kicks in with that one. I mean, that was one of the last things we did, and that would've been a great starting point, if the album would have opened with that song. On that one, Glenn and myself were there solely for the musical side, whereas Rob was really reaching out, on an international level, really, to be heard with his lyrics."

There's really not much to the lyrics, and they are quite abstract, but indeed Rob has explained that they are inspired by the crude oppression represented by the Berlin Wall. He recalls being in Berlin one year in November, unable to sleep and going for a walk in a watchtower-type area where he could see over the wall. He's struck by the contrast of lit-up and partying West Berlin versus East Berlin which was pitch black, "just dead," the only sign of life being soldiers peering at him through binoculars.

But the West wasn't treating Priest with much enthusiasm. Press for the band Stateside—good or bad—was still thin on the ground, even if Circus' Michael Bloom managed a fairly lengthy (and tepid but encouraging), review of the record, calling *Sin After Sin* "a very balanced album with the right amount of raunch, no real rough edges, and a ballad just where you need one to mellow out—in short, a joy to any A&R man's heart." Bloom then singles out Simon Phillips, calling him "one of England's top five drummers, a sort of heavy Phil Collins with an unbelievable double bass drum roll and other behemoth chops. So this is the best drummed record of its kind in history."

That last point was particularly perceptive. *Sin After Sin*, in large part because of Simon, can be seen as one of the cornerstone albums of progressive metal, along with all of the '70s albums by Rush save for the debut, and for other reasons, the likes of *Demons and Wizards* and *The Magician's Birthday* and perhaps also *Sabbath Bloody Sabbath* and *Sabotage*. Still, for those who stress the metal in progressive metal (and against Sabbath, particularly, those who stress progressive), it might come down to *2112* or *Sin After Sin* as ground zero. Even, at a stretch, *Sad Wings of Destiny*.

In the same issue of Circus, a short piece ran on the band, with Rob talking about wanting to move to New York and live in a skyscraper, as well as wanting to dance for a living, like Fred Astaire, a comment I recall as following him closely for a few years, causing no end of grief to this writer as a young pup, a junior headbanger who saw this new heavy metal band as the best in existence. The writer of the article, Hannah Spitzer, as well as Rob, briefly acknowledge that punk was garnering all the attention in the music industry. True, *Sin After Sin* was issued smack at the point of punk's peak, yet history would record the genre more as a curious cultural movement, with the record and ticket sales still going to all those bands we call classic rock today. Also of note, the piece erroneously listed Alan Moore as Priest's drummer.

In a grouped review including Angel's *On Earth as It Is in Heaven* and BTO's *Freeways*, Melody Maker said that Priest had, "carved out their own style, relying as ever on the thundering rhythm section and bursts of flamboyant lead guitar. You've got to tip your hat to them—not only do they have the wit to write a song called 'Let Us Prey,' (geddit?), but they also have the cheek to do a heavy version of Joan Baez's 'Diamonds and Rust.' In a musical form where the protagonists take themselves far too seriously, humour goes a long way."

For the *Sin After Sin* tour, Priest would end up collaring one Les Binks to pound the skins, Les being a percussionist of similar technicality to Simon, also a double bass drum player, a rare commodity back in the late '70s. Binks, curiously as Simon did, would also claim earlier Roger Glover connections, having worked on Roger's *Butterfly Ball* project, as well as pounding the skins for Eric Burdon. *Butterfly Ball* morphed towards Eddie Hardin's *Wizard's Convention* project, and Les was there for that too, as well as two records with obscure pop act Fancy.

Binks provides the background concerning his entry to the band, while also filling in some of the blanks on the hiring on of David Hemmings as management, a decision to figure in his controversial departure from the fold a couple years later.

"I joined the band right around when punk and new wave was coming up," begins Binks. "Bands like Black Sabbath and Deep Purple, I think some of them had split up at the time, although temporarily—they got back together eventually of course. But it wasn't a good time to be in a heavy metal band in England, because record companies thought the punk/new wave stuff that was happening then, that was going to be the next big thing. But they weren't that enthusiastic about metal at that point in time."

"Judas Priest had made their first two albums on a very small label called Gull Records, and they had a local guy called Corky—that was his nickname—who was a friend of the band when they started out. And he became a local promoter and kind of was unofficially their manager at the time. And between the first album and the second album, they'd changed drummers already."

"So at this point they were having a hard time financially and were on the verge of calling it a day, when they were approached by a guy called David Hemmings. Not the actor, by the way, but this guy was originally tour manager for Black Sabbath, and I think he was from Birmingham as well, so he kind of knew the scene up there. And he said look, I've got in partnership with these other guys, and we formed a management company called Arnakata. And he said, if you sign up with us, we'll get you out of your old record deal with Gull and we'll set you up with a new worldwide deal with a major label. Which they did, in fact, and it turned out to be CBS/Columbia. And they were facing bankruptcy probably, or going down that avenue, so they jumped at it."

"And so the first album, they brought in Roger Glover to produce it. They'd parted company with the second drummer, who played on *Sad Wings of Destiny*, but all the studio time was all set up and everything and Roger suggested bringing in Simon Phillips, and he was the first guy to use double bass drums in Priest. Simon was brought in just to do the album as a session guy. I think he was only about 19 at the time and he had a lot of drums."

"Funny story on that; I met up with Simon recently, in London and I told him this story (laughs), because, we used to cross paths. We used to work at a lot of the same studios in the '70s, when we did session work. And I remember going into a studio in London. I can't remember for the life of me which one it was, but the engineer was setting up mics around my kit, and he says to me, 'We had this guy in the other day, and he had so many drums on his kit, that we didn't have enough mics to mic them up. We had to send out a guy for more microphones.' And I said, 'Who is that?' He says, 'A young guy named Simon Phillips.' But he used to play something called the Ludwig Octopus kit, which had two bass drums and eight single-headed concert toms and an 18-inch standard floor tom. So that was the setup he was using, and that's what he used on the *Sin After Sin* album."

"But Simon was going on tour with the Jack Bruce Band and so he was just passing through," continues Binks. "He was never intent on joining the band as such. And so after the album was completed, they suddenly realised they gotta tour. The management had already set up a tour to promote the album. And they suddenly realised, hang on, we haven't got a permanent drummer. We haven't got anyone. So they went back to Roger and Roger recommended me, because I played on his solo album, and we did a big concert together at the Albert Hall, with Ian Gillan, David Coverdale, Ronnie James Dio, all those guys, Jon Lord, Glenn Hughes. So I went along and had a blast with them and they asked me to join."

In terms of an audition, there was no loose jam session as such, no bashing out of Cream and Hendrix tunes and a 20-minute blues shuffle in C. All business, it was straight into the polished slide rule-and-protractor metal of *Sin After Sin*.

"Well, they sent me the album, so that by the time we actually got together, I had an idea of what they expected me to play. It would be no point turning up and not having an idea of the material. So they sent me a pre-release copy of *Sin After Sin* so I had enough time to spend listening to that and learning drum parts on it. So by the time we got together in a rehearsal studio, we could pretty much play a lot of that material straight off because I had learnt it, as such."

Seasoned pro that Les was, there was a bit of a scramble happening to get this gig nailed. "Yes, I had dabbled with double bass drums before, but I didn't use them the majority of the time. Not every circumstance or every situation that I was involved in required them. On this occasion, when they played me the *Sin After Sin* album, they had an acetate of that, a pre-release copy. And so this is the stuff that I had to learn to go out and promote the album. And of course Simon played a lot of double bass drum stuff on that album so I had to quickly get another bass drum and learn all his drum parts. The very first time we got together to rehearse some of that material, I still hadn't got the second bass drum. But I had a little, tiny 18-inch bass drum. So I set that up just to get through the rehearsal. But it wasn't long before I added the second bass drum to the kit, and the kits got bigger and bigger and it's still quite huge today, in fact. I like playing multi tom-tom setups because the type of fills that I do only come off when you're playing a range of tom-toms that goes from very high to medium to low. And you can't really pull that off to the same effect on a kit with a limited range of tom-toms."

Out on the first leg of the British tour, perhaps spurred on by getting away with his "Raw Deal" lyric, Rob was raising eyebrows with his flamboyant dress, his prim shortened coif, his eyeliner and his stage moves. But the crowds were eating it up.

Recalls Les, "Yes, the one thing that did impress me with Priest when we did the very first British tour to promote *Sin After Sin*, was the foundation that they had already built up at that point. They'd only made two albums before that, but they had already established quite a good fan base. And it was the loyalty of the metal fans that impressed me. A lot of them would not be content with just going to the venue at the town that you came to play in that happened to be the town where they lived. A lot of them would follow you around the country and stay in hotels and go to the next venue. So you'd see the same faces sometimes; you'd recognise some of them from previous gigs. So that impressed me. I thought, what a great fan base to have. And of course, that's built up tenfold, maybe more, since those days."

Bob Catley from UK prog rockers Magnum recalls their 1977 support slots ahead of the Priest as career-defining for his band. "We had recorded the first album, *Kingdom of Madness*, but it wasn't due to come out for some reason, until '78. And we thought it was a good idea, you know, let's get out there. We were doing residencies and our own gigs around the Midlands, and then Jet Records got us onto the Judas Priest tour, which was their first major European tour. And we had a great time, 'Oh, here we are, we've arrived, we're on a proper stage with a lot of people in front of us.' Not a lot of them knew who we were, but we went down very, very well. And it taught us a lot about how to get on in the business. What we do now, we take for granted. You make an album, go out on tour and you do interviews and all that, but we didn't know about any of that at the time. It was all new to us. So it was a bit of an eye-opener, the Judas Priest tour. I used to have a couple chats with Rob Halford on occasion, when they were sound checking, and when we went in to sound check ourselves. We would talk on occasion and have a beer. But you don't really mix, you know? You have your own band and your own crew and kind of leave people alone. Nice guys though, all from Wolverhampton. And over the years, you meet them again and you talk about stuff you'd done together years ago."

The *Sin After Sin* campaign left England in May '77, Priest finding themselves supporting REO Speedwagon as part of their first trip to the States. The 1977 Superjam found Priest opening a show at Busch Memorial Stadium in St. Louis, 45,000 fans in attendance to witness the band's brand of math metal in advance of headliners Ted Nugent and REO Speedwagon, both regional favourites.

Dates were also logged with Foreigner, Head East and Starz, with the highlight of the trip being Day on the Green in San Francisco, playing to 60,000 at a show at 11:30 in the morning, later headlined by the mighty Led Zeppelin. It is said that Robert Plant personally had asked for the baby band from his hometown of Birmingham to help fill out the Bill Graham spectacle, and in retrospect, Priest look upon their two shows with Zeppelin as the crystallizing moment of the band's career, despite Rob getting himself a hail of boos by greeting the Oakland crowd as San Franciscans.

Notes Les on that first US campaign, "CBS were a much bigger organisation, obviously, much more professional, and that definitely gave the band what it needed at the time. And crucial was the opportunity to go and tour America for the first time. If you cracked it in America, then you don't need to worry about the rest of the world, really. That's where you have to focus on."

"I'd toured America before, with a band called Fancy, and so I kind of knew what to expect. Because it's very different—it's such a vast country. They call it the United States, but it's like a whole lot of little countries all stuck together and they all speak the same language. The accent varies, of course, from one state to another but also the laws change. You have to be 18 in one state to drink alcohol or go to a bar while in other places it's 21, so you have to try and remember what the deal is when you're moving around."

"And also, in order to crack it in America, for a band to become successful in America, you can be really big in one state and still not so well known in another. San Antonio, in Texas, warmed to the band straight away; we were always really, really popular there. And then you have to sort of work your way around, do a few tours to build up and make it in each different state. And the thing about America is, as opposed to the UK, you had these big stadium gigs. Plus they took musicians more seriously than in the UK, at that time. I think it's all changed now, but you still get that old attitude here."

As for the bands they played with and how they were treated, Les says, "We did shows with Foghat, we did some with Foreigner, we did some with UFO, REO Speedwagon. We didn't see that much of the headliners. We would turn up and do our thing and then head back to the hotel. We never had any particular grievances with any of them. I suppose a lot of people who hadn't seen Priest before didn't quite know what to expect. And when we were playing along with, say, a band like Foreigner, who are more sort of melodic with harmonies, an FM radio-friendly band, it was a bit of a mismatch. We were a lot heavier, a lot more hard-edged and they were a lot softer. But we just did what we did; it wasn't preconceived or premeditated—it came from the heart and soul, really."

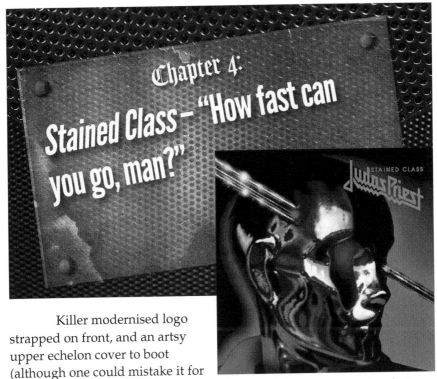

Chapter 4:
Stained Class – "How fast can you go, man?"

Killer modernised logo strapped on front, and an artsy upper echelon cover to boot (although one could mistake it for a disco album), *Stained Class* arrived February 10th, 1978, proving that the technical metal madness of its predecessor, *Sin After Sin*, was a mere half-step along a plane reserved for the masters smack in the middle of a near super-human run of creativity.

Les Binks, touring drummer for the last record, would distinguish himself on the new album as a more than able replacement for Simon Phillips, and all around him, the band was intent on intense fireworks to match his heat, start to finish.

Says Ian of *Stained Class*, as introduction, "That was Dennis MacKay that recorded that; it was done in Chipping Norton, Cotswolds, that beautiful place (laughs). And on that album of course was the infamous 'Better by You Better than Me,' which actually Dennis didn't produce that one. That was an extra track that we ended up putting on as the album was a little bit short."

Dennis MacKay (also credited as Mackay in places, but it's MacKay on the original UK issue of this particular record) had engineered for the likes of Supertramp, David Bowie and Jeff Beck, but his productions were more in the jazz world—Al Di Meola, Stanley Clarke and Mahavishnu's John McLaughlin all benefited from his deft touch. Since Priest, he's produced a varied resume, with Pat Travers and Tygers of Pan Tang being closest to Priest genre-wise. In essence, here we had

Priest repeating history. A jazzy drummer helped turn *Sin After Sin* into an up-market oddball of a record, a pioneering note-dense heavy metal album of high construct. For *Stained Class*, it would be a producer from that same world that would serve much the same function, and oddly, most pertinently in the drum area, for this was not the way you produced heavy metal drums, and yet the heavy metal world was somehow better for it.

Providing a bit of back-story on MacKay, Binks says, "I'd been working as a session musician, so I'd been in and out of all the studios in London, working for other artists. And one of the studios which was quite famous was called Trident Studios, and a guy called Ken Scott used to work there quite a lot. And he's quite a famous engineer, who worked on *Abbey Road* and a lot of the Beatles stuff. And later he started to do a lot of things for the jazz fusion guys, such as John McLaughlin and Billy Cobham and people like that. Billy Cobham, as a drummer, was a big influence on me as well, although he's in a different genre. He kind of crossed over between jazz and rock, as with the jazz rock fusion thing he did with Tommy Bolin."

"So Dennis had been working with Mr. Scott at that particular studio, and he was kind of one of his understudies. So I liked the work that they had done; I'd heard a lot of that stuff and I like the production and the sounds that they got, especially with the drums. So I was keen to use Dennis and everybody else was in agreement. So we met up with him and the choice was made and off we went to a little studio up in Oxfordshire, in the Cotswolds, a place called Chipping Norton. Sadly, that little studio doesn't exist anymore. The building is still there but it's no longer a recording studio. It was a live-in studio; it had accommodations and you stayed there while you worked."

"Everything went very, very smoothly," continues Binks. "When you choose people to work with, you have to choose people you're compatible with. And that applies to producers, engineers, all the people that are involved in getting the final product together. And obviously the musicians as well have to be able to enhance each other's playing, bring out the best in each other. In fact, all of the stuff that we did together was very harmonious. We never argued about how it should end up. We just put in suggestions and everybody was quite open-minded and cooperative—we had good chemistry."

The recording of *Stained Class* took place October and November '77. The mix would be handled by Neil Ross at Trident. The aforementioned "Better by You Better than Me" was produced by James Guthrie after the original sessions. It is said that label wanted to try their luck again with a cover version, so the Spooky Tooth obscurity was recorded after the original sessions, at Utopia in London, at which time,

Dennis MacKay was unavailable for the job (the mix was handled by Ken Thomas and Paul Northfield at Advision). Still, the sound, for all intents and purposes, matches up, the entire album stepping politely out of the speakers with upper crust high fidelity, featuring meticulous separation, scintillating treble, measured, pinpoint bass, and in totality, a level of precision not associated with heavy metal records.

Stained Class opened in explosive fashion with a legendary Les Binks drum intro, featuring a barrage of double bass drums—rare in that era—after which "Exciter" proper kicks in. Widely considered one of the early speed metal classics (as mentioned, "Fireball," from '71, trumps it; as does Priest's own "Call for the Priest"), "Exciter" builds to a screeching crescendo, all the while Glenn and K.K. turning in classy, artful riffs and rhythm charges and changes, Rob showing his thespian skills, range and intensifying lyrical sophistication—a lot of words, many of them quite big, are stuffed into this road racer of a track. As well, the religious overtone and feel of Rob's pomp-filled phrasings lend the song the gravitas it needs, or else it would likely fly off the rails.

The first influence that comes to mind for Les Binks when asked about double bass playing is the aforementioned Billy Cobham. "Yes, well, the thing about Billy Cobham is, I was from the jazz background, especially in the younger day. Billy is in his 70s now, so he's a lot more restrained, shall I say, in his playing. But back when he was with Mahavishnu Orchestra with John McLaughlin he was very, very fiery. He had a lot more fire in his playing than he has these days. And he was one of the few drummers from a jazz background to use double bass drums. I've never been a huge jazz fan, but Cobham, I could listen to all day. If you listen to his solo album, *Spectrum*, the double bass playing on that is pretty much up there with the metal stuff you know?

"But looking at "Exciter" specifically, it was really inspired by Mr. Ian Paice and the song "Fireball." That's the first time I ever heard Ian playing two bass drums, and that surprised me because he normally just plays a single bass drum. So I wanted to do something along those lines."

"And it was just one day at a sound check with the band, it just came into my head and I just launched into what ended up being the opening drum pattern for "Exciter." It was just a spur of the moment improvised thing that I came up with, and Glenn's ears picked up when he heard me play it. He asked me to play it again and he joined in with a guitar riff. And that was the birth of that song—everything else developed from that."

"'Exciter,' that's just a classic Priest track," muses K.K., addressing its speed. "I think that one and 'Hell Bent for Leather' would be synonymous with the name Judas Priest. I think we just set out to write the fastest track ever written (laughs). And the one before that would have been 'Call for the Priest' on *Sin After Sin*—that was the progenitor of it all, I think. *Stained Class* also saw the change of the band really going for the leather and the studs. We're very, very proud of that record, and proud of everything we've ever done. We had great times, obviously, recording the record. It was obviously full of great songs."

"Why did Glenn start playing 'Exciter?'" queries Rob rhetorically. "It all comes from the riff. He just… how fast can you go, man? How fast can you play? And like what I do in 'Freewheel Burning,' I try and see how fast I can say something within a song. It's a bit like a challenge, a sense of daring, of trying to do something that you've never done before. How fast can a drummer play? How fast can a guitarist play a riff, but it can still be articulate? How fast can cook through it being a blur? Doing the song that you've never done before." Live, Priest would open "Exciter" with the same cascading, descending power chord barrage that they would later give to us officially as the intro sequence to "Hell Bent for Leather" from the album of the same name.

Tipton composition "White Heat, Red Hot" follows, with Glenn turning in another complicated ambiguous but decidedly apocalyptic lyric for the band, both tracks on the album thus far fitting of the stated theme from two records back on *Sad Wings*, namely "big changes are gonna come." Tipton's riff is a circular classic, and the guitar sound is gorgeous. Priest change it up for a venomous double speed chorus, before settling back into a funky groove the band's last drummer might have appreciated.

Next up is the Spooky Tooth cover, written by keyboardist Gary Wright. It dovetails so nicely with the rest of the material, one might not even suspect it was a cover. It's quite riffy, the chorus is aptly grand and "religious" of vibe like many high-minded Priest moments, and with those gorgeously tuned toms of Binks (much like Peart), the song bears enough of a Priest stamp to not disrupt the sequence of events. The track was issued as a single a month before the release of the album (backed with "Invader") but failed to chart.

The title track is next (countless times in the press, this album was called *Stained Glass*) and once again, Priest stuff a pert and perky, modern metal rocker with all sorts of "A" riffs, shifts in tempo, corners and creases. Rob does some of his highest singing, also using some of his sing-songy vocal melodies he had written seemingly effortlessly back in the golden era of the band. At the lyric end, Rob is clearly proving that he has raised his game. Thespian, eloquent violent imagery careens and rattles around the tight frame of this song like a polished steel pinball in its garishly-lit prison. Once more an epic struggle is occurring, one that could be Biblical, medieval, paranormal or extra-terrestrial. Mash what Priest is doing together across half the songs on each of *Sad Wings*, *Sin After Sin* and *Stained Class* and there's a panorama of filmic possibilities, all of which would cost out as enormously expensive.

At the musical end, it's hard to miss the crisp percussion work of Les Binks, in particular, his use of many toms, tuned to perfection like Neil Peart. The intro sequence to "Stained Class" represents a clear example of this, and all told, this characteristic to Binks' playing provides a nice through-line from what Simon Phillips had established on the previous record.

"I had basically two kits," recalls Les, asked about his hardware. "I had double-headed tom-toms and single-headed tom-toms. And I had a set of concert toms, which ranged from six, eight, ten, 12, 13, 14, 15, 16, and then an 18-inch floor tom. As I say, I like to use a lot of tom-toms (laughs). Because to me, it's like sometimes when I sit in on someone else's kit and they're using a more basic setup, that's fine—it depends on the music you're playing. Ringo's kit was very basic: bass drum, mounted tom, floor tom, snare drum, a high-hat and a couple of cymbals and that was it. It was all he required for the music. And sometimes when you have less to play on, you have to be more inventive to come up with something interesting."

"But when I sit in on someone else's kit playing a more basic setup with your regular tom-toms and so on, I feel like a guitarist playing with three strings. Or a piano player playing with only half the keyboard. Because with me, I have all the drums set to a different pitch and a different voice, and I have all that in my head, and so when I want to bring those sounds out, if they don't exist in my kit anymore, I'm frustrated because it's not in a voice that I have anymore."

"I was using Pearl drums at the time," continues Les, "which are made in Japan. And that kit had two 22-inch bass drums. I sometimes used just all the concert toms and a floor tom to go with it. Which were all single-headed. And then other times I would mix them up and I would use a 12, 13, 14, mounted over the two bass drums, and then a 16 and 18 floor tom. And I would have just the first four high concert toms on my left over the high-hat. So that would be the six, eight, ten and 12. And so that's still a lot of tom-toms, and more than ample for what I wanted to do. So it varied; the kit did vary slightly between those two setups."

"Invader" offers more of the same post-Deep Purple modern metal perfection we've heard thus far, Priest finding groove, goodly and godly riffing while Rob turns in an amusing lyric on a subject dear to metal hearts, alien invasion, Halford yet again adding to this landscape crowded by all manner of being. Who will win, we'll never know but there's never a dull moment as we take our ringside seat.

Opening side two of the original vinyl was "Saints in Hell," Rob again using mostly the high end of his prodigious range. Lyrically, this is a colourful one with all manner of man and beast joining in yet another apocalyptic battle, one that seems to involve good and evil in a religious sense, but also, true to form, beings and creations from science fiction. Increasingly it is possible—although as I say, in a bit of an anarchic muddle—to see most of the songs as part of the same fiery, astral tale, with the slick graphics of the album cover even helping to flesh out a vibe Tipton was wont to call "cybernetic." And really, the thorny, precise musical mélange chosen, action-packed at every turn, serves as perfect aural metaphor to the sky-straddling metaphysical battles depicted.

"Savage" is next, and it's a bit of a departure, heavier and darker than the rest of the album, almost Sabbath-like, with Rob writing a classy lyric mourning the white man's vanquishing of "savages" and their lands. It's a smart, poignant lyric, helping underscore this band and this album as something a few notches above standard heavy metal fare. And true to heavy metal form, at the core of the problem is missionary Christianity. "Savage" features K.K. Downing's only stand-alone solo, with K.K. also taking the second break in "Beyond the Realms of Death." Other than that, all the solos are either Glenn alone or Glenn in dovetailing duet with Downing.

Tipton also begins to assert himself as the main songwriter in the band, figuring on six tracks, with K.K. credited on only two.

Notes Binks, "'Savage' was one of K.K.'s songs. Ken and Glenn had slightly different writing styles, although when it all blends together, it all sounds like Judas Priest, you know? And I think with a singer so distinctive as Rob, he always puts his stamp on it—when you hear his vocal on it, it couldn't be anybody else. But those two, it was kind of 50-50. Glenn was more methodical and quite melodic; I love the solo he plays in 'Beyond the Realms of Death;' it's still a classic solo and very unusual. He put that together very tastefully; I was quite impressed with that, to this day. K.K. Downing on the other hand was more influenced by Hendrix and all that kind of use of whammy bar, etc, which Glenn didn't really do. K.K.'s playing was more wild and freaky. So the two styles complemented each other, and I think to this day, it's a unique guitar duo that they created."

Next up was "Beyond the Realms of Death," a dark and pure heavy metal "power ballad" of a serious type that would give rise to classics from Metallica like "Fade to Black" and "One." "That was the one that got us into trouble," recalls Glenn, of the song that brought the band a lawsuit when on December 23, 1985, 18-year-old Raymond Belknap committed suicide and 20-year-old James Vance, attempting suicide, was gravely maimed, dying three years later. It was alleged the two friends were inspired by Priest's lyrics to end it all, with the suit taking its toll on all involved before ultimately being dismissed. Scrambling for answers, debated at the time was this track, "Heroes End" and "Better by You, Better than Me," concerning subliminal messages and the trendy at the time bugaboo called backmasking (lyrics played backwards that supposedly reveal Satanic messages).

"That's what thinking about that album brings back to me immediately," continues Tipton, "all that hullabaloo and nonsense surrounding it. I had to go to court every day in a suit, because they wouldn't let us in without a suit. And we had to listen to bare-faced lies. But we were victorious in the end, so in a way we flew the flag for heavy metal. Because every book, film, article afterwards would have come under fire. It would have been unbearable for everyone, had we lost."

Adds K.K. speaking more so about the album as a whole, "That was the one with the so-called subliminal messages and the court case, so obviously, I don't know if the band has grown to distance themselves from that album (laughs). Well, we wouldn't musically anyway, because they're all our babies."

The song's mournful, passionate, despondent catatonic depression and suicide theme would be cited as the fuel behind the arguably spontaneous suicide pact from which, as I say, one friend died and another was greatly disfigured, dying later of a drug overdose. *Stained Class'* cover art was even called into play, with the bar pattern (some call it a laser beam) seen as the path of a bullet. Strictly speaking, it was "Better by You Better than Me" that was cited for subliminal messaging—i.e. backmasking—with "Beyond the Realms of Death" collared for its forward message.

Notes Al Atkins, "The big riff in the middle of 'Beyond the Realms of Death' sounds very much like a song I wrote called 'Life Goes On.' But it was a long time ago and I don't lose any sleep over it." Indeed, that is one monster of a riff of which Al speaks, a ferociously angry and heavy break in a song that is mostly a ballad, although heavy and Sabbath-like come chorus time. Oddly, the song is credited to Binks/Halford, reason being that indeed Les penned it. K.K. has said it's the one and only time he'd ever seen Binks pick up a guitar, going so far as to say that Les wrote all of it, save for the solos!

"I live in London and the guys were all based in Birmingham, which is where the band was born," begins Binks by way of explanation. "And so it was more practical for me to go up there and rehearse with them when we were working on new material for the next album. And there was a little sort of demo studio up there, that some friends of theirs ran. And so we thought it would be a good idea, once we had the format for each song, to go in there and sort of demo the album before we actually went into a major recording studio with a producer. And also it gave the perspective to whoever we chose, in terms of giving them something to listen to so they could see how the album was developing and hear the songs before we got into the studio."

"And after we'd got most of the songs recorded or demoed, I came back to London, because I was travelling back and forth. And I thought there's something missing, you know? From this. Because most of the songs were pretty much up-tempo tunes. And when you're performing live, it's nice to introduce a little bit of light and shade, especially midway through the set."

"So I thought it would be nice to have something that started off gently on acoustic guitar, almost, and then build up into a big heavy riff. So I had a little Revox at home, a reel-to-reel machine, and I just picked up an acoustic guitar, started messing around and came up with the opening chords, plus the riffy section, the midsection, the middle eight, the solo, everything else."

"So I made a little home demo of it," continues Binks. "I just put a little beat box that I had then, on there to keep the rhythm. And I played the guitar parts all myself. I even put a bass line down as well. But I wanted somebody to put a solo on it, just to finish it off. And a friend of mine,

U.K. Tour 1978

who lived near me, at that time in West London, I invited him to come around and play guitar on it. And that was a guy called Steve Mann, who is with Michael Schenker these days; in fact, he's living over in Germany now, I think. He also has another band which is called Lionheart, which I actually was in on the birth of. And we did a one-off tour with Def Leppard at the time. But that's going off to another story (laughs)."

"But I had no lyrics at all. That's one of the hardest things I find to do. I can come up with lots of melodic ideas—that's not a problem— and rhythmic ideas, obviously. But when I'd listen to all of the songs that they'd written so far, I thought, well, let Rob do that because that's his niche, you know? That's his forte, what he excels at. And it also gives more of a Judas Priest style to the song. I thought Robert's writing style was quite diverse; it could be dark but it could be quite positive as well."

"Anyway, so I just made the home demo thing. And when I got to Birmingham again, the rehearsal studio, I said, 'Guys, I've got this song. Have a listen to it. I've written no lyrics, but see what you think.' And they sat around, well, what are the chords? And I'm a bit hack-handed when I play guitar. It's never been an instrument that I took all that seriously. And I'm right-handed, but I play guitar left-handed. I never got around to buying a left-handed guitar, so I play a right-handed guitar left-handed, or upside down, if you like. So my chord shapes are different. If you're looking at someone who's playing a guitar conventionally, you have to approach it somewhat differently. So they were looking at me playing the guitar upside down and trying to figure out what the chords were that I was showing them. But eventually, they got the hang of it and really liked the song."

"So Rob just went away and came up with the lyrics, etc., and obviously, the song title. And it was quite a surprise to me, really, because the song has quite a dark meaning. It's basically about suicide. It's quite a haunting lyric, and it works well with the melody. So it's now become a Priest classic. And I think it holds up today. It works great on stage too, because as I say, I felt all the songs that were presented for *Stained Class* were pretty much all up-tempo, and this one started off slower and gentler and acoustically and then builds up into a big, powerful riff. And it was undeniably Judas Priest."

"I love that song because whenever I sing it, emotionally it takes me on a wonderful journey," reflects Rob on this morose and funereal classic. "I think about a lot of things when I sing that song. Obviously I think about my times with Priest. I also reflect on some of the unfortunate situations that happened with people in rock 'n' roll, and of course to some extent the fans, people who have difficulties in life and for one reason or another, want to end their life in different ways. But also it's a song that has a lot of strength because it's talking about an individual surviving those difficult times."

Stained Class ends with "Heroes End," an ingenious inverted or backwards-sounding riff placed on a bed of halting, marching rhythms, over which Rob delivers a Glenn Tipton lament concerning the untimely deaths of a trio of talents (Janis Joplin, Jimi Hendrix and James Dean), and how their passing transformed them into immortals. Indeed,

Glenn dedicates two quite perceptive and concise stanzas to Joplin and Hendrix each, and then for the final verse, a single stanza for James Dean. Embedded late in the sequence is a haunting sort of death march, over which Rob sings low and churchy about how, essentially, a rabid public craves the tragic tales of heroes dying young, simply to keep their dreary selves entertained.

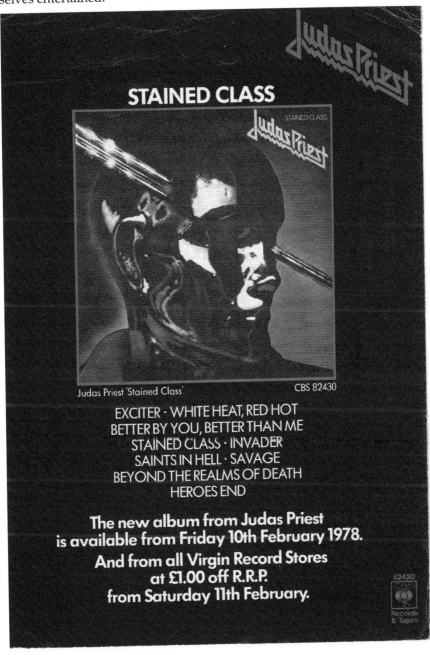

Halford's vocal is suitably indignant (at the waste), and is a big part of the song's success, as is the additional, typically high quality riffing that adds dimension to the track. In fact, there are a number of progressive metal surprises that present themselves across this somewhat lengthy opus, including some truly unholy guitar tones. As mentioned, "Heroes End" was also brought into the fold of the aforementioned notorious suicide pact case, the argument being that the song glorified death by equating it with heroism.

Out in the marketplace, *Stained Class* failed to light the world on fire, reaching No.173 on the Billboard charts (and No.27 in the UK, a slight drop from *Sin After Sin*'s No.23 placement). Nonetheless, once fame hit, the album was pushed past RIAA gold status, the band earning their *Stained Class* plaques on November 10th 1989.

Hitting the road, the band played a little over half the record, with the omissions being "Invader," "Saints in Hell," "Savage" and "Heroes End." The rest of the set was split evenly between emerging *Sad Wings* and *Sin After Sin* classics, with *Rocka Rolla* ignored in its entirety. January and February of '78 saw the band blanket England and Scotland.

The band's stop at Sheffield City Hall on January 23rd took on added historical significance given that Def Leppard's Joe Elliot and Pete Willis wound up meeting future second guitarist Steve Clark at the gig, convening after the show and comparing notes on their favourite bands. Priest would later take Def Leppard on their first round of American tour dates in 1980. As well, both the band's debut album, *On Through the Night* and Priest's *British Steel* would be produced by Tom Allom, and both at the same locale, Ringo Starr's Starling Studios, first the Leppard and then *British Steel* immediately after.

Spring saw Priest venturing over to the US. Glenn has bad memories of supporting a none too sociable or helpful Foghat—30 minutes, no spotlights and nary a word spoken to the affable support band—after which five milestone dates would be logged in Japan from July 25th to August 5th 1978.

Frustratingly, Priest were still an underground act, ironically flying over everyone's heads as it were, with metal too smart for the masses, apparently. It would be time for another re-think, and this time, with a solid foundation of timeless classics already written, recorded and waiting to be discovered, the Priest would soon prevail.

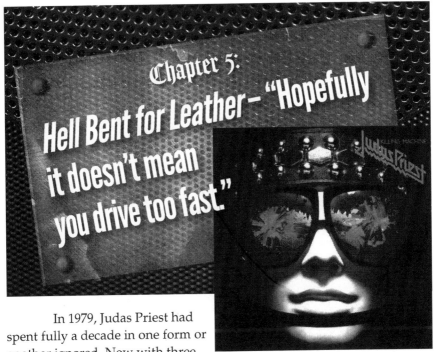

Chapter 5:
Hell Bent for Leather— "Hopefully it doesn't mean you drive too fast."

In 1979, Judas Priest had spent fully a decade in one form or another ignored. Now with three superlative, ground-breaking heavy metal masterpieces to their name, they were still pretty much without commercial success. Dismally, the band's next record, called *Killing Machine* in the UK and *Hell Bent for Leather* for the US market, wasn't going to change that situation appreciably. But what it would do is provide the band with a bridge concept, the bridge to a sound that would give them the success they so long deserved.

How much the band in retrospect appreciated the beauty of *Hell Bent for Leather* is essentially... not much. Perhaps blinded by actually making some money for once, the guys tend to look upon its dumbed-down follow-up *British Steel* most fondly. In this writer's opinion however, some of the greatest records in rock are such bridge albums, records that seem to contain the underground striving vibe from earlier records combined with some sort of new spark or excitability that is all the richer, because it finds an old band making new discoveries. Ergo, I consider *Hell Bent for Leather* to be the greatest Priest platter of them all because it possesses the perfect blend of the band's feverish old school technicality, and the sturdy, chopped-down songfulness—the new "discovery"—of say, *British Steel* or *Screaming for Vengeance*.

What's more, I consider this record to be the best sounding Priest album of them all, for the first time, heavy, but wholly exempt from the trendy '80s and '90s production traps the band would stumble into on every record going forward, save for *Angel of Retribution*, one last quite organic display before what is now a trio of records too digital and too compressed despite much good material across them. Indeed, the sound on *Hell Bent for Leather* is carnal, dirty, but still loaded up with all the frequencies you want covered, even bottom end, which to some extent was missing on its two prim predecessors, less so, oddly, on *Rocka Rolla* and *Sad Wings* which are almost more "correct" production-wise than the extreme, eccentric third and fourth from the band.

Killing Machine would be recorded in August 1978 at Utopia and at CBS studios in London, with the mix also handled at Utopia. The album was produced by James Guthrie, making a return trip after handling the one late, errant track on *Stained Class*. Shortly, he would distinguish himself as the producer for Pink Floyd's *The Wall*, and later Queensryche's full-length debut *The Warning*. The album was issued two months later in October of 1978 in the UK and Japan, February of the following year, with the new title and one extra track, in North America. "Ironically enough," notes Rob, "we were told by the label that *Killing Machine* was too much of a heavy statement to use in the US and Canada, so they suggested *Hell Bent for Leather*." The framing at the time was that the title's "murderous implications" would have been too much for the large record retailers to want to put the album on its racks.

"James Guthrie, I believe, was recommended by Columbia," recalls Rob, switching tack. "He came highly recommended because of his engineering and production skills. I think if you look at those three albums back to back, there is a tremendous growth; from *Sin After Sin* to *Stained Class* to *Killing Machine*, there's an incredible sense of adventure going on. So we wanted a producer who would be able to accommodate all of the things we were thinking of doing. If you look at some of the songs on there, they are pretty diverse. I mean you put 'Hell Bent for Leather' against 'Killing Machine' or 'Burnin' Up,' and those two songs especially are a real stretch from songs like 'The Ripper' or 'Victim of Changes.' I think the band was just showing its muscle and capability to go through lots of different dimensions and parameters and we wanted a producer who could come on the same journey with us and not just some guy that was stuck in one particular mode of production ideas."

"I know that that record by its own merits, stands alone," adds Rob. "They all do, they all have something special about them, and something different to say. And I just recall that it was a really cool experience recording with James Guthrie. It was just another one of those things where the band was specifically at, at that moment in time."

The cover art for the *Killing Machine* record was gorgeous, yet tough. Brandishing a slight update to the Priest logo debuted one record back (as well as slight text colour variations between the two territories), the sleeve included an introduction to the leather and studs of heavy metal, but through a classy, artistic, oblique presentation thereof.

"That was done by Roslav Szaybo, from the art department at CBS in London," notes Ian. "He did a couple of them. On *Hell Bent for Leather*, for that effect with the sunglasses, he actually got an air rifle and he had dozens of pairs of sunglasses and shot them with the air rifle until he got the right effect. And then he lit it from behind to get all the colours right."

Muses K.K., "We were talking about the artwork for that album, and how it probably was the archetypal beginning of it all, with the leather belt around the head of the figure. I think that probably is the definitive beginning of heavy metal—maybe. Maybe I'm wrong, but definitely for Judas Priest, that says it all. Here we are, the ultimate metalheads."

Delving into the music, *Killing Machine* opened with a shattering anthem of confidence, "Delivering the Goods" being a masterful display of pacing, riffing, surges and hanging back, growls and seductive crooning. It is perhaps the perfect Priest experience, the track delivering the goods of which Rob speaks in every way, from overall production, to effects, guitar sound, heavy and grooving drum performance, and above all water-tight construction—witness both its smart start and the "Rock And Roll"-inspired drum barrage finale from Binks. On any given day, this writer's favourite Priest song, one need only

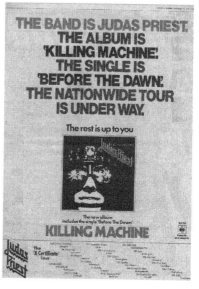

THE BAND IS JUDAS PRIEST. THE ALBUM IS 'KILLING MACHINE'. THE SINGLE IS 'BEFORE THE DAWN'. THE NATIONWIDE TOUR IS UNDER WAY.

The rest is up to you

KILLING MACHINE

listen to "Delivering the Goods'" Mensa-mad pre-chorus riff, or even Ian's bobbing, delicious bass line, to realise this was a Priest inspired. There's a modulation to the solo section, followed by a break (with tambourine!) and then a whole new song's worth of gorgeous riffing, before another round of modulation brings us back to the original verse riff—genius song architecture, and accessible enough that the band really didn't need to pander further, as would be the case for all of the 1980s.

"Rock Forever" is next, and again Priest triumph. Tight, technical yet evocative of the blues, this one's a corker, technically a shuffle, driven by a little bit of deftly placed double bass drum from Binks, as well as Rob's passion-filled metal-loyal vocal. Saxon and a dozen New Wave of British Heavy Metal bands would take this defence of their music concept further, but with this quick, perky number, Priest were setting the stage for a decade permeated with metal music, telling us why we all love metal in the first place and then writing a feisty, compact rocker that sounds like something either Michael or Rudolf Schenker might have written and been damn proud.

There's even a twin lead, and a somewhat unconventional one, quite southern rock-sounding, signalling perhaps that something from their unhappy stint supporting Foghat might have rubbed off on the boys after all. Indeed, there's similarity lyrically between "Rock Forever" and

Foghat's recent minor hit "Stone Blue." But of course, Foghat's talking about how rock 'n' roll pulled them through, and Rob needs "the beat of a heavy kind" to jerk him out of those "blue days." There are other soulful moments on this record—funky and fleeting but there nonetheless—that have me reminiscing fondly about "Slow Ride" as well, but let's not get carried away with the analogy.

"Evening Star" arrives mid-side, and a vanilla-safe comparison to Deep Purple's "Never Before" is in order. Rocky but not all that creative or even attractive from a hook point of view, it is a song that seemed destined for launch as a single by those who wanted to play it safe—a little melody, a little hard rock, not much of anything. Lyrically, the song can in fact be classed as a Christmas carol, addressing the journey of the Magi.

On the positive end musically, Ian's bass line is a funky blast, as is that opening tom fill from Binks. Turns out there's a bit of a story about the song's opening percussive salvo.

"Yes, this is before electronic drums became quite common," begins Binks. "We were in Los Angeles, and I had heard the theme tune to a Bond movie, with Carly Simon, 'Nobody Does It Better.' The drummer on that track is Jeff Porcaro from Toto. Jeff was a session drummer as well. In fact, everybody eventually who made up Toto were session musicians that worked together and just decided to form a band. And so when I heard that record, it opens up with, I think a piano intro, and then the drums come in with the tom-tom fill. And I thought that's a unique sound. It was like a sweep on the toms with these sonic drops."

"And it turned out that he'd used something called Syndrums, which were one of the first successful electronic drums to come out. And they were built by a company based in Los Angeles. And when we were in Los Angeles, I tracked the company down who made them. And I rang them up and they invited me around, explained how they operated, gave me a demonstration of them. They were used to death on all these disco records at the time, but the way I use them is the way that I had heard Jeff Porcaro use them, and that was to blend them in with the acoustic drums. So I would play a fill on the acoustic toms, and then I'd set the Syndrums up and I would tune them so that they blended in totally with the acoustic toms. And with the Syndrums, you could get that swoop, that bend in the notes. But when you blended the two together, it sounded like one drum. You'll hear that on the opening of 'Evening Star.' And that's the only time I used them with Priest."

"I got a set to take back to England and I used to hire them out," chuckles Les. "At that time you couldn't get up there because they were just brand-new; no one had a dealership here where you could buy them. And the way things used to work in recording, especially for session musicians, if there's some new gizmo, everybody wants to use it. You can always tell when you're listening to records these days, what year they were recorded in, by the instruments on them. Later came the Simmons drums, which are those octagonal shaped drum pads, and you'd plug them into a electronic brain; they sounded a bit more convincing as drums. If you listen to a lot of stuff from the '80s, there were these Simmons drums on so many records and now nobody wants them because they're old hat."

Next up is the album's short shock rocker, "Hell Bent for Leather" being note-dense speed metal with attitude—something missing from previous fast ones from a band often a bit behaved and looking down their spectacles. Opening with an effects-drenched assault of drums (as alluded to, previously used live in front of "Exciter"), the song settles into a brisk Purple-ish recline, an over-the-top pre-chorus and a hugely anthemic chorus. Come solo time, Priest give us a nod to their religious-toned past, their melodies here almost baroque. Of note, it is said that the title might have been a lift from the Blues Brothers, and that project band's covering of a song called "Rawhide."

As for the song's memorable and composed finger-tapped guitar solo, a technique usually attributed in the main to Eddie Van Halen, Ken says he picked it up from a band in England, even though he can't recall their name. "There was a three-piece band playing somewhere in London, and it was long before Eddie Van Halen came along. This is late '70s, I'm guessing, and I forget the name of the band. But the one guitar player there actually showed me this finger-tapping thing. He said that it came from a guitar player... not Chet Atkins, but somebody like that implemented this technique in their performance, and I remember him kind of doing it, and I thought, well, that's just a bit of fun. It just didn't seem like metal to me, you know what I mean? At the time. And then obviously, I suppose Eddie was the great one who came along. But obviously, it has its uses. When you are constructing a solo, to put anything together, any technique to string the parts together that creates interest, and different dynamics, it's all good stuff."

"Well, you either finger-tap or you've got a six- or seven-inch-long little finger," laughs Glenn. "So it makes playing those sort of stretch things a lot easier. I just fell into finger-tapping. I honestly can't remember the first time I started it. I do quite a lot of it still, and it's just something that always seemed natural to me. But exactly when I started to do it, I honestly can't remember."

As an interesting side-note, Van Halen's earthquaking self-titled debut album was issued on February 10th 1978, the same day *Stained Class* hit the shops.

Asked about the need for speed that results in a song like "Hell Bent for Leather," Glenn counters that, "Well, first I have to say, Priest aren't all fast music. Obviously, there's a lot of diversity in it. And it's great to play tracks like 'Angel' as opposed to tracks like 'Freewheel Burning' or 'Hell Bent for Leather.' But obviously the excitement in a heavy metal band, the double kick, you know, the whole chaos of that speed element, is very exciting. It's great to play on stage. Great to listen to in a car when you're driving along; hopefully it doesn't mean you drive too fast, you know. And really, that's what metal is all about. It's about speed, I suppose, in a sense. But at the same time, we like to feel we've got a contrast. And when we do a quiet number, it makes something like 'Hell Bent for Leather' just rage when it comes on. So there's that element as well."

"I will say that we've drawn blood, I think, playing some of our riffs," laughs Downing. "It's like setting the tempo, with myself and Glenn giving it this edge. If anybody out there has any difficulty keeping up with some of the riffs, let me tell you, it's not that easy sometimes." Adds Glenn, "I think that sums it up—on the edge."

Closing side one of the original vinyl was "Take on the World," another metal-is-all anthem, set, innovatively to propulsive drums, a bit of guitar, no bass and lots of layers of vocals. The song ended up a bit of a soccer stadium staple, much like its brethren anthem from Queen, "We Will Rock You." Asked about "Take on the World," Hill explains that "these types of songs weren't really recorded as singles. They were just recorded as rock anthems. The fact that they were  commercial is because of the lyric, 'Take on the world.' 'United,' same thing. But we never consciously went out and wrote a single per se."

But this one in particular bears increased importance, given that it's the first of these for the band, of a handful to come in the '80s, each providing diminishing returns, save perhaps for "United," which raises eyebrows with a crushing verse riff. But here is Priest unwittingly kicking off what would be a New Wave of British Heavy Metal, through the writing of the movement's first "anthem," a subtle distinction, anthem perhaps in this case meaning "boring song," like the old "God Save the

Queen" but most definitely not like the Sex Pistols' "God Save the Queen," which is not boring. So right here in this record, "Rock Forever" and "Delivering the Goods" are anthems too, but not by this narrow definition, namely a song allowed to be boring.

"Actually, we were before the new wave," affirms Hill. "Maiden and Def Leppard and all that lot. But heavy metal was very much more popular in Britain, I think, per capita, I should imagine, than it was in the States. There was the famous TV pop show on BBC called Top of the Pops..." and that's where Priest really drove home the point of "Take on the World." "Right, we were on there, and Donny and Marie were on there at the same time. So it was all very varied in those days."

"I believe 'Take on the World' was recorded in CBS,"

recalls Les Binks. "That was really Glenn's idea. Because it was around the time that Queen had a big hit with 'We Will Rock You.' There's actually no drums at all on that record; it's just the percussive sound that they got basically sitting on a chair and banging your feet on the floor for the bass drum and then slapping your thighs for the upbeat—real simple. And they just tracked that loads of times so it sounds huge and probably made a tape loop of it at the time."

"Glenn wanted to do something along those lines, which is rhythmically simplistic, but this time on the drums. But on 'Take on the World,' there's no bass, which also is the case with 'We Will Rock You.' 'Take on the World' is just drums, guitars and vocals. And so we just messed around to see what we could come up with. I had come up with that drum pattern, and to make it sound really huge, I multi-tracked the drums, so there's maybe, five or six drum kits all playing the same thing. And I played double bass drums on that, but not that fast. I played what, sixteenth notes on the bass drums, and, hang on, eighth notes on the floor tom and two and four on the snare, and then on the next bar... something like that. Anyway it was very simple rhythmically, but a percussive track. And we put that out as a single and it was a hit for us, the first hit single we had in the UK."

"Heavy metal music is full of anthems," explains Rob, asked by Sam Dunn about "Take on the World." "It's full of these great songs, resounding songs that really capture what is the heavy metal spirit. Again, you gotta bring the fans into the picture. 'Put yourself in our hands,' something, something, 'and together we will take on all the world.' That's not just the band saying it, that's everybody saying it. It's a statement of confidence. Like we're not going anywhere, this is who we are and we believe in what we do. And so that 'Take on the World' track is again just a shout, a real demand for attention. And to get on a show like Top of the Pops, some of the fans didn't like that. They didn't like that at all. It was like selling out onto a commercial TV show. We said no, no, no, we're spreading the metal. We're spreading the gospel of metal and the best way you can do that is through something like Top of the Pops, which without a doubt really helped the band grow."

"But again, that's a great show. When we did Top of the Pops, it was like you're in junior high school again. It was the longest running music show, and you saw how that show grew and developed. Top of the Pops was in transition from '60s pop into this heavier thing. And the metal fans, as Top of the Pops progressed and grew, you saw the change in audience. A lot of the bands and band managers were like, get the fans into the show, because it's gotta be relevant and connect. But definitely those early, vintage TV appearances, it was new grounds for everybody. You look at that old footage and half of you wants to scream and pull your hair out if you got any, and then the other half is like this is great. This is really important and valuable, and there's a story there. There's your band on TV, believing in itself plus your audience. We were prepared to take that risk, and grow step by step by step."

"Lyrically, there's the great tradition and heritage and history of metal. Priest were always aware and always grateful for those early days. Even now, that the only way you can progress is with the people that support you. The people that buy a ticket to your show, buy a record, buy a T-shirt. That all goes in the pot that keeps the whole machine moving. So you recognise that. You look around and you see these fans and you go, God bless these fans because we can't do this without the fans. We are without a doubt united in that heavy metal spirit."

"So you think about how you can make that connection. When the band is singing those words, the fans are singing those words, we are all singing about the same thing, the same idea. For this heavy metal community, this spirit of the whole thing is something we experience together and it just makes that bond stronger. We recognise each other, and that this is really important to us. And from those early days and even now today you get the detractors that look at it and go, what is that?

Well we don't care what you think. This is who we are, this is what we love, and this is how we're combining our forces to support each other."

"Take on the World" ends abruptly—hauntingly even—with an epic gong crash, which, according to Binks, gets onto the record in amusing fashion.

Judas Priest tears off the cloth and puts on the leather.

Judas Priest brandishes the leather and makes you like it on their third blockbruiser, "Hell Bent for Leather."

Ten dominant ditties including their English smash-single "Take on the World" and a killer cover of the original Fleetwood Mac's "The Green Manalishi (with the Two-Pronged Crown)" comprise an album that is, we confess, the final catechism in stomp-rock.

Lead singer and whip wielder Robert Halford, flanked by the twin lead guitars of KK Downing and Glenn Tipton, flays up enough excitement on stage and on record to get everybody quivering…on the beat. **Down on your knees and repent if you please! Judas Priest is bent! "Hell Bent for Leather." On Columbia Records and Tapes.**

"We were getting all the drum tracks down, and usually in the middle of the night sometimes, you'd get a phone call to come in and do the percussion overdubs. They had to fit it into what time the studio was available—this was Utopia, I think. And so I got a phone call; they said, bring the gong in, because we want to put the gong in at the end of this song. I had lots of percussion gizmos and gadgets and stuff. And at that time I didn't drive, so I ordered a cab to take me to the studio, with all my equipment. The drums were already there at the studio. But I had all these percussion bits and pieces, and one of them was a 36-inch Paiste gong."

"So somewhere between three or four in the morning. I get a phone call to go into the studio to do these percussion overdubs. And so I ordered a cab and it's what we call a mini cab here, which is a private hire company; they're not like licensed cabs. So the doorbell rang and I went to the door and I was surprised that it was a woman, because normally, especially at that time of the night, you don't expect that. And so I said, 'Oh, I've got all my stuff, this percussion equipment to go to the studio.' So I started to bring it out and load it into the car and she said, 'Oh, I'll help you.' I said no, that's alright; I didn't want a woman lifting anything heavy, you know."

"So we get in the car, and I'm sitting in the front seat, the passenger seat, and there was a load of music cassettes sitting on the dashboard. And we took off and this person was driving like crazy, driving like a lunatic. And then as I looked across at the person and looked at her more closely, and I could see in the moonlight—because it was dark or whatever—I could see a little bit of a five o'clock shadow. So the penny dropped and I realised it was a bloke, it was a guy. Dressed as a woman. You know, with a wig. So I thought, oh shit; this guy, obviously, was a cross-dresser or a transvestite, and when he went out mini-cabbing at night, he would dress in women's clothes with a wig and all the makeup on and everything. And he wasn't very effeminate looking either; he didn't do a great job of it."

"So he turns this corner, and like I say, he's driving really fast and erratically. He turns this corner and all the cassettes slid across the dashboard and all around into my seat. So he pulls over and he says, 'Oh, sorry, sorry,' he bends over and starts groping around my legs, you know? And I said, 'No, don't worry, I'll pick 'em up, I'll pick 'em up.' So when we got to the studio, I said, 'Have a look at this cab driver.' And he picks up this 36-inch gong and carries it like a builder would carry it, you know, big, muscular bloke. It was hilarious, you know? Absolutely hilarious. The guys took the mick out of me the rest of the evening."

Explaining how this gong technique works, Les says, "It's simple, very easy. You just get a container, like a big plastic tub, and fill it with water so you can semi-submerge the gong into it, maybe halfway up at the most.

And so you hold the gong in one hand—it's got a loop-holder at the top of it—and you strike it with the beater and then you lower it slowly into the tank of water. And it bends the pitch of the gong; it suddenly makes a strange swishing noise. You mic it up; you can use as many mics as you like, a couple takes, not too many, until you get it right."

Cross-dressing cabbie dispatched and the throb of "Take on the World" subsiding, come side two of *Killing Machine*, another lesser heralded Priest classic drips with magnetism. "Burnin' Up" is groovy, melodic, yet still supercharged with rock-solid guitars. Again, there's a confidence and a swagger there, as musicians, frontman and producer conjoin for an upper crust metal experience. The break is a bit of a psychedelic respite similar to "Whole Lotta Love," from which the band emerges vicious and delicious, molten guitars battling and caterwauling until one final, victorious lapse into a reprise of the song's magical first verse.

"'Burnin' Up' is quite funky, actually," muses Les. "If you listen to the drum part of that, it's almost a funk pattern. I came from a session background, so I was required to play many different styles, and I used to quite like listening to some of the black American funky drummers. We were talking about Billy Cobham earlier on, but Lenny White was another guy, who worked with Chick Corea, Return to Forever. If you doing session work, you need to be able to expand and listen to a lot of different musical styles. Because sometimes you're hired to go into the studio and you really don't know what you're going to be asked to do when you get there. The guy might have a demo of a song or it might be just a chord sheet or on some occasions, they've written out all the drum parts. So you can't turn around and say, no, I don't like that. You're there to do a job. You're there to try and play a drum part that fits the style of the music and enhances the song. And usually producers and songwriters will kind of leave it to the drummer, because, you know, their brains don't work the same way. So they leave it to the drummer to create the drum parts to a certain degree and that is pretty much what happened with Priest."

Fleetwood Mac's "The Green Manalishi (with the Two-Pronged Crown)" comes next in the sequence, but only on the North American issue of the album called *Hell Bent for Leather*. Again, unsurprisingly, the label thought it might be a good idea to record a cover to float as a single. "Better by You, Better than Me" came about this way, as did "Diamonds and Rust." Priest figured they would only keep the song if they had put their personal stamp on it and that was accomplished in spades. This leaden heavy metal behemoth barely resembled the early Fleetwood Mac original. Its celebrated Priest chug is an instant invitation to headbang, and it's been a live favourite ever since.

Quips Glenn, "It was a song we liked. Peter Green has always been a bit of a hero to me anyway, a great white English blues guitar player and a great songwriter. I don't know whether I suggested it. In fact, I don't think I did. But it would have been one of us, I think, as opposed to 'Diamonds and Rust,' which I think was suggested by the record company, and then we kicked it around."

Adds Ian, "I know at one time we were going to do 'Race with the Devil' by a band called Gun, the Gurvitz brothers, and that's one of the extra tracks we recorded that we didn't use. We went away, and again they were asking us to do a cover version with a view toward getting it on radio and somebody came up with that. We thought, yeah, that's great. We were all into Fleetwood Mac and Peter Green. And I think it was Ken and Glenn who got their heads together and revamped it." Rumours persist of the band also, at one time, working up "Play with Fire" by the Rolling Stones.

"Again, this all came off the back of the experience we had with songs like 'Diamonds and Rust,'" recalls Rob. "I think because that was so well-received, and since the label, particularly from America, was hoping to get some music that they could use as a crossover into American radio, we were approached with a number of different possibilities. And someone suggested 'Green Manalishi.' My recollection is that that was the one track that we were excited about approaching."

People have speculated that Peter Green's "Manalishi" lyric is in reference to the seductive allure of money, and that it was part of what was pushing the enigmatic guitarist into mental illness. A strong argument can also be made that it refers to acid and acid flashbacks, Green once saying that he "took acid and never came back." Turns out the story with the most substance contains a bit of both. Green once intimated that the Manalishi was an elastic-banded wad of paper money he once saw, proffered as payment for a gig. The wad was stood up on end and then fell away in two directions, looking like a crown, after which the word "manalishi" came to him. In other interviews, Green has more plainly explained that it was simply a song about money, about a working guitarist getting more of it than he deserved, more of it than he personally could handle.

The band's original title track came next, "Killing Machine" being another one of these lesser-known Priest gems, the band going for a minimalist, down-wound rhythm, again, illustrating the adventurous nature of this album, this idea that, as Glenn has enthused, the record contains an astonishing range of emotions and styles. Part of the charm of "Killing Machine" is the stereo effect, with the guitars panned hard left and right. Another interesting feature is that it is slow and atmospheric, often a challenge to pull off in metal. There's also no chorus, or at most a very brief and heavy one, with Halford growling "I got a contract on you" amidst other lyrics outlining the on-the-job rewards of being a contract killer.

K.K. seems to intimate that the band had attempted too much on records previous to this one. Asked if *Hell Bent for Leather* represented a move away from the fast, scientific writing all over *Stained Class*, he concurs. "Yes, an easing off a bit. Because you can actually try too hard in the studio, that's for sure. You can become a victim of your own endeavours, really." Too clever, perhaps? "Yeah, exactly (laughs). They always say you can get sucked up into your own ass if you're not careful in the recording studio. And there's a lot of truth in that."

Asked whether he viewed *Hell Bent for Leather* as more of a flamboyant record versus its predecessors, in terms of letting certain aspects of his lifestyle emerge, Halford is reticent. "You know, even today I'm pretty uncontrollable with where I'm potentially going to go next. I think it's just because I have this mental ability. I have a very, very broad mind for anything that's interesting or I could find potentially entertaining as a lyric, both from what goes on inside of me as a person and from what I've witnessed in the rest of the world, whether it's on the street, the TV, or the radio, conversations with friends. I'm just absorbing all of this stuff. So I think that's where it was with the music at that time and how it affected me to write songs like 'Burnin' Up' and 'Hell Bent for Leather.' You just sit there and think about the possibilities. I mean, there's no rules. That's what I like about it. There really are no rules about what you can do with lyrics in music. But even though there's always been a certain portion of metal, being this kind of escapist, fantasy, illusion world, I was always looking for some real issues to talk about."

"There was always that in Priest," says Rob, asked if there was any degree of friction in the band during the *Hell Bent for Leather* days. "There was always that there. Everybody wanted to do everything else. I would have liked in Priest, at that point, to go in the direction of a band like Queen for example. If you really sit down and have a complete understanding of the mind and the music of Judas Priest, it's very much that kind of Queen-like approach. You can do anything. Just look at what Judas Priest has done, the different kinds of music that we've created. It's remarkable, really."

"I think a lot of people miss that. They just look at it from album to album. But if you look at the diversity and all the adventures that Priest has had, it's remarkable. I don't think there's ever been, or will ever be, another metal band that can make those kinds of things happen and make them stick. When you look at what Priest did in terms of the great writing and the experimentation that it pursued, there were similar elements to what Queen was doing. There is always a moment where you can go further. I've always believed that you don't set rules for yourself. You should be prepared to push and stretch and take risks. And that's what that band did continuously. Although in their mind, Queen weren't taking risks, they just continued to do what they do. But they were carefree about what people thought about where they went with their music, and I just admire that."

But disagreements of direction reared their head within Priest time and time again, even though given the band's reticence in interviews, you rarely heard about them. "All the time, yeah. But that's the way it should be. You can't just sit down and nod your head and go, 'Yeah, okay, let's do this.' You've got very strong characters and personalities in any successful band. I don't care who they are. It's never smooth sailing. It's always about pushing for what you want to hear, and what you want to try and getting the other person to think the

same way as you do, to make a good song better. That was always the approach. We always said, 'Well, okay, I'm not quite getting this yet, but let's work on it a bit' and we'd massage it and make it complete. One thing I do recall is that over all my time with Priest, when we went into the studio, we said let's start from scratch. Let's see what we can do with new ideas, although we would pull a riff from a previous Friday and work it into something new. But essentially it was okay, it's a new record, let's start fresh."

"Running Wild" comes next in the record's canny sequence, and you can pair this one with "Rock Forever" as a crystallised, compact statement of metal intent, the band coming up with a gorgeous yet brief rocker light on its feet, efficient of construction. I could picture this as an Accept song, and indeed a dozen tracks of theirs and a dozen tracks of Priests, I could see swapped. There are considerable differences between the bands, but there are a number of convergences as well. This one is in possession of that same joyful pure metal spirit found on Accept's 1982 album *Restless and Wild*, with other songs on this record sounding very much like some of the material on its predecessor *Breaker*.

"Before the Dawn" is the record's token ballad, and it at least retains the sombre nature of Priest and what the band was busy building. Not unlike "The Last Rose of Summer" or more so anything funereal and quiet from Sabbath, why this was picked as a single is a bit of a mystery.

Killing Machine closes with "Evil Fantasies," another lumbering Sabbath-like number in tone and tune with "Killing Machine," earlier on the same side. Again, the band is confident enough to play very slowly, rife with spaces and pregnant pauses. Top-notch riffs are all over the place, as they are on the rest of this solid but varied and well sequenced record. The song's almost Nazareth-like double time finale is an excellent way to close out this bruising, insistent, dynamic record, representing a bit of an outro jam.

Notes Les on this one, "The studio we had used for *Stained Class*, for my liking, was a little bit dead in terms of acoustics. I like to record the drums in a big ambient room. And if you listen to "Evil Fantasies," it's got a big open ambient drum sound, quite a contrast with the drum sound on *Stained Class* or some of the other *Killing Machine* tracks."

"And that's because that track was recorded, I believe, at CBS Studios in London, in a huge big room with parquet wooden floor and, so you could put mics at the other end of the room, ambience mics, to pick up the drums from a distance and actually blend that in with a closed mic drum sound. So you've got a big Bonham-esque kind of live drum sound that wasn't achievable at Chipping Norton Studios, because it was a smaller room that the drums were set up in. And it was all carpeted and everything was quite dead acoustically. So for that album, we had to go for more closed mic sounds than we did on the next album."

"Now there was also Basing Street, which is Island Records, who had a studio, and we recorded there as well. There was Utopia, Basing Street and CBS Studios, so there were three studios used for that album. I actually like *Hell Bent for Leather* better because of that, because we used

Martin Popoff

lots of different studios. I got to experiment more with the drum sounds, especially when we got into the bigger studio, CBS. You will notice slight differences in the drum sound from one song to another there."

"All told, I'm pretty much happy with all of it," says Binks, asked about moments of the record he is particularly proud of. "Because whatever song you're playing, you have to approach it in a manner that whatever you play has to work for the song. Some people practice this lick and practice that lick and they're determined to get it in regardless of whether it fits with the song or not. And that's really an immature way to approach playing a song. For instance, you get a track like "Exciter," there's a lot going on there from a drum point of view. Other songs just required a more simplistic approach."

As for being part of a rhythm section with Ian Hill, Les figures, "Ian was a very solid bass player, easy to work with. He'd lock in with the drums sympathetically. And I think he's the only guy in the band who's been in it from day one, if I'm correct. And you know, pretty much everything was live in the studio. I mean, we would get the basic track down with a guide vocal, including bass and rhythm guitars, and then they'd add guitar solos on and in some instances I would add percussion on afterwards as well."

All told, with "Evil Fantasies" in the roller-coaster sequence, and indeed with the subtle charms of what happens within the song, Priest proved that they could no longer be ignored. And with what they had single-handedly accomplished for the genre through four records head and shoulders above any of the band's competitors, neither could this newly cock-sure strain of heavy metal, which was about to manifest and replicate throughout the NWOBHM, kicking off ten intense years of commercial success for this exciting and ever-evolving genre.

Hitting the road, however, Priest would be in support of a record that had hit a mere No.34 on the UK charts and a paltry No.128 on America's Billboard rankings. Not for lack of trying, the label floated a variety of singles. "Evening Star," frankly a fence-sitter, was issued, backed with a live version of "Beyond the Realms of Death"(from The Agora in Cleveland, May 9th 1978); the band was rewarded with a No.53 placement back home with the nifty clear 12" version of this one, an item that included "Green Manalishi" as its third track. The US chart placement on this track would be No.67.

Then there was "Before the Dawn," backed with "Rock Forever" and also "Take on the World," featuring "Starbreaker" live as its flip, from that same Cleveland show, reaching No.14 Stateside—the UK 12" issue included a live version of "White Heat, Red Hot". Into May 1979, CBS issued "Rock Forever" backed with "Green Manalishi." One might argue that until "Rock Forever" was trotted out, CBS had given priority to the three worst tracks on the record. "Rock Forever" may have even been a bit too obscure and obtuse of melody—and too heavy—to have a chance. In this writer's opinion, it is "Burnin' Up" that should have been lead single. It's a well-written song, it's not too fast, it's about a universal theme, namely sex (but it's light, tongue-in cheek), the vocal is not too in-your-face, and it's incredibly hooky. Sure, it's squarely heavy metal, but the choices across Killing Machine are slim pickings in this regard.

Lip-synched videos from Top of the Pops were produced to support "Take on the World" and "Evening Star," the latter receiving a cheap Christmas ornament-style star for on stage spice. A lip-synched live footage "Take on the World" was also whipped up, as were staged/semi-live clips for "Rock Forever" and "Killing Machine."

Recalls Ian, "'Evening Star' was out of the blue, really. It was an album track, and CBS decided that it was commercial enough for a single, so we ended up on Top of the Pops, playing it. On two occasions when we did Top of the Pops, we were playing our hometown, Birmingham, on the same evening. And on both occasions we were late. They forgave us the first time, but I don't think they ever forgave us the second time, the following tour, when exactly the same thing happened. They said, 'We'll get you on first; we'll record your part first, and you'll be able to get back.' Because obviously, the recording was in London at the BBC studios there. And the last time, they had helicopters and aircraft standing by but the weather was too bad. It was a nightmare really (laughs). We were a good couple of hours late. But the audience, God bless them, they sort of sat there and waited for us."

For the Top of the Pops version of "Take on the World," the miming was obvious. Rob claps (his wrist!) while holding the mic loosely to his lips and Les Binks is barely touching his drums. Glenn can be seen working on his red leather image, but it is Rob who has really moved it along, looking a bit like a Nazi brownshirt who's combined the fashion sense of his superiors with nods to S&M. K.K. looks fairly metal in big black leather boots, but both Les and Ian… well, they could have dropped in from a Nashville hootenanny.

But there was no bullwhip. Donnie and Marie Osmond were scheduled for the same episode and Marie had said that it was either the whip or them, despite Rob charming Marie in the dressing room, telling her she didn't need any makeup, that she looked great without it.

For "Evening Star," Rob is now clean-shaven, with his hair bleached almost blonde. But he's decked in leather, as is K.K. and Glenn, who is sporting his red pants, black jacket, white shoes look. Rob had said he always had had a problem with the band's wimpy attire, butted up against such loud, forceful music. Fed up with stealing things out of his sister's closet, it dawned on him that two worlds he was part of—the heavy metal and the homosexual—wore the same clothes. Into a leather shop in London called Mr. S, and the proprietors started loading Rob and K.K. up with gear that sent the image even further, into the world of S&M. Priest's trademark look was born.

"Well, we all knew he was gay," explains Ian, on this interesting dimension Priest shared with Queen, "and we just treated him like a normal human being, the way gay people should be treated. That's about as far as it goes. It's probably the worst kept secret in rock 'n' roll (laughs). To be perfectly honest, I don't know if people were that particularly interested. I mean, what Rob eventually did, by announcing it to everybody, what's the big deal?"

"In the artistic world, sexuality means absolutely fuck all," adds K.K.. "If you have an artistic temperament, you have an understanding about a lot of things. And it's just been there from day one. We've done so much traveling and roughing it. Jesus Christ, we used to sleep in the back of the van in Norway and Sweden and Germany, and we used to clean our teeth all together in the fucking snow. We were all doing the same thing and it just wasn't an entity, know what I mean?"

Both Rob and Glenn have spoken repeatedly about the empowering quality of putting on the gear and hitting the stage, the synergy that happens between the costume and the music coming together. Toward that end, the leathers keep getting heavier and the studs keep multiplying, even to this day, near to the point of distraction, especially when it comes to Rob and his celebrated mirror 'n' metal jacket. Rob has also stressed that given the competition in the world of rock 'n' roll, if you don't have great songs as well as an instantly identifiable image, you're going to be dead in the water.

And back at the *Killing Machine* tour, attention paid to image was helping spice things up. Rob's use of his whip in "Genocide" had one critic up in arms thinking Rob was actually whipping the audience—eventually there were buttons being circulated that said, "I was whipped by Rob Halford." "Genocide" also, for a brief time, featured Rob firing off blanks from a real machine gun, the stage winding up littered with shell casings. It was all too much for fire marshals and the prop was short-lived.

The UK tour began in late October '78, pretty much intensive until November 24th. In terms of a set list, much of the album would get played, save for the surprise deletion of "Evening Star," along with

"Killing Machine" and "Before The Dawn" (understandable in both cases) and "Burnin' Up," a bit of a surprise as well, given that track's sturdy melody and metal heft. An interesting wrinkle was the persistence of "White Heat, Red Hot," a deep album track from *Stained Class*, nestled in the middle the set.

Four dates in Japan were notched in mid-February, from which the live *Unleashed In The East* album would be cut. After that, through to May 6th, America was assaulted, Priest grouped with a host of bands struggling in and around their level, including Pat Travers, Point Blank, Wireless, Angel, and UFO, the latter two verified as headlining over Priest.

In March, Priest played their first Canadian date, supporting Rush. Asked if Neil Peart's finely tuned tom-toms were an influence on him, Les says, "To tell you the truth, I never listened to very much Rush at all. I could hardly tell you any song titles. Actually, we did a gig with Rush at the El Mocambo club in Toronto. We came across the border at Buffalo. I remember going to Niagara Falls and checking that out. I'd never seen Rush before or heard any of their music. The one thing that I noticed was that they had banks and banks of Marshall amplifiers, Marshall stacks, right? Loads of them on stage. And when they were on performing, I stood at the side of the stage and I noticed the guitarist's guitar lead was going behind the Marshall stack, and it was plugged into a Fender twin reverb mic'ed up. That's what he was actually playing through, and all these banks of Marshalls were just there for show."

"But I never really listened that much to Neil Peart, and I always thought the bass player, Geddy Lee, sounded a bit like Jon Anderson from Yes, with that girly voice. The musical style was a bit between prog rock and metal, not really metal as such."

But a double bill like that surely represents two sides of the progressive metal coin, Rush more prog, Priest more metal, but both fairly complex and note-dense. "Right, okay," muses Les. "It's quite difficult, for musicians, when you've been involved in the creative process and putting it out there, to realise what it is. I don't think you really realise it at the time. It's only in retrospect, taking in the comments the people make later on, that you understand the impact that we had on metal. That era kind of put the stamp on Priest as a fully-fledged heavy metal band."

"But we didn't really think about it at the time. You come up with ideas for songs, you get together, you rehearse them, go in the studio, record them, try to make them sound the best as possible and then you move onto the next thing. It's only, as I say, in retrospect, that you realise a lot of people were influenced by those albums. A lot of the bands today, they grew up listening to that stuff. It inspired them to pick up a guitar or pick up the drums and do it for themselves."

"It's been such a long time since I played on those records," reflects Les, "and I've done so much more since then that nobody knows about. But it's the Priest fans that keep referring to me. And it surprises me, because I can be playing with someone, trying to be as anonymous as possible, and someone will approach us and find out who the drummer happens to be and they'll produce a load of albums and things for me to sign. That's always a surprise. But going back to Rush, everybody perceives it in a different way; everybody has a different perspective on it. Like I say, I'd never really heard much of Neil Peart's playing. He's a very good drummer, but I was listening to people like Billy Cobham and Steve Gadd."

JUDAS PRIEST

Back in the UK in late May, Priest were supported by NWOBHM oddballs Marseille, flipping back into support position for their jaunt with AC/DC in Europe. In Dublin, Ireland, July 1st, 1979, as direct support on a four-band bill to Status Quo, Priest were in a stand-off with the local authorities over the use of the motorcycle. The police thought that it might incite violence, but Rob proved them wrong by bringing it out anyway, with no repercussions other than a happy headbanging crowd getting exactly what they wanted.

Back on the road in America, Priest supported Kiss in the fall of '79, for the first month of a two-and-a-half month second US leg. Kiss records weren't selling so well any more, but the shows were still huge and hugely successful. K.K. remembers the situation somewhat that way, noting that Kiss were on the wane and Priest seemed to be on the rise, intimating that the pairing might have accentuated this idea that a changing of the guard had been set in motion.

Fortuitously for all involved, September 24th 1979, Priest was to hook up with Harley Davidson, Rob debuting in Milwaukee with a Harley for the first time, this being the area where Harleys are manufactured. Previously the band had used a Triumph Bonneville, but Harley was in a slump, getting ready to mount their much celebrated and publicised ascension to the intense brand recognition they enjoy today, and they were looking for ideas. Priest's management, Arnakata, were able to buy Rob's first Harley for a single dollar, and a marriage made in heavy metal heaven was born.

Chapter 6:
Unleashed in the East – "30 guys
in white overalls
turned up."

Judas Priest's first live album, *Unleashed in the East – Live in Japan*, was to paste Rob's S&M image and the ultimate heavy metal prop—Rob's ride—firmly in mind as the visual actualization of Priest, all they stood for, metal all the way, hell bent for leather.

"We just got on with our own thing," says Ian Hill, asked whether there was direct kinship with the burgeoning New Wave of British Heavy Metal, a profusion of bands exploding the same year *Unleashed* launched Priest into wider rock 'n' roll consciousness. "We didn't feel part of a movement or anything. We were aware of other bands playing heavy music, but we didn't feel any sort of affinity with them. We were quite happy that the genre was becoming popular, but other than that, we just got on it."

The band's first Harley was given away in a contest a year after its heavy metal use. Rob claims to still have the second one proffered, although an early one was also on loan to the Rock and Roll Hall of Fame in Cleveland. At the height of their fame in the early '80s, the band visited the Harley Davidson offices and was presented with custom leather jackets for all they had done to elevate the name of the brand.

But Priest were still courageously and mainly about the music. While firing on all sixes with what are now considered no less than four of the greatest heavy metal albums of all time (not that anybody had noticed yet), the band briefly touched down in Japan to record this landmark live album.

Unleashed in the East would find Priest making an important hook-up, namely Tom Allom, who was brought in to produce the album, as much as a live album could be. Allom was signed to the same management company as Priest, and had been involved in the first four Sabbath records. Tom explains that his early assignments tended to be with bands managed by the Arnakata, these including Strawbs and The Tourists. Tipton has said that it took a few rounds at the pub to get in synch with Allom, the hard luck, rockscrabble upbringing of the band chafing against Allom's upper middle class sensibilities, Tipton adding however that Allom turned out to be an asset due to his diplomacy amidst the band members, and his ability to get sounds.

Another key happenstance would be that the album would be mixed at Ringo Starr's Ascot-based Startling Studios, (Starr had bought it from John Lennon), soon to be the cradle of the band's breakthrough album, *British Steel*. Like the ubiquitous Manor Studios owned by Richard Branson, this facility was housed in a mansion nestled in acres of countryside, the perfect setting for a band wishing to re-focus and retool.

In any event, the retooling would be later. For now, Priest was all about underscoring all that had come before, presenting with all their hard-won experience, an astonishing raft of great metal songs performed with formidable skill and explosive intensity. *Unleashed in the East* would contain eight Priest classics, but in Japan, the album—rechristened *Priest in the East* and with altered cover art—came with a bonus EP of fully a third more tracks cut from the same cloth.

Fortunately, "Rock Forever," "Delivering the Goods," "Hell Bent for Leather" and "Starbreaker" would be tacked on as bonus tracks when Sony reissued all of the Columbia albums in 2001. Initial shipments of *Unleashed in the East* in the UK also included an EP, featuring three tracks, "Rock Forever," "Hell Bent for Leather" and "Beyond the Realms of Death," the latter also showing up as a b-side to "Rock Forever" two years later. Finally, "Evil Fantasies" would show up as the b-side on a "Living after Midnight" 12" in 1980. "Take on the World" and "White Heat, Red Hot" are the only set list inclusions that remain unissued.

Recalled Glenn of that inaugural round-the-world trek, speaking with Circus, "That was a trip and a half. It took us 14 hours to get there, and by the time we arrived, we were totally exhausted. The first gig was in Tokyo and when we got to the hall, none of it was set up. We were all ready to start ranting and raving when about 30 guys in white overalls turned up. Before we knew it, everything was up."

Mused Halford, "Japan is still one of the most fascinating countries in the world that I've ever been to, and I find it remarkable that heavy metal is so big there. In those days, we used to start the show with our backs to the audience and a stage full of dry ice. As the curtain went up, all these bouquets of flowers, presents, balloons and streamers came flying across. When we turned around, it was like Beatlemania!"

Not many drummers would put up with this today, but quite incredibly, Les Binks would be performing on what has become lauded as one of the greatest live albums of all time using a drum kit he had never before laid eyes upon.

"Yes, well what happened was that the second time we went to Japan, by that time… on the first trip I had brought my own set of Pearls. But I introduced myself to Pearl, the Pearl drum company, and I signed an endorsement deal with them. And so on the second trip over, I didn't bring any drums—they supplied a brand-new kit, all maple shells. And that was actually the kit that I used on the live album, *Unleashed in the East*. I just brought cymbals with me and that was pretty much it."

"When we arrived in Tokyo, for the first gig, I got a call from Pearl saying that they are delivering the kit directly to the venue. So I had to go down there with my drum tech in the afternoon and get everything set up the way I wanted it and tune it the way I wanted it. And normally I have a small hole cut in the front bass drum head, the logo head in the front, for mic'ing up. But we didn't have time for that, nor the tools. And so we just went and recorded the bass drums with the full head on the front, with just a little bit of foam dampening inside."

"And the thing also was, they'd introduced a new line of pedals as well. You know, most drummers, they use pedals that feel comfortable to them to use. And when you switch over to something new, it changes the whole feel, when you connect up with them. So I had all these new pedals as well—new kit, new pedals—so everything felt completely different. But everything worked eventually and it didn't make much difference to the end result."

The original *Unleashed in the East* is usually the lone single-record album that shows up on the list of greatest heavy metal live albums of all time journalists crank out periodically (myself included). The others, as I've alluded to are all doubles, namely UFO's *Strangers in the Night*, Thin Lizzy's *Live and Dangerous*, Blue Oyster Cult's *On Your Feet or On Your Knees*, Scorpions' *Tokyo Tapes*, and of course, Kiss' *Alive!*. In contrast, Priest keeps it tight, taut, rock-solid, yet bullet-barraged and worked with fire, which must have helped push the album to optimistic chart placements—No.10 in the UK and No.70 in the US.

The record starts fast, with a carnal, much less polite version of "Exciter." "Running Wild" is a surprise second selection, the band then settling in with "The Ripper" and "Sinner," then pummelling the kidneys with "Green Manalishi." Requisite hit "Diamonds and Rust" gets as heavy as it can—which is not much. Still, this arguable low point was issued as a single, backed with "Starbreaker." Finally, the *Sad Wings* trilogy, "Victim of Changes," "Genocide" (with pointless extended intro) and "Tyrant," finish off the crowd.

"Sinner" was a particularly interesting song to figure out how to play, says Les. "Sometimes guitar players write riffs or lines in songs where they're not thinking how it would look on paper, if it was written out. And quite often, it changes the time signature. So from a drummer's point of view, you have to sit down and analyse it, and sometimes the easiest thing to do is to learn the riff, what the guitar player is playing, in your head. That's the easiest way to remember it without having to count it. There's a section in 'Sinner' where it goes into 3/4 time, and then a 2/4 bar, and then another couple 3/4 bars, and rather than counting it, it's best to learn it from a guitarist's point of view, and think about what they're playing and then just play with it. Which is a more musical way of playing it, rather than making it more mechanical by counting it in your head."

When all was said and done, inclusive of the records above, no greater one hour of extreme metal classics had ever been assembled to date. Sabbath could have done it, yet at that point, they didn't have a live record. And then again, one wonders if at any point in their career they could have executed with this much flash. Deep Purple could have done it, but through two live records, they chose to attach themselves to the dreary early '70s template, offering boring jams doubly lethal due to being stuffed into some of their sleepiest numbers. Zeppelin and Rainbow charted the same course, and thus *The Song Remains the Same* and *On Stage* are usually banished from the above list, although, to be fair, a large and vocal throng, including Yngwie Malmsteen, cites *Made in Japan* by Deep Purple as something special (unfathomable to this writer).

Still, shoving Priest into that double-record pack, it was obvious which band represented a new guard. Amusingly, Priest were as old and experienced as any of them, but the band, through hard luck, ended up being forced to shape their sound in the corridors, spending five years traveling the motorways before putting out a debut album, and then, in doing so, making a pretty good one.

"Very little!" is Glenn Tipton's response to accusations that the record was heavily doctored and not that live at all (earning the nickname *Unleashed in the Studio*). "This rumour came out initially because... why there was work done on it, was because when Rob did it, he was sick; he had a cold. And we really had to give the vocals a little bit of attention, which is unusual, because Rob has a great voice. But he sung that show and he really had the flu. So he did a little bit of work, not a lot, on the vocal side of it. And we touched a couple of guitars up, but very, very little. And this rumour came out that it had been redone in the studio. But if you listen to it, you can tell it wasn't. It really caught Priest as they were, as they played in Japan in '78. All in all, it was a great live album, and a very honest live album. Some people strip everything off and then put it back on again. We wouldn't do that. But there will always be rumours."

To be fair, ardent Priest fans have compared the album with a bootleg of the February 15th show and found it to be quite similar to the finished record. However Rob had been spotted back at Startling Studios out on the patio, with headphones on, singing away, and the rumours caught fire from there. Issues have even been taken with the crowd noise, but again, a comparison with the bootleg shows a similar idiosyncratic Japanese crowd effect.

"*Unleashed* was a difficult record, because it was really badly recorded," explains producer on the project, Tom Allom. "They recorded several shows; Sony recorded them, in Japan, and they recorded them all exactly the same, and so they were bad in exactly the same ways (laughs). I had a terrible business mixing them. And I remember that it must've been towards the end of the tour and Rob's voice was very tired."

"We weren't able to do any... we didn't do any guitar overdubs. I mean, it would have been absolutely impossible. I've tried to do this with other live stuff, where you try and match the sound of a live recording and it's terribly difficult. More or less impossible, actually. What we probably did... I can't really remember now; again, it would've been a lot harder to do then versus today, taking a piece from a different show and slotting it in, guitar parts or whatever. It would be dead-easy to do with ProTools now, but it would've been frightful then. We just had to bash on with what we'd got."

"So it was some vocals but nothing major," continues Allom. "I remember it used to be called *Unleashed in the Studio*, and it's absolutely not the case (laughs). And I've done over this last couple of years two or three live things for the band; about five years ago we did the Budokan thing, and no overdubs on that. Also no overdubs on the *British Steel* live thing that we just did. There was a nice little album that came out in the spring last year called *A Touch of Evil: Live*. That was a selection of different shows during the close of the touring; they did a couple of years touring. Didn't even see the band, actually. When we were doing the *British Steel* thing, Glenn came down for an afternoon, for a little bit of input. We had a little bit of trouble with the tuning on some of the tracks, and we had to bend it a bit."

Back to *Unleashed in the East*, the cover art however was indeed done back home, bearing the handiwork of top snapper Fin Costello. Esteemed Sounds scribe, Geoff Barton, on tour at the time with the band in Chicago, asked K.K. if there's any truth to the rumour that the front cover shot was taken at Dunstable Civic Hall in front of a bunch of old age pensioners playing bingo (Barton knowing full well it was, because his buddy Fin told him so). KK plays it deftly, tongue firmly in cheek: "Where did you get that information from? Dunstable Civic Hall? A total fallacy. Who do you believe, readers? Me or your favourite Sounds writer? Fin? Never heard of him. From a professional point of view, I totally deny these accusations. I just don't know where you get your information from. Fin Costello? When I get to see him, I'll give him a shunt up the arse. No, the picture was taken when we were playing in front of one of our favourite audiences in Japan. Good shot, isn't it? Except for Glenn. His face looks like a bruised tomato."

Downing had been participating in this eye-winked back-and-forth with Geoff Barton amidst tour dates in the US, where Priest were supporting Kiss, K.K. remarking upon the headliner that, "Those guys are multimillionaires, but before I go out on stage, I'll generally see Paul Stanley sitting on a flight case, just dressed in ordinary jeans and a T-shirt, and he'll say, 'Have a good gig.' That sort of thing means the world to me; it's not what I expected. I mean, we've actually opened for English acts, namely, Foghat, and never even got to see the fucking geezers. There's been like this big barrier. Even Ted Nugent had more to say than them. One of the nicest people, though, is Eddie Van Halen; he's terrific, not stuck up. He even admitted to me once that Van Halen used to play 'Victim of Changes.'"

When Geoff tells K.K. that Rob is one of David Lee Roth's favourite vocalists, Downing reflects, "Ah, yes, Rob. Well, who else is there at the moment? You've got your bands—Scorpions, Mahogany Rush, UFO—but who's got the vocalist? We have. I've been in rock 'n' roll a long time, and I would match Rob against anyone. I mean, the guy's got an incredible voice. He can sing Frank Sinatra, Robert Plant, Bing Crosby, you name 'em."

An interesting wrinkle about the *Unleashed in the East* cover is that Les Binks isn't pictured. This was because at the time of the shoot, he had already left the band. Notes Ian, "He was a fine drummer, Les. But I don't know, I think he had run his course. I think he was a little bit tired with it, all the road work we did. He'd had enough I think (laughs). He'd moved on."

That's the polite face on it, but another cooked-up reason—and only a shade stronger—is that Les wasn't all that powerful live. A studied listen to *Unleashed in the East* doesn't proffer any indication of this, and if Binks does indeed lack power or groove, he certainly makes up for it in matching the band's sense of flair, whack for whack. Sure, there's that bizarre lost-my-mind disco beat in "Starbreaker" (which isn't even part of the original album), but other than that, Les is a huge part of *Unleashed*'s wow and prowess.

Still, the party line ossifies in the minds of those who were there, such as Glenn... "Les was a fantastic drummer, you know. If I had to criticise Les, I think technically he was capable of playing anything. And he stepped into the situation and filled the gap admirably. But he didn't quite lay it down enough on stage. It was in time and it was note-perfect, but there was... I think for what Priest needed, just a slight lack of physical energy there. And I think that is eventually why we parted company. But funnily enough, I met someone the other day who knew Les, and none of us can really identify the moment when Les left. You know, there is a strong possibility that Les could still be with us, because none of us is really sure when we parted company. He was a vegetarian too, and that maybe didn't ring too well in the Priest camp (laughs). We're big meat-eaters here."

Adds Halford, "Les' involvement came about off of the back of the work that Simon Phillips did for us on the *Sin After Sin* album. Simon Phillips is a very technical, very inventive drummer. And the two previous drummers we worked with, John Hinch and Alan Moore, were very kind of straight down the road, very economic, simple, tasteful drummers. And I think the reason we got so excited about using somebody out of the Simon Phillips style of drumming, was that we could just see again, at least at that time from the writing point of view, the advantage of having a drummer that could be very flamboyant and busy and hitting a lot of things, that kind of approach. So Les was with us for two albums, *Stained Class* and *Killing Machine*. After we had been through those two writing modes, and we eventually had the experience and hooked up with Tom Allom, the band was suddenly writing in this *British Steel* format. There was just this feeling that we wanted to get back, if you will, to that very simple, steady, solid, almost Bonham-esque style of drumming. And we found all of those things we needed in Dave Holland."

But all of the above is a bunch of bollocks, according to the man at the centre of the storm, Les Binks himself. Says Les, it's a pile of excuses,

Martin Popoff

although, to be fair, the guys might have been genuinely guessing at what the hell happened to the drummer that made *Stained Class*, *Killing Machine* and *Unleashed in the East* three of the most beloved Priest albums according to the fans that go deep.

"Well, the problems all started back in Japan, really," begins Les, recounting the narrative that leads to his walking away from the band. "I noticed at the time, that when I got the drums all set up and tuned, that there was a 24-track mobile at the back of the studio, and the engineers were running in cables to record the gig."

"Now don't forget, I was pretty much still freelance. I wasn't contracted to the management and I wasn't contracted to the record company. And so the deal I had with them was, I would go into the studio with them and I would get paid session fees for the recordings, plus I had negotiated wages for when we were on tour. It's not to say that I would've been opposed to signing to the record company but I never really was offered that. But the thing that made me decide to leave the band was the fact that, you know, the management they had at the time was a guy named Mike Dolan and he was basically a crook (laughs). You know, me and the guys, we were all young in those days and a lot more naïve, especially about the business side of things. And there were too many sharks around in the industry that were preying off people like us."

"Our previous manager, David Hemmings was dead at this point. David Hemmings, at the time when I was with them, they had Annie Lennox and Dave Stewart, and they were in a band together called The Tourists, before they formed Eurythmics. And The Tourists had had a hit here in the UK. So they were under the same management, and the other guy that was under the same management was the Pat Travers Band, Canadian guitar player, still around today. And I think David Hemmings decided he was going to move and set up on his own in New York and he was going to take total control over the Pat Travers Band. So they all agreed to that and he moved to New York and he had a girlfriend at the time, set up an office there, and he was looking after Pat Travers and I think he committed suicide, for whatever reason."

So in comes Mike Dolan. "Yes, and he had a brother for a partner, and the brother was called Jim Dawson. Two different surnames, you know? There's something dodgy there (laughs). My brother has a different surname than me. How did that one come about? So it was those two, but we never had much to do with the other guy, Jim Dawson. But yes, after David Hemmings left, Mike Dolan took over as personal manager for Priest."

And back in Japan, "Management was with us at the time," continues Binks. "And I pulled management aside and said, 'What is this about a recording? We haven't discussed it in advance. I need an arrangement for making a live album.' And they said, 'Oh, no, no,' tried to brush it off, 'Don't worry about it. It's just for CBS, Sony's sake. If we want to do anything with it we'll sort it out later.'"

"So after we came back and did a British tour, we took a break, because we'd been touring nonstop. And I was the only guy in the band who was musically active outside of the band. So as soon as we took a break from touring and whatever, I was phoning up my session contacts saying, 'Look, I'm back in town, I'm available for sessions, have you got anything you need me for? By all means give me a call.' So I'd been working in studios and doing stuff for other people when the band was off the road."

"Then one day I got a call from their manager, Mike Dolan, saying, 'Hi Les, come into the office. I wanna have a talk with you about the band's next move.' So I said okay, fine. I went in the office and sat across the desk from him, and he said, 'The guys are down at Ringo Starr's studio, Startling Studios, in Ascot,' which, you've probably seen that place. It's featured on the 'Imagine' video. You know, with John Lennon and Yoko going through the big white building with all the things white inside. And he sits at the piano and plays it. That's where the guys were. They were coming down from Birmingham."

"And this is the first time they hooked up with Tom Allom, as producer. I never met Tom Allom because I never went into the studio. Obviously, all my drum parts were recorded in Japan. So the manager says to me, 'The guys are all down at Startling Studios and are listening to the tapes from Japan, with producer Tom Allom, and it sounds really good.' He said, 'We've had a lot of inquiry from fans, when is the band going to release a live album? So we think this could be the new album, you know.'"

"I said, 'That's great, that's fine, just do me the same as you paid me for the last album.' He said, 'Well, that's what we're thinking; it would be a nice gesture on your behalf if you would waive your fees on this occasion.' So I was completely gob-smacked, you know? I thought, how can someone have such a hard neck to suggest that I take no payment for this, you know? How am I supposed to pay the bills? So this was when the proverbial shit hit the fan. And it all got very nasty."

"Now I never saw the guys again. I never had any contact with them, because I was never invited to the studio to have a listen to the tapes. The first time I heard that album was when it was released on vinyl. And I was a little bit annoyed that nobody in the band called. Communication in those days, of course, was all by landline and we all had each other's phone number, but nobody phoned me or got in touch and said, 'We hear you're leaving the band. You know, what's the problem? Are you upset about something? Is there something we can work out, because we don't want to lose you.'"

"That never happened. That conversation never took place. So I just made the assumption that they knew what their management was up to. But in retrospect, I don't think they did. You know, they just thought I decided to leave and give them no excuse, no reason. And of course, the manager was in between. He was probably giving them some cock and bull story, you know? I doubt if he would've given them the truth on the matter. So the manager was telling me, 'Waive your fees,' not the band. A lot of people think, you know, when someone leaves a band, they're leaving because they're not getting on with somebody in the band and they're having problems. That was never the case with me. We never had any arguments or any cross words at all."

This final point is key. It kind of screws around the idea that Priest deliberately changed direction so abruptly for reasons completely unrelated to who was drumming for them. If you think about it, with Les still there, one would think they might have carried on closer within the frame of what they had just accomplished across *Stained Class* and *Hell Bent for Leather*.

"Complete bollocks," answers Les, asked to comment on the idea, widely reported, that Priest at this point desired a drummer who played more straight ahead, less "jazzy." "Think of it logically, right? I explained to you the reason I left the band, right? Now, if they'd been honest and said, why has Les left? How would that have looked to the fans? 'To be honest, it was because we didn't want to pay him for our latest album.' How ridiculous would that have sounded to their fan base? There were all kinds of made-up excuses and reasons put out to the media, after I left, to try and give some smokescreen, to put up something out that people would buy. If they'd said Les left because we didn't want to pay him, everybody would've gone, that's ridiculous, you know? They would've got a really bad reaction to that."

"So they had to think up other reasons. And the thing was, who comes along to replace me? Dave Holland. But Dave Holland couldn't play like me. He couldn't do all that stuff that I did. He didn't play a multi-tom kit and he couldn't play those sorts of fills and stuff that I did. They had to think of an excuse as to why they had such a radical change in the style of drumming. So they came up with, 'Oh, Les was a lot more technical.' Well, of course I was, but so was the music—it fit the music."

"Dave Holland, I never really heard his playing. I heard a live recording recently, actually, of just after he joined the band, where he's playing some of my drum parts, or attempting to. And his style was a bit more… what's the word, a slightly more basic style of playing, you know? He had good time and he was a pretty decent drummer, but he had a simplistic approach to the songs. There were certain things that I played that he never even bothered to attempt. I don't think he ever played 'Exciter' live. I may be wrong, but I don't recall. I think they dropped 'Exciter' from the set, and not because it wasn't popular. It was very popular with fans, but I don't think he could adapt to that style."

"So at this point it all got rather nasty with the manager," continues Binks. "First off, I felt hugely insulted. Hugely insulted and completely undervalued and disrespected, that someone would come out with such a suggestion. And it dragged out for months. I could've dealt with the situation in a completely different way. Because I wasn't contracted to the record company, the record company couldn't have released that album without my consent—because I'm not signed to them. When we made an album, I had to sign a release on it; you know, accept the session fees for it. So they couldn't release that album without my consent. And that meant they had to pay me something."

"Oh, and the other thing was, my drums at the time, the kit that I'd just picked up from Japan, the end of the British tour, all the back line equipment was being held in storage by the lighting company, on their premises. My kit was in there with all the rest of the back line. And I had another kit at the management's office. And I made a tragic mistake. I had already decided, this is ridiculous, they're treating me as if I'm a disposable piece of… you know. I'm not important. So I'd decided and realised that this guy was a rip-off merchant anyway, their manager, and I just couldn't work with the guy. That if that's how he was going to treat me, if he thought this was an acceptable way to treat the drummer—or any human being, for that matter—I decided that's it, I'd had enough."

"So I made the mistake of calling at the office and picking up that kit first. Because I needed it anyway, because I was doing session work—I needed my drums back to use in the studio. But the other kit, I had to hire a van, and I went up to the lighting company's premises in Watford or something, and the guy who did the tour with us, a guy named Ronan, it was his company, he came to the door, and I said, 'Oh hi Ronan, I've just come to collect my drums; I've got some sessions lined up.' He said, 'Well, we've had strict instructions from the band's manager not to let you take any of your drums off the premises.' So my drums were being held ransom basically. So in the end, you know, I could've got lawyers involved and slapped an injunction on the album and all that sort of stuff and got really nasty. But to tell you the truth, I just wanted to get as far away from it all as possible. I had a real sickness of being messed about being ripped off."

What amounts to an emasculation of Les Binks within the Priest fold extends to his favourite badge of honour concerning those days as well. "The same guy also stole my publishing for 'Beyond the Realms of Death,'" explains Les. "I don't get the publishing on that now. At the time, they had a publishing company as well as a management company. And so as I had just written this one song, I thought, okay, well, I'll go with the same company that Rob is with and the rest of the guys are all signed to, which was the management company's, Arnakata Music Inc., a limited company. Limited liability."

"And so Rob and I signed effectively the same contract. So we split the royalties 50-50. But we were really young and naïve at the time, and the deal we were getting, they were taking 40% of the publishing, from the publisher, and 60% to the writer. So Rob and I were only splitting 60% for the song. So we got 30% each, and they got 40%. A ridiculous contract to sign. But, you know, young and naïve."

"Then shortly after I left the band, they stopped sending out the royalty statements and the checks stopped coming. And so I rang up the office and I said, 'Look, I'm due a statement. There's no check, nothing; it's several weeks late' or whatever. 'Oh, don't worry, it's just an administrative error.' 'The check's in the post,' all kinds of stories. Actual fact, what was happening was, the company was being put into liquidation. And they weren't going to tell me about it. At this point, David Hemmings was dead. All right, so, at that point they had to find new management. And that's when they switched over to Trinifold with Jayne Andrews and Bill Curbishley, who are still with them today."

"And so I just wanted to make a clean break," says Les. "I wanted the album to come out as well, because I thought it be good for me as well. To get my name out there. So I didn't cause any big stink, as such.

In retrospect, you know, sometimes I think I should have. Because I got ripped off on that one as well. So anyway, when the royalty statements stopped coming in, I tracked down who currently had the publishing of the song and it was a company called Metro Holdings. And who should be running Metro Holdings—Mike Dolan. So I rang him up, and I said, 'Hi Mike, I believe you're publishing my song.' I said, 'I haven't received any royalties from you.' He said, 'Oh, well, we went back to the receivers, the official receiver, the liquidator,' and what happened was my half of the song was left on their catalogue of songs that they... and that was seized by the liquidator as an asset. To bring in money, to pay off their debts."

So he said he went back to the liquidators and said there's some songs on the catalogue we would like to buy back. And so he said, 'We took legal advice at the time and we're not liable to pay you anything. Your contract is with the old company. In liquidation. You don't have a fight with us. We're not liable to pay.' And I've been fighting this for years."

It's a tale that is typical of this business, and unfortunately, one that is marred and scarred by a crucial lack of communication between the parties that could have potentially fixed it all—the five members of the band.

What Priest might have accomplished with this classic lineup still firing on all sixes for another few albums, we'll never know, rock 'n' roll history is far worse off for it. Les' last album with the band, *Unleashed in the East*—no doubt helped by the touring of it, despite it being a live record—would rise to an impressive No.10 placement in the UK charts, while stalling at No.70 in the US and No.73 in Canada. More importantly, as fans slowly realised how top-shelf Priest was—even with Dave Holland on the drum stool struggling to play what Les had done—the album would achieve platinum status in the States, quite the accomplishment given that half the material hailed back to the band's murky and medieval second album from three years previous.

Chapter 7:
British Steel – "We're metal, but like, don't be afraid."

"All through the 70s, we were journeymen, really. We were trying to build, trying to get the acceptance of metal. The reason why that particular album, *British Steel*, is such a special album, is because with Judas Priest, whatever you want to call it, luck or judgment or talent, the timing was right. Timing is very important. I've always said that in music, anyway. *British Steel* was the exact perfect record. For once, Judas Priest fucking got it right. The timing was right for that record, more so than any of our other records."

Those are the words of Priest's most forthright member, K.K. Downing, or I should say ex-member, now retired from the band to his pastoral estate, and good for him if he thinks that's what he wants for the rest of his quite charmed life.

"One of the wonderful memories that I think we all have about Judas Priest is 1980," seconds Rob. "Because here, we have the start of a new decade. You look at what happened in 1980 alone with all the other releases that were happening, it's a remarkable year. It definitely is that New Wave of British Heavy Metal movement. By then of course we've had a few records established, but *British Steel* has become a masterpiece for a lot of people in metal for lots and lots of different reasons, but I think it's a case of a band truly finding their defining sound."

"We also at last had found the look and the imagery. It was kind of filtering in with *Hell Bent for Leather* to some extent, *Killing Machine*, but by the time we were into *British Steel*, we'd got it. We knew absolutely everything about who we were, what we were trying to do and be. We knew there was still a lot more to do, but that was just a great start to an incredibly important decade in metal—1980 and *British Steel*. So 'United' is there, all those great songs, 'Rapid Fire,' 'Steeler,' 'Grinder,' you know, 'Breaking the Law' and 'Living After Midnight'…. every track has something really important to say about the concept and messages of metal as we were thinking about them in 1980."

With the exclamation point of the live album out of the way, Priest set about making new inroads into accessibility. Finances were dire, despite the triumphant signals that the front cover of *Unleashed in the East* might loudly be sending. Reaching back even further, *Hell Bent for Leather* might conceivably be viewed as a first step toward some far off songfulness that would finally garner the band some sales. But it would be the band's fateful

association with producer Tom Allom that would unlock a box filled with the psyches of a headbanging army of fans latent for years and now ready to burst with pride. Indeed Allom had just recorded Def Leppard's competent and youthful *On Through the Night* debut, at the same homey home studio he was taking Priest into, so the vibe was there to take Priest commercial.

"I think it was one of the simplest records that we made," muses Halford on *British Steel*, understating the fact by a multitude of multiples. "At that point we were all on the same page; we were all thinking in the same way. Because that album is literally written from scratch. So it wasn't a case like, where in some of the other instances, we would sit at home with our tape recorders and come in together and throw our ideas on the table. With *British Steel*, we really wrote that together. That was the first time that me and Ken and Glenn wrote as a trio."

"And when we saw how successful that was, and how much fun we were having doing that, we decided from that point on to write as a trio. But the friction still existed in that healthy competitive manner. Ken and Glenn both had two very different styles of guitar playing. So it was just a question of give-and-take really. I mean, I can only speak as an observer. I would never put words into their mouths, but just from what I experienced, there was just this constant type of situation of essentially wanting to do the best things, but having that kind of healthy, robust competitive edge in what one would present to the other and back and forth (laughs). It was like a tennis match, volleying riffs at each other."

As regards Tom Allom's production job, with *British Steel* taking a mere four weeks to record, Rob explains that, "as far as the end result is concerned, you are responsible for the final things that come out of the speakers as much as the producer. Because at the end of the day you kind of nod your head and give it the green light and say, 'That's good; let's move on to the next track.' But I mean, producers have their own style and way of capturing the sound. That's why we were so thrilled to work with Tom. He suddenly came along and captured all of the dimensions that we felt were right for the sound we were creating, and that's why we had such a long experience with him."

Rob has also said that the sound of the album has an almost stainless steel quality about it, and that the album was to the point, sharp and direct. Tom Allom further claimed that the album's lively sound came from the fact that he and the band quickly decided that the confines of the studio itself wouldn't work. On a search for sounds, they fanned out, recording in various rooms of the manse, with the expansive marble-floored hallway becoming key for the drum sound, hanging ambient mic'ing and all.

"It was done at Startling," says Tom, referring to Ringo Starr's "home" studio. "I've made quite a lot of my records there. I had actually, at the time I made that album, I had only done one Judas Priest record, which was the live *Unleashed in the East* album, which we mixed at Startling. But the reason we did that there was because I was using the studio quite extensively with other bands. And then I did the Def Leppard album there, and then the next thing immediately after that was *British Steel*. Leppard was either side of Christmas that year and *British Steel* was the whole month of February."

Oddly and even frustratingly to this writer, when asked how he had changed Priest's sound, Allom, in a manner, draws a blank. "I don't think I did, to be honest with you (laughs). To be perfectly truthful, I may have helped them get their live sound on record, but I don't think I changed their sound at all. I wouldn't have considered that I did that. I think I captured it."

What was the significance of the change in drummers then? How did that change the sound?

"They had been through a couple of different drummers by the time I worked with them. The only drummer who was actually a member of the band, that I'm aware of, was Les Binks, who I actually did finally meet once. Because the last time they made an album with him was *Unleashed in the East*; he didn't attend the studio at all, I don't think. And then of course, Dave Holland played on all the albums I did with them. But I don't think there was a conscious decision to commercialise. It just happened that they came up with two really commercial tracks, 'Breaking the Law' and 'Living After Midnight.' I mean, it's extraordinary, really, because the whole album is not only recorded in the 28 days of February, I'd say that somewhere between 80 and 90% of it was written in that time too. They just came into the studio, as I recall, with some ideas for guitar riffs and little more."

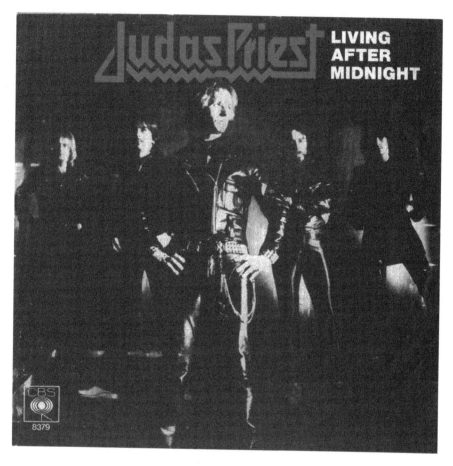

Comments K.K. on Tom and his methods, "He would rearrange the songs. Tom was the type of producer who would, if he particularly could, make a song simpler and punchier and to the point—he was more that way inclined. We only had about six weeks to record the album, so that was conducive to getting the job done. And yes, sound-wise, we actually recorded the drums in the staircase, as you would, really, to get the best ambience and room sound. It was kind of weird really, because I was in the library, I think Glenn was in the dining room, Dave was in the staircase. We were all split up in these different rooms for separation. But I really liked it in the library, because it had a wooden floor, which is fantastic for guitar playing, any room with plenty of wood. So you get these really nice warm real sounds. It's kind of weird, you've got your headphones on and you can hear everybody talking, but you're spread out all over the house."

Unsurprisingly then, the guitars sounded good, even great. Even if there's a certain lack of warmth from the drums, and maybe not enough bass on *British Steel*, to be fair, Tom Allom's idea was to get the guitars upfront and prominent, which he did. Another key hard rock producer of the era, Tom Werman acted much the same way, diminishing, arguably intentionally, thump and thunder for the electricity of a supercharged guitar (or two or three or five). To that end, as alluded to, both K.K. and Glenn were recorded in large rooms for what they considered a live or raw sound, with close mic'ing as well as mics 20-odd feet away. K.K. joked that he spent the whole month in the library, and not with any good books to read either. Only "poor Ian" was in the actual studio.

"Tom was just a bundle of fun," says Ian, "and he was a great producer. We had a great time with him, mainly in bars (laughs). No practical jokes. I don't think anybody pulled anybody's leg, really. Apart from, I don't know, not spiking your drink, but putting ketchup or something in your Bloody Mary." Additional hijinks included fishing in Ringo's swimming pool and riding motorcycles around his garden.

But, adds Ian, neither Tom, nor new straight-eight drummer Dave Holland, nor anybody at Columbia, had been the major causal factor of *British Steel*'s stark simplicity versus previous records. "There have been very few extra forces. Obviously Ken and Rob and Glenn write most of the songs but it's all very straight out of their heads rather than being pushed into it one way or another via anybody. The only influence we've ever had is when somebody else would suggest doing a cover version and then it's been left up to us which one to do and what we do with it."

"And the commercial tracks... like I say, they weren't consciously recorded as commercial tracks—they were album tracks. We've never set out to do a single. We just got on with it and played what we felt. And like I say, we left that up to the record company. If there was a commercial track on there, they would obviously put it out as a single. *British Steel* was a bit of a landmark. It was the first album that we headlined in the States. We had opened for different bands and special guested until that point, with the net result that up until then it was the most popular album, the biggest seller. And in fact I think it outsold *Point of Entry*. It was an important album but again, just a progression from *Hell Bent*."

"*British Steel* was an album that we actually wrote a lot of in the studio," confirms Glenn. "We did it in a very short amount of time, went into Tittenhurst Park, which was Ringo's house, and I think we wrote probably about 40% of that when we were in the studio. We don't normally do that, but it did work out really well because *British Steel* was a classic album." The studio was available because Ringo had ended up moving to France, due to crazy British income tax laws that turned many rock stars into "tax exiles." Rather than letting it sit empty, he decided to rent it out as a working studio.

British Steel was classic yes, but decidedly commercial compared to all that came before. At the time of its birth to the public, it was actually a sharp shock to the party faithful, considerably less note-dense, all the bitty parts gone, no flash drumming on display, lyrics teenaged, hot and bothered.

The biggest shock came with advance single "Living After Midnight," unleashed on the public in March 1980, one month before the album proper. Like a stinging slap in the face, this modest anthem emerged from radios around the world with bravado, yes, but framed as little more than a Kiss song. Band lore has it that Tipton had been working on the riff through the wee hours (two or three Marshall stacks are mentioned—could it be anything but?) while Rob slept away in the bedroom directly above the studio, only to emerge in the morning worse for wear but with a lyric that came to him in his sleep.

"We were expected to do a commercial track," says Hill, dangerously close to contradicting earlier statements. "And Rob had this great lyric, living after midnight. And it just fell into place. It was one of those things. It was one of those tracks that was worked on with an eye to being commercial and radio-friendly, and it turned out to be a very popular track. It's still in the set today (laughs). That's one of the tracks you can't drop. People will go to the live show expecting to hear that and if you don't play it, they'll walk away disappointed. So 'Living After Midnight' was actually written in the studio. We came up short with material. We'd just come off the end of a very long tour, a two-year cycle, and Ken and Glenn and Rob hadn't got the time to write a complete album, so that one and 'The Rage' we wrote in the studio."

"But 'Living After Midnight' and 'Breaking the Law'... the radio station started to pick up on those songs, and it started to gain us fans from areas we wouldn't necessarily pick them up from. Maybe people who'd never go see us live, or bothered to be into the things we were into at the time (laughs). So it probably started heavy metal on its way to its popularity. So I guess up to that point, it made for the definitive heavy metal album, and it also crossed over into other areas. But when you finish a record, it's very rare that it sounds anything like it was intended to sound like when you first set out. Once you finish it, it takes a few weeks, or a month maybe, for everything to sink in."

"It was a very hectic schedule," continues Hill. "It was write, record, tour, write, record, tour, maybe with a couple of months off in between. That's all. For us to write a song, and then not use it was almost like sacrilege."

Parse Ian's words, and he seems to be saying that *British Steel* was metal enough so that every metal fan, or at least ever Judas Priest fan, bought it, but commercial enough that there was a further layer of buyers, open-minded but maybe not identifying as metalheads, that showed up and pushed it over the top.

"Living After Midnight" is indeed a form of anthem, and back in 1980 it was a smash hit, the calling card that was presented to prospective buyers of this new version of Priest, a band for the '80s. It was indeed the happiest song the band had written to date, and who can fault making people happy? It also had a catchy, very simple groove, one that wouldn't be out of place at an AC/DC show.

JUDAS PRIEST

Glenn and K.K. fully admit that the song is less sophisticated than much of their material, but that it's a blast to play live, which transfers over to the audience. On other levels it excites as well. The end result—success in America—was an intoxicant. The guys just loved how they could hear the song playing on stereos and on radios across the expanse overseas, and how, subtly, the sentiment enclosed was more of an American thing than British, this idea of being relentless, being possessed by a determination to have a good time and in the process, going all night long, and then disappearing like a Wild West hero. As K.K. is wont to say, "Who says you can't sing along to the Priest?"

"There was a certain commerciality with the *British Steel* record," affirms Downing, "even though we perceived it to be—and always wanted it to be—heavier and whatever. But don't forget, we had been coming to America, and as much as people are passionate about their rock and their metal, we didn't want to be The Grateful Dead, you know what I mean? We are people who like to rock out and have some fun, drink beer (laughs). Hence 'Living After Midnight' and 'Breaking the Law'—fun things! And the good thing is, it was a record that moved on, wasn't it? Boom, boom, boom, nothing too long-winded, nothing too pretentious, fucking long-winded solos, intricate stuff. It was, for the time, just in-your-face, here we are, we're here, we're metal, but like, don't be afraid, we're here to fucking party out."

Invited to headbang with abandon, one almost forgets certain aspects of the song's construction, namely that the verse riff is pretty heavy, and that in actuality, it starts with the chorus, rather than the verse. Also, the song is opened by the band's new drummer, Dave Holland playing alone. Holland would become the lightning rod in the band around this issue of paring down, or put in more of a negative light, dumbing down.

Looking back, after years of conditioning by drum tornado Scott Travis, Glenn comments that, "Dave is a very solid drummer, but he never had the ability to operate fast kick pedal patterns, which, you know, we did suffer from, there's no doubt about that. But when it came to laying down tracks like "Living After Midnight," he was a very solid drummer."

Dave Holland had joined Priest in August 1979 at the age of 31. Citing Johnny Kidd & The Pirates and jazz as early influences, Holland started on piano but got his first drum set when he was ten years old. Debuting with a psych band called Pinkerton's Assorted Colours, Holland's main pre-Priest gig by far was with Glenn Hughes in Trapeze, for which he recorded all of the original studio albums plus later live material. On the side, he guested for Justin Hayward, Glenn Hughes and in the middle of his Priest run, Robin George.

"We auditioned drummers for Trapeze," begins Glenn Hughes, asked to assess Holland as a drummer. "We were called Finders Keepers before, and Dave was in that band with the ridiculous name—it was a pop band, and they had a big hit in England. Dave is an amazingly good orchestrated arranging drummer. He's really funky, unlike what you would imagine for Judas Priest, which is a really great band. But in Trapeze he was a really great arranger of great songs. In Priest, you know, I think Glenn Tipton ran that band on the musical side. Rob obviously was very in control of the vocals. But the music is run by Glenn Tipton. In Trapeze, Dave was a great drummer. I think for Priest, he wasn't. I mean, I think on a couple of tracks he was, but he's certainly greater on the Trapeze stuff. I mean, Dave spoke to me many times about... I think he had a lot to do with the arrangements of some of the songs for Judas Priest. Dave is really good at that."

"Dave was always a good drummer," adds Trapeze lyricist Tom Galley. "Strange style—he just belted. But if you've ever watched him, you were always wondering whether he was going to come out of the roll sometimes, because he's got a strange technique. But whatever he was, live he was great; recording he was very good."

"I don't know what happened with Les," muses Ian, on the departure of the reclusive Les Binks, a drummer, now legendary for his status on fully three of the band's most revered records, two studio and one live. "One day he was with us and the next minute he was gone. I don't know why he wanted to leave, simple as that. To tell you the honest truth, I haven't seen him since. I know he's moved around musically with things, but I've never run into him, and I don't know if the other guys have. I think Dave... We were lucky with Dave. We knew him by

reputation from Trapeze. Dave was a very good solid rock drummer, but also a very technical drummer. Well, if you listen to some of his drum patterns. And his name was mentioned. He wasn't doing anything at the time. So we contacted him one way or another and met him in a pub in Carrick in Staffordshire (laughs), and ran through a couple things and said, yeah, he's well capable of doing what we were doing at the time. Took him on."

But alas, no more double bass drum for the newly lean Priest... "No, but Dave covered it in other ways. He wasn't very good with double bass drums, although he could play a single bass drum as fast as anybody I ever heard (laughs). But he still couldn't obviously play it as quick as someone playing with two feet. But he covered the songs. Put it this way, nobody came up to us afterwards and said it was crap (laughs). But it was a little bit simpler if anything; a lot more direct. Again, it wasn't a conscious effort. It was what the songs needed. And of course, there's the reggae start to open 'The Rage' (laughs). That was something we'd never done since, and never done before."

Again, whether it was Holland's dead-plain drumming or a host of other signals, *British Steel* was simply all right there, plain for all to see. Even a speed metaller like opening track "Rapid Fire" is drummed stripped-down and old school, in lockstep with the song's smeary, almost dreary riffing. The production matches up with Dave's playing style—

Holland's drums are dry and there is a dearth of bass, but as with the guitars, there's a neat immediacy.

Staying with "Rapid Fire," only Halford is exerting himself performance-wise, spitting out his words like a drill sergeant, having a ball with what he calls his Olivier moment, being Shakespearean, being a Brummie, even going so far as to make up a word (desolisating). However, the break section is infinitely guitary, with K.K. and Glenn turning in one of their patented shredding trade-off solos, separated geometrically by Rob's vocal. According to plan, the song does stick to the memory circuits, aided by Rob's flash lyric that marries his old sci-fi themes to characteristics of heavy metal.

So yes, even a fastback rocker, like "Rapid Fire" sounds like it was steered toward something that just might be a hit. And yet, Ian reaffirms that scoring hits just wasn't part of the radar.

"I don't think so, no. In those days, it was very, very different to the way it is now. The record company would actually look at an act and say, 'This will make us money over a period of time.' It's not going to earn us anything overnight. We have to wait for this. We have to nurture the popularity of the band. In fact, heavy metal in general, and heavy rock, fell into that category. There were very few… Zeppelin, that was basically blues rock, and Sabbath, they were at the top of their game in the mid-'70s, I suppose; they were making it big, but very, very few others. We were all sort of long-term projects. But there was never any real pressure. I mean, even *we* thought it might be a good idea to have something a radio station might be able to play (laughs). So make something short and snappy, something under five minutes long, so it might get picked up. But other than that, there was no pressure. CBS, as it was then, have always been very, very good in that respect. They still are."

"So *British Steel* was just the direction we were going in anyway," continues Hill. "The compass was set, and that was the direction we were going. We just tried to take that step forward. A lot of bands will stick to one format and people love them, but we've never done that. We will try to push the envelope a bit instead of just stagnating. It was basically that—another step forward."

Asked to comment on K.K.'s view that, hey, rock 'n' roll is supposed to be fun, Ian figures, "He's got a point. Especially in 'Breaking the Law' and 'Living After Midnight.' 'Living After Midnight' is the rock 'n' roll lifestyle (laughs). 'Breaking the Law,' I don't know if you've ever seen the video for that, but that was a lot of fun. I mean, it might be a bit cringe-worthy these days, but at the time, we had a blast doing that. It was a little tongue-in-cheek. It wasn't taken as deathly seriously as it had been before. Maybe we were offering a bit of a lighter side; it was evolving. We were getting across to the people who we wanted to get across to, which is basically people like ourselves. That's who we were playing to. As long as we had an audience, and we were keeping them happy, that was the most important thing to us. And as I say, it was just the two radio tracks, or three maybe, that set this album aside, broke us into another audience, another area."

Ergo simplicity. "Yes, there's generally passages that are too long, things that can be cleaned up, shall we say. Parts that are relevant to the song, clever parts, maybe, but it doesn't quite sit properly. There is always something you can cut out, but conversely, there's always something you can throw back in (laughs). The people that I had spoken to have universally liked *British Steel*. As I say, the audience was maybe changing. The definitive heavy metal live audience was just coming into being then. If we would've gone the more self-indulgent route, we would've ended up another Mahavishnu Orchestra

(laughs). You could go complicated—that was one route; you can go to a jazzier style—or you can do what we were doing."

And in this spirit of simplicity, or possibly because of it, "We put the record together pretty fast," recalls Downing. "You probably heard, some of it was put together in the studio. I think the whole thing from beginning to end was well under two months, six or seven weeks or something like that, and that's what kept it fresh. Now, surprisingly, when I listen to the record, I'm thinking it almost sounds like a live record. The recording process these days can be a bit sterilised. But when you are with a tight schedule and a tight budget, you get in there, and it's real and you are playing together. You are laying the songs down as a band, which we did, right up until the *Painkiller* album, I would say. So you stand together. And you miss those times where you get like a four-minute song, and at 3:58 into it, somebody fucks the ending up and you go, 'You bastard!' And you would be so nervous, and you're running through the song again, 'If I fuck that up again...' you know what I mean? 'Those guys are just going to kill me.' That sort of pressure—you kind of miss that."

"Metal Gods" is another song that demonstrates the directness of the new Priest, but with solid success. Holland's two-fisted high-hat beat supports handily an instantly memorable riff, which turns dark and increasingly heavy for the song's modulation to a sturdy pre-chorus. Halford again is thespian, fully convincing, yet the song closes with an extended musical passage over which the metal gods themselves do battle. Says Ian of the clashing sword effect, "That was a dropping of a cutlery tray, plus there was a golf club making swishing noises, banging of radiators, and dropping bottles, which was in 'Breaking the Law.' All sorts of stuff went on there. It was the dawning of production pieces."

"Homemade, handmade, by the guys in the band," laughs K.K., "including the smashing of the bottles on Ringo's house, whatever. Those audio effects, they're real recordings. We tried everything. We put light bulbs in microwaves to see if they made any noise exploding. We did a lot of zany stuff. That was the fun part of that recording. These days you've got such a catalogue of sound effects, you just dial it up. I remember, on the one song, and I forget what album it was on, we actually had a gong, we bashed it, and then lowered it into a big vat of water (ed. an old Sabbath trick, that one, circa *Master of Reality*). Yeah, but you know, the cutlery had been a secret for a long time. But the way the world is now, everything comes out. Because if we didn't say it and we lied about it, you know, 'Yeah, man, we were just smoking a bit of dope and these aliens came down with all this machinery and we put a mic on it, man...' (laughs). Sooner or later somebody, the tea boy from the studio, 'No, not quite. Someone was shaking a cutlery drawer.' And then you look like a real twat. So if I've learned one thing in this industry, tell it as it is, because, for better or worse it's going to come out sooner or later."

"Metal Gods" certainly got the thumbs up from the record's producer. "One of my clear favourites," says Allom. "I've always been a thumper for 'Metal Gods;' I love it to bits (laughs). It's a classic. And it's real heavy metal. And it sounds so big live— it sounds enormous. I've mixed live versions of it and I've always loved it. I remember 'Metal Gods' was certainly written in the studio, but it's the core structure and the key that it's in that makes it sound so large."

Asked about the inclusion of Tom Allom to the fold, Ian explains that, "He was suggested to us by the record company at the time. When we first met him, we thought there's no way this bloke could be a heavy rock producer. He was very public schoolboy. He came from a well-to-do family, and spoke very Queen's English, sort of thing. We thought, this isn't going to work. But he mixed the live album, *Unleashed in the East*, and he did a tremendous job on it. So he was with us for over ten years there, right up until… Well, from '80 to '88, was the last one we did, *Ram It Down*—he was with us all that time."

"Colonel Tom Allom," laughs Ian. "I think he was from a military family. I think his first job was producing the marching band in the regiment, something like that. The jokes abound, you know what I mean? Funny instances, yeah. It was our younger and wilder days. First and foremost, he was an excellent engineer. And he sorted out the sounds of the various instruments, and that was the basis for the sound, obviously, of *British Steel*."

"And he was also a good mediator. Because if a couple of lads wanted to do something in the band one way and a couple the other, he was very pragmatic. He would look at the pros and cons and he would go to the most sensible suggestion—he was good at that. And his mixing technique was very, very good, and production, and all the noises, the production sounds. There was no such thing as samples in those days. We had to invent them. But he loves his work. Like they say, if you find a job you love, you don't have to work ever again (laughs). And that's Tom

Allom. But Tom would make suggestions to us, 'Why don't you try this? Why don't you try that? Play double time, single time.' That's part of the process of Judas Priest recording. Ken and Glenn would come in with all the ideas of the songs, and obviously a basic format, and the rest of us would put our two pennies in."

"Breaking the Law" was in fact spruced up by the boys dropping some of Ringo's beer bottles and milk bottles out back on the patio. The siren in the same track is produced entirely by K.K. on his guitar, through bends on his Strat. Rob was particularly pleased with the outcome of this sequence, which, he says, tells the story with sound, adding that he likes to do much the same with his lyrics, paint a little picture that leaps to another medium, such as the movies.

The thunder at the beginning of "Metal Gods" was nothing more than the slamming of a heavy door, magically transformed into something more epic in the studio. The swishing noise within the song was obtained by Rob swinging a pool cue quickly, with Allom twiddling a few knobs—essentially increasing the compression—to get it up to a heroic, god-like level. A whip effect proved problematic for one of Rob's own whips, so a guitar cable was used instead, against a flight case.

The main effect in "Metal Gods" though is the repeated clashing sword sound, which, as Ian has indicated, comes from trays of cutlery. Tom Allom has in fact explained that it was obtained by multi-tracking ten or twelve times, the dropping of the cutlery tray on the stone floor in Ringo's kitchen, courtesy of himself and Rob. Added in are some mic stand spikes to the floor with the base removed.

"If there was ever a great song in metal and if there was ever a metal anthem it would have to always be 'Metal Gods,'" says Rob, in his amusingly verbose, circular manner of speaking. "Talking about the robot scythes and the laser-beaming hearts and the molten breath, it's a great caricature for metal. It's almost like an animation idea put under cover of a piece of metal music. And when everyone sings along with that song, I think they feel that they are a metal god too. It's just a great song that connects with people on an emotional metal level."

One must suppose that Rob's love for the song also derives from the fact that he quickly became known as The Metal God, just as Glenn Hughes is called The Voice of Rock, or Bruce Dickinson is deemed the Air Raid Siren. Further, Rob has talked about the song being influenced by old horror movies, in particular *Day of the Triffids*, and monsters like the Kraken. The idea was to imitate one of these big robots stomping around, which is underscored by Rob's robot walk stage move during the song, that amusing bit of choreography tied to the song's instrumental close being a highlight of any Priest concert.

If "Living After Midnight" was to be *British Steel*'s light-hearted calling card, it was "Breaking the Law" which would emerge as the album's biggest hit, its full-on anthem, perhaps the band's perennial key spot of magic up there on the live stage. Backed with "Metal Gods" and served in a limited gatefold sleeve with arch-NWOBHM patch, the song vaulted to No.12 on the UK charts. Its tale of alienated youth fit perfectly with post-punk Britain, the nation having seen all too many years of economic recession. Rob stresses the track's universal relevance, that it is a song about being promised all these things through working hard, finishing school and whatnot, and then finding that success isn't achievable—so you break the law.

A campy, light-hearted video for the track was produced courtesy of Sex Pistols documenter Julien Temple, who had also put together the clip for "Living After Midnight," which featured the band live at Sheffield City Hall. Rob looks like a natty Joe Jackson, which helped underscore the punk verve of the new Priest, an element wisely not emphasised, but one nonetheless brought up, Rolling Stone comparing the band (or at least the energy of the band) to the Ramones and The Damned.

The album cover also offered a bit of punk in the form of a razor blade, although frankly few Priest fans made that connection at the time. Recalls Hill, "I think the cover that attracted the most discussion was British Steel and the razor blade, only because it was a symbol of the punk movement at the time, which we obviously weren't a part of. And obviously it's turned out to be one of the classic Priest covers, instantly recognizable. But there was some concern about that, that maybe people would think we turned to punk."

The British Steel cover was the work of CBS artist Roslav Szaybo, returning to heavy duty after his iconic image for Killing Machine. Along the lines of a band calling themselves Metallica and Venom using Black Metal as the title for their second album, British Steel presumed a sort of last word in heavy metal status for Priest. But it was also the name of a steel company from the Midlands, one in fact, that employed a Mr. Glenn Tipton for five years, Tipton recalling his years there as drudgery in a grey, dour setting not unlike something out of the industrial revolution. Credit for the name goes to Ian Hill. Rob pushed the overall concept along by noticing the name Sheffield Steel on some razor blades that he had.

Besides the aforementioned punk bit, additional controversy came in the idea that the razor blade was actually cutting into the hand. The imagery was toned down, and rendered without blood (or at least in shadow), to the deft point where one could see it both ways, as a hand merely holding the blade, or the blade beginning to slice into the fingers. A subtle point made by the band in various interviews was that a bonus implication was that, given the lack of blood, it was safe to be into this kind of music.

Says Ian, "In fact, the title British Steel came out as sort of a light-hearted joke, because there was a huge steel company in Britain called British Steel, and we couldn't come up with a title, and they were on strike at the time, and I said, 'How about British Steel?' as a bit of a joke. Everybody laughed a bit, and then the giggles died down, until they realised, you know, that sounds pretty good."

"You couldn't escape it in the Midlands," continues Ian, on the subject of heavy industry up north. "In the '80s, things were starting to wind down a little bit, but when we were growing up as kids, they called it the Black Country for a very good reason. I mean, there were foundries, factories, coal mines, you name it, everything in probably, I don't know, 30 square miles between Wolverhampton and Birmingham and everything in between. And it was very, very industrial. You would go to school and you would go past three or four foundries, spring works, all kinds of things. British Steel ended up… I think the government bought everything out, the different steel companies, and nationalised it as British Steel. In fact, not long after, they went bump anyways. We might've had something to do with that, I don't know (laughs)."

But that title… It really did bring everything together for Priest. "Yeah, that's where I was going," muses K.K.. "Because even though Priest had the attitude, had the music, we were always wanting to make the record that epitomised what Judas Priest is, you know, like the look and the sound. The look was the thing that we were still struggling with a little bit. But it all came together, for the *British Steel* thing. The record came together, and the look and the image of the band. Suddenly it was leather, studs, motorcycles, fucking whatever. And that's what happened—suddenly we had that. We had just found what the future for Judas Priest was, in the beginning of the '80s. We came over to this continent in '78, I think, or it may have been '79, but there were hints of things that we were doing. But everybody was clad in leather and studs, and that was it, we couldn't get enough of it. More leather! More studs! More motorbikes, more all of this. Rob Halford and the bullwhip and this, that and the other."

"Just fell into it, really," laughs Ian. "We were wearing all kinds of things, velvet, satin, denims, a whole eclectic look at one point. I think one day Rob walked in wearing a leather coat, a biker jacket, and we thought, gee, that looks pretty good, and we all got one. I think it was as simple as that; we just fell into it. It fit perfectly with the music we were playing."

As for the razor on the front cover, adds Ian, not much mind was paid to punk. "I don't think so, no. The punk thing had been going for about five years or so, but we were never here to see it, per se (laughs). We were always out on the road or in the studio. The thought of us going out and catching a show in those days was alien to us. But obviously, it was in the music papers at the time, New Musical Express and Sounds and Melody Maker and things like that."

As Ian says, punk was already long in the tooth. In another, parallel world it had morphed into post-punk, but more focused was the new metal tribe issuing indie singles and air-guitarin' and covering their jean jackets in the patches that came with those indie singles.

"Yes, and the direction our music was going sort of attracted a certain audience anyway. We didn't attract girls for instance (laughs). We used to at one time, but with the leather and the studs and the actual power, the raw aggression of the music, it was not something that was attractive to the female audience. So most of our audience were boys, really, teenage boys, which we all were ourselves at the time. We were sort of in our mid-20s at the time, maybe 30, but yeah, that was when the typical heavy metal fan, if there was such a thing, started to evolve. In terms of the uniform, I think even today, it's T-shirts and jeans, just the universal rock uniform. Sprinkled with the leather coats. But very few people dressed up in the full studs and everything, the whole nine yards."

"Most metal bands have said when we are on stage we are with our fans," explains Rob, talking with Sam Dunn, on how the metal uniform is a symbol of unity. "We don't consider it to be a separation; there is an identification. The way that your fans want to relate to you to some extent comes from what you dress like. So you get down to the flea market, you get an old denim jacket, or you get an old biker's jacket and you cut the sleeves off. I can't remember how that first began but I mean it did somewhere."

"Again, it's this identifying look. Okay, how can I walk around? I could be down the pub and people look at me and go, he's a metalhead or she's a metalhead, you know. And so bands were selling the patches and somebody says, well I'm going to stick this on this jacket. Sticking it on someone's denim vest whatever. It's like, you wear the colours of your band, don't you? It's like your soccer team or whatever it might be. You want to dress in the colours of your band. And so the fans I think were just as excited to try and create their own image, while also representing the bands. Again, looking back at those very early days of Priest, we were developing that image at the same time the fans were. So we were both growing together visually at the same time."

"Much like the music grows and develops, there's the feeling of, well, how can we make that sound take on an appearance that is relevant? To the point where you look at yourself before you go on stage and say, 'That's how my music sounds, that's how the power and the energy of the metal would look if you could put it into some kind of visual and wear it on your body.' Whether it's spiked wrist bands or leather pants. It just felt, for us in Priest, like a very natural place to go to. And obviously we got it right because almost immediately it was picked up around the planet. That's it—now we have something to wear. So if you're walking down the street, people see it and go, 'There's a metalhead.'"

As K.K. alluded to, 1980 was the perfect year for Priest to issue a record called *British Steel*, and to issue any record, really. The fact that it was celebrating the glories of headbanging made it all the more relevant for that juncture year.

Addressing the timing of it all, Rob explains that "the New Wave of British Heavy Metal was creeping up from like '76 through '79. You could read little bits and pieces in the papers about this band, that band, this pub or that club or whatever. You could sense that everybody was going, 'Hey, have you heard about this new sound? It's called heavy metal. It's gonna be great.' This generation of music fans now had something to run to and identify with. As we know, in rock 'n' roll, everything happens at the beginning of a decade; I don't know why it's that cycle but it is. So I think it's fair to say that the New Wave of British Heavy Metal, including Priest, which was also part of the old wave, we all came together and it was like dynamite going off—1980, bang, we're here, let's go. This is now going to be a worldwide event and it was."

"And it was tremendously exciting," continues Halford, "because suddenly you are surrounded by these bands as well as the fans, who are feeling the same way you had felt for a number of years before that moment, before 1980. So you just feel, I guess, satisfied, maybe a sense of relief that it's not just us. This is great! Look at this band, there's Maiden, there's Motörhead, like we're all in it now."

"But we believed in it in Priest right from day one. We knew something was going to happen, but we didn't know exactly when. So when all these other bands started to connect, it was tremendous. It was a great boost because there were still those detractors. Everybody was trying to crush it. 'Metal sucks, metal is rubbish, it's going nowhere.' And we're like no, no, no. We're going to stick through this. We're going to get through it and we did."

"Just before that new wave of metal thing exploded, we had to deal with punk and new wave and the New Romantic moment, because suddenly everybody went, 'See ya! We're going over here now.' A lot of bands like Priest were left to get on with it by themselves. I mean, it's very important to remember that media, press, any kind of exposure, is vital to a band's growth and development. Suddenly we were left with nothing. Nobody was interested, couldn't get an interview, couldn't get a photo shoot."

"But we sensed that the punk moment was going to be turbulent and short-lived. Some great things happened at that time but that's the thing I love about metal. It's like the blues or jazz—it's always gonna be here. It's not like a type of music that is going to fade off into the sunset. It will always be here and that's how we felt through that turbulent period with the punk/new wave thing. We knew metal was gonna survive, and 1980 was the start of the match."

But it was a long slog and it's still a tough slog, frankly. I mean, I can tell you stories from just last year where it's me, Ken and Glenn and Scott and Ian, and we're wandering around the docklands in Scandinavia because the ferry dropped us off and we can't find the van. We were wandering around in a blizzard and we can't find the van. You know, we're looking at each other, what's going on? We've been doing this for 40 years and we still can't find the tour bus? I mean, I was just roaring on the floor; it was like a bunch of lost old men bumping into each other. It's brilliant. That's a part of everything that we love about heavy metal."

Asked by Sam whether the sudden deluge of competition that came with the NWOBHM gave the boys in Priest any cause for concern, Rob figures, "Love it—it's great. It's the best thing any band can have. It's just your time to have a go, type of deal. You know, come on lads! Especially if you are in a festival. When we did festivals, I was always checking out the other bands. It just fires you up, gets you into fighting spirit. You play harder and stronger. It's not like, oh let's blow them off; we are better than they are—it's none of that. It's the sense of effort and pride that every band has. Every band in metal is proud of who they are and what they are trying to be. Everybody's like wait 'til we're on there and we can show you what we can do!"

"And so we couldn't kind of sit back and go hey, we've done it all. You've still got to get out there and prove to yourself that you've still got what it takes, that you've still got the guts and the passion and self-belief that you had right from day one. And I know we do that in Priest. That's what we do every time we go out on stage. It's not like, oh, this is a drag doing 'Living After Midnight'—no, we're doing 'Living After Midnight' like it's the first time we ever played it."

Martin Popoff   **Judas Priest: Decade of Domination** | 161

With Rob nicely bringing us back to *British Steel*, "Breaking the Law" would be instrumental in pushing *British Steel* gold, the band's first "record of metal," hitting that plateau within two years of its issuance, albeit with official platinum designation not to come until 1989. Of note, the song's prominence was recognised early: it was the opening track on the original North American vinyl issue of the album, but "Rapid Fire" gets the pole position on later reissues, with a reversion to the original UK sequencing.

British Steel rose to No.4 on the British charts and No.34 on Billboard, Priest finally finding a spot of success on which to hang their hats. And "Breaking the Law" was the soundtrack to that success, its slightly mournful, poignant melody, its pulsation and verve, and its various sections—the next always raising the stakes—combining with the band's new plainspeak attitude to form what is arguable Priest's first highway song. Again, the widely seen video reinforces this road trip aspect, with the band singing along while driving to make a heist at Barclay's bank, packing guitars instead of guns, going after gold records instead of money. The overall effect is indeed a sing-along, with producer Allom even going so far to say that the song has a pop groove to it.

"'Breaking the Law' is just one of the great metal songs of all rock 'n' roll," muses Rob. "It will be as strong as it was when it was created in '80, '81, and here we are 20 years later playing that song at Rock in Rio, and all the people are singing it word for word. It just says everything above what rock 'n' roll represents. It's a real high energy, anarchic, gang-type number. It just brings everybody together because of what it talks about, namely that we go through our early stages in life and we feel that we are being made a lot of promises and then when those promises are broken, we react, and that's something I think everyone can relate to. It's a fun song too. It has a serious tone but it's a great, fun song to experience and I'm aware that when I play that song around the world it gets an incredible reaction."

"Grinder" is another classic of heavy metal economy, with the band strutting along to an insanely catchy back rhythm from Hill and Holland, the lyric almost a continuation of the character sketch plotted in "Breaking the Law," that of a young male cranked full of hormones and ready to make his mark on the world. Halford again growls menacingly, finding new dimension and confidence in his multi-varied voice.

Twisted Sister's Dee Snider was one of many metal legends on which Halford was to make an impression, Snider also perceptive in noticing Rob's rough side as well as the obvious and penultimate soar above his roar. "Halford is a great singer, but I don't know if vocal styling-wise, he was someone I really emulated. The one thing I definitely learned… I came from that era where high singing was what people wanted to do; people wanted a high singer. I got into Twisted Sister auditioning on Led Zeppelin stuff. The more you sang high, the better it was. I think Halford actually started that way too, but he came to realise he was more effective by staying low, and then kicking it up, for accenting. As opposed to 'Exciter,' which is all high, and it just wears on you, I looked at something like 'Grinder,' and I went, ah, I get this—he's seasoning with his high voice, and it's more effective, so I really learned that from Rob."

Reminiscing about hearing Priest for the first time, Dee mentions "Grinder" again, noting its effect on where the Twisted sound was to originate. "It was probably 'Exciter' that I had heard in a club, back in like '78, '79, New Jersey. And I thought, 'What the fuck is that?!' My God! We used to play that as our opening track, our intro track for years, just because, man, it's one of the most intense songs. 'Fast as a Shark' is another one, 'Kill the King' by Rainbow—I should make a list."

"So I started to nose around, and it wasn't the one with 'Exciter' I bought, but it was *Hell Bent for Leather*, with that album cover. That record, with the shattered goggles and the blood—that record was just staggering. At that point I really started to study them as a prototype of a two-guitar band. Twisted Sister was a two-guitar band; there were two guitars joined, and I don't think we had a role model per se, but when Priest came along, we started to define how the two guitars would be used. You know, not playing two separate guitar parts like Aerosmith or whatever, or Guns, which was later, but playing unified guitar parts, doubling each other, for the intensity, the effect of it. The perfect example is 'Grinder'—all of a sudden the second guitar comes in, just as strength. So that really helped define Twisted—the way Priest approached two guitars."

Glenn's "Grinder" solo is particularly tuneful, Rob commenting that many of Tipton's patterns are near to a vocal, or a singer's pattern. As a result, says Glenn, the solos become an integral part of the song—forever, and for the most part, can't be altered in a live setting, given that punters will be expecting to sing it in their heads, and in many cases, hammer out a bit of air guitar to reinforce the effect.

"United" saw the band doing Top of the Pops again, which broadcast August 28, 1980, five days after the release of the single and

12 days after Priest performed at the very first Monsters of Rock at Donington Park, headlined by Rainbow. Priest never played Monsters of Rock again, although they were asked in 1987. The band declining, with K.K. wondering who in the world would ever want to support Bon Jovi? In the band's ten-song set were three selections from the new record, "You Don't Have to Be Old to Be Wise," "Grinder" and "Living After Midnight."

An endearing video emerges from the Top of the Pops visit, one that captures the ground floor excitement of the NWOBHM, here applied to—and in homage of—one of the bands that built that house, volunteering their services in a sense, given the lack of pay the band had to endure for well on a decade at this point.

Tom Allom called this one the record's anthem. Even though "United" emulated the trudge (and drudge) of "Take on the World" and "We Will Rock You," this time Priest was smart enough to place prominent guitar signposts along the muddy path of the march. "It speaks for itself, really, 'United,'" says Ian. "Stand together, the camaraderie and all the rest of it. It was a good source for a single because of the lyric content. So the record company thought it might have been a good idea to put it out." Backed with "Grinder," "United" rose to No.26 in the UK charts, adding further steam to *British Steel*'s ascendance, the single issued on cue four months after release of the album proper.

Articulating the spirit of "United," Glenn reiterates that, "It's never us and the audience when we're on stage, it's the whole thing. The audience sings along with our choruses, verses, and even lead breaks now. So tracks like 'Take on the World' and 'United' are fantastic for the audience to sing and join in with, and that's something we love. When we do a concert, it's not all about Judas Priest, it's about Judas Priest and our fans together and the atmosphere that creates. I suppose we consciously do compose some music with that in mind."

"Don't Have to Be Old to Be Wise" (the "You" was added for later reissues) parties it up very much like "Living After Midnight," both tracks in essence anticipating the first wave of hair metal to hit in '83, a couple years past the launch of MTV. Again, Rob plays the role of a jean-jacketed headbanger misunderstood and ready to grab the reigns of his own life. Rob sells the argument effortlessly, while the band plods along with a happy, humpy set of chords. Grudgingly old fans took to it, while new fans showed up in droves, pumping their fists along with this new everyman's version of Priest.

Ian Hill goes reggae for the fleeting and inconsequential opening sequence witnessed on "The Rage," an under-rated epic rocker, one of the little discussed tracks on *British Steel*. Halford delivers an enigmatic lyric about some sort of huge conflict, while the band Sabbath-stomps toward... one more round of reggae. "The Rage" was one of the last things whipped up for the album, and the band definitely welcomed its sense of adventure, the guys all joking that the lyrics were definitely grand, even if no one—Rob included—knows what they're about. K.K.'s solo is a bit of an anomaly for him, Downing calling it bluesy and emotional, against his usual wild style. Glenn has called "The Rage" one of his favourite Priest tracks of all time, admiring the fact that it employs a key Priest characteristic, this idea of a preceding light passage bestowing upon the subsequent riff a greater sense of power through contrast.

Additional pairing up of styles can be proffered, with "Steeler" bookending "Rapid Fire" for OTT, or "over the top" content on the album, an essential double dose of speed metal, although, as befitting *British Steel*'s safety features, mild speed metal. Still, this one possesses more of a carnal attack than "Rapid Fire," especially given some of the violent turns later in the track, past the fairly benign root riff, the break signalling a branching out into darker terrain, studded with chopping riffs, wild soloing and Rob barking malevolently.

Over and out pretty quickly, *British Steel* wound up a pretty short album. "I think we were comfortable with it," figures Ian. "I can't remember at the time, but maybe we were a little bit concerned. Generally, albums in those days were 40 minutes. Any longer than that, I mean, you're talking about the days of vinyl records here. The more stuff you put on, the more grooves there are in the record, and the shallower the groove, the less quality to it. The deeper the groove, obviously, the stylus was sitting lower in the groove and it could pick up more information there. So, 40, 45, a real push, and you're starting to lose quality."

Just to stir up a bit of controversy, unbeknownst to the band apparently, Priest's PR point man Tony Brainsby cooked up a story that the album's master tapes had been stolen from Coronet Studios in New York and put up for a ransom price of $50,000. The first the band heard about it was in the papers, and Glenn quickly moved to have the story quashed.

The *British Steel* tour would finally put Priest over the top. Oddly, both "Metal Gods" and "Breaking the Law" wouldn't be part of the party, only getting added to the set list the following year. Even more oddly, "Don't Have to Be Old to Be Wise" was firmly in there, as was "Steeler" along with the expected "Living after Midnight" and "Grinder."

Rob was sassy in long-ish blond hair as Priest warmed up at home in March 1980, leading up to the release of the album with an ambitious young band called Iron Maiden in tow for early dates. Maiden saw themselves as the next big thing and rightly so. Featuring the same five-man, two-guitar lineup as Priest, two words to their name, Maiden were indeed like a loose-bolted, punkier Priest, a NWOBHM proposal, the proposal being, we're here to take over.

"Well, let's just say that a lot of our fans turned up," recalls Maiden bassist Steve Harris, "and we were a bit surprised, because obviously they were a British band, and nobody expected us to be... you know, I think a lot of people bought tickets that were Maiden fans, without a doubt. And so it definitely showed in the reaction—it was fantastic. I still think they're a great band, but we did really make it hard work for them. They had to work really hard every night, and maybe they weren't used to that, I don't know."

Adds noted UK journalist Garry Bushell, "Maiden had already come through. They'd obviously been signed by EMI by then and they'd had *The Soundhouse Tapes* and that, but that was a very important tour for Maiden. It was a chance to play to an audience who hadn't seen them before. And, of course, Priest have not got the pace. Obviously very heavy, but they've not got the pace that Maiden had. Maiden were much faster, if I recall."

"They may have given them a run for their money," reflects NWOBHM DJ and industry insider Neal Kay. "But Iron Maiden went behind Judas Priest on their first major tour with the release of their album. I mean I knew them well; they were friends at the time. They'd come to the Soundhouse for me. We did a video for them, "Living After Midnight," in which I loaned them Rob Loonhouse and the Headbangers. And there's a scene in that video where they come to the solo and Rob Loonhouse replaced K.K. Downing, and plays it on his hardboard guitar."

I knew the Priest camp real good, and I went along to see some of those shows, and as good as Maiden were... look, you suddenly don't become a rock 'n' roll hero overnight. You need to learn the profession. You need to tread the boards, learn the ways of rock 'n' roll. Priest were brilliant, and probably still are. They were a very experienced band back then. They'd replaced their drummer Les Binks—he'd gone. They had a new twin guitar-driven fast feel. Their earlier stuff had been a little stodgier, but well-put-down, well-driven, well-respected."

"The newer stuff from Priest was dead heavy metal. You know, there's no question, and they were the perfect band for Maiden to support on tour. They let Maiden on board without any tour fee. They trucked their stuff. I mean it was a nice relationship that was going on. I'd just come off tour with the Canadian band, April Wine, I think, in Sheffield. I'd been with April Wine and some others and I knew that Priest and Maiden were playing the city hall or somewhere and I was there and I went that night and saw all the boys and everybody. The thing was that Maiden were very good, but Priest, for me, were still the more polished because they had more time at it."

Chris Collingwood, reviewing the pairing for Sounds, also saw no cause for concern, writing, "After the lights went up when Maiden had finished their support slot (and how long is it before that becomes a headlining one?), I thought, especially as Priest hadn't been that convincing the previous night, that it could be another Lynyrd Skynyrd/Golden Earring situation where (as you know) the support band (Skynyrd) blew the headliners off stage. Is this possible? No chance, mate! Having dropped 'Exciter' from the set (the rumour being that new drummer Dave Holland couldn't master the beat), Priest opened with 'Hell Bent for Leather,' with Rob Halford being allowed, unlike the last time at Hammersmith, to ride his motorbike onto the stage. K.K. Downing and Glenn Tipton must be the best pair of heavy metal guitarists in existence. If you don't agree, try name another duo that excites on stage like these two. Tipton handles most of the solos, and I think that it's fair to say that he is more of a soloist while K.K. is more of a riffer. But they both complement each other, unlike twin lead guitarists who tend to get in each other's way sometimes. The light show has to be the most impressive I've ever seen, and that includes Rush's. Priest own it, and I can see it becoming yet another one of their trademarks along with the twin guitarists, the leather and the vocalist with the incredible range."

Adding fuel to the fire, as Ian alluded to in our *Hell Bent for Leather* chapter, Priest were late getting back for an all-important gig, March 26th, in their hometown of Birmingham, and this was the second time this had happened. They had been filming the video for "Living After Midnight" and indeed eventually arrived back and played the gig. Problem was, many punters had to catch the last train out and missed the gig entirely, with a couple of angry letters about the debacle winding up in Sounds magazine. Both letters rubbed it in, saying support band Iron Maiden were great on the night. And just to stick the knife in, there was a third letter saying that Maiden blew Priest off the stage at the Edinburgh Odeon. The devastating and well-written notice from "High Priest Alistair" summarised that, "All in all, getting good vibes out of Judas Priest is about as easy as stuffing half a pound of butter up a sparrow's arse with a needle."

Other than the healthy competition with Maiden, Rob exposing himself on stage at The Rainbow on April 1st, the band being late for a gig yet again due to their "Living after Midnight" Top of the Pops filming, and Tipton trashing his equipment at Sheffield Town Hall, the tour went off without a hitch. West Germany and one gig each in France and Belgium were next, but then in May, it was off to America, where Priest would politely state their case and emphatically stake their claim.

The US tour would feature support from Def Leppard and Scorpions, two bands that went on to sell more records than Priest ever would, something Iron Maiden, UK seat-warmers from a couple months back, would manage as well (if worldwide sales are taken into account). May and June would find the band making a Texas stand, before taking the show west through June. A festival was logged in St. Louis on June 29th. Called the Grand Slam Super Jam, the bill featured Priest along with Sammy Hagar, April Wine and Shooting Star, none of the four acts all that big at the time, but each with a hopeful pocket of fans, a career so to speak. Into late July, a handful of shows were logged with Scorpions, Heart and the drugged and doomed Joe Perry Project supporting their very, very good *Let the Music Do the Talking* debut.

As mentioned, second to last date of the tour, August 16th 1980, was to be a highlight, Judas Priest playing second on the bill to Rainbow on the very first Monsters of Rock festival at Castle Donington. New mates Scorpions and April Wine were along for the ride, as were Saxon and US baby bands Riot and Touch, the latter no doubt there due to their Bruce Payne management, a shared circumstance with the headliners. It was a wet and muddy day of new heavy metal, and with Rainbow on the ropes with a less than classic lineup, it was Priest that would win the day, hands down.

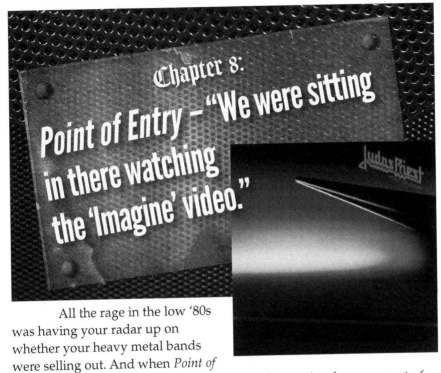

Chapter 8:
Point of Entry – "We were sitting in there watching the 'Imagine' video."

All the rage in the low '80s was having your radar up on whether your heavy metal bands were selling out. And when *Point of Entry* emerged, all melodic and bouncy and demurring from any sort of attack stance, a rapidly expanding new army of punters wrinkled their noses, still having not gotten over how the last Led Zeppelin album we would ever hear was stuffed full of keyboards.

So here was Priest waving hello again, the first thing to hit radio being something called "Don't Go," which most certainly perked ears that something was afoul in the Priest camp, a departure if you like, a point of entry. Indeed Glenn had said as much, intimating that this new record was an introduction to Priest circa the '80s, a Priest ready to shed their '70s moves.

The sessions, conducted in exotic Ibiza, Spain, were actually fraught with difficulties. The studio was situated in an old farmhouse way up a long and treacherous driveway that only the band's high-up rented Renaults could commandeer without getting beached. The owner of the place was having financial problems, so he kept running out of diesel fuel, which was needed to keep the generator going that provided the electricity. Add to this that water had to be brought in from a well, and you had a rustic scene indeed, charming, but not without frustrations.

Out on the town, the band got into a bit of a brawl in an upscale club with some Germans, prompted by the hunting horn/plastic trumpet incident in which Glenn picked up a trumpet that had been there and started playing it, much to the chagrin of the tony patrons. Back at their rural retreat, horn still in their possession, Tom Allom would be fed beer and cigarette butts through it as he belted out "When the Saints Go Marching In."

Asked whether there was pressure to go more commercial with *Point of Entry*, Ian Hill figures, "It wasn't so much pressure. We always had artistic license or artistic rights where if we didn't want to do something we didn't have to. But these people do know their business. If they come to us and say, 'Listen, I don't think there's anything on here that's going to get you onto rock radio; how about trying this?' We'll obviously listen and pay attention to  that. It was only ever suggestions. That was the first album we recorded in Ibiza. There were lots of distractions, but I don't know about influences (laughs). We spent most of the time on the beach, or in nightclubs, or driving motorcycles through the mountains. It was great fun. So maybe that influenced us."

I asked Ian if he would have wanted to be included more in the writing process. "Well, it would be nice, yeah. But the thing is, there was a great team there with Ken and Glenn and Rob and it worked well. You know what they say: 'Too many cooks spoil the broth' and all that, so I backed off and let them get on with it. There's a great relationship there. They got on with it and I was quite happy with what they were coming up with. I could obviously put my own bass lines to it and the drummers could put their own beats to it; everybody had their own parts. But those three did a great job and I saw no real reason to intrude on that. We were all getting along really well. We're all comparatively easy-going. There are no prima donnas. The chemistry has been there all the time, with the possible exception of drummers who keep leaving for some reason. But it's one of the major reasons we've been able to keep it together for so long. If there's an arsehole in the band, sooner or later he's going to cheese somebody off and the band's going to split."

Tom Allom confirms Ian's hint or inclination that the band might have been receptive to the idea of making themselves one step further accessible, over and above what they had purposely put in place on the previous record.

"Well, coming off *British Steel*, having had one or two sort of reasonable singles, if I cast my mind back, CBS Records probably said, 'We'll have some more of that commercial stuff, lads' (laughs). And *Point of Entry* was possibly the only album—no, the *only* album—that I was involved in with them where they consciously tried to write singles. As a result of which, they didn't write any (laughs)! Although in many ways, musically, *Point of Entry* is one of my favourite Priest albums, if not my favourite. We made it in Spain, although it was mixed in December at Startling, just after John Lennon was shot. God, that was weird. We went back there and mixed it and I remember we were watching the news, that new year, and they were showing little clips of all the famous people who had died in the previous year. And they showed part of the 'Imagine' video, which was shot in the sitting room, the big white drawing room at Startling. No longer white, but we were sitting in there watching the 'Imagine' video on the BBC news, sitting in that room, which is very spooky."

JUDAS PRIEST

And of course drummer Dave Holland, back for his second record, was an acceptable fit for the simple music all over *Point of Entry*. "Yes, the feel then was to have a pretty straightforward solid beat," reflects Tom. "And if you listen to most of those tracks, there's nothing very complicated going on with the drums. *Screaming for Vengeance*, you know, a little bit more elaborate. But they just liked the idea of a really solid, uncomplicated drumbeat. And I think that was kind of, if you like, what he was instructed to play (laughs). And it worked for the music.

Martin Popoff

Quite distinctive. I mean, he was a good drummer. His time was pretty good and he didn't play enough elaborate stuff to... an awful lot of drummers speed up when they do the drum solos and all that stuff—he didn't do that. He was pretty solid, although sometimes it was difficult to get exactly what we wanted. Once he'd settled on the way he was going to be, or settled on the way he was going to play a track, he was pretty good at sticking to that and not wandering off on an irrelevant tangent."

As for a production philosophy down at the drum end of things... "We used the same sort of technique to record the drums on all of those first three albums that I did. We used a lot of room mics, natural ambience mostly. Particularly in Ibiza. *British Steel*, we recorded them in the hallway at Ringo's house, put the mics up the top of the stairs, and we tried to re-create that on *Point of Entry*. There was an unfinished stone room in Ibiza, and it was too big, so we had to sort of pile up a load of breeze blocks across the middle of the room and hang blankets and things to try to deaden it a little bit. But that was the thing, to get as natural a drum sound as possible."

"Tom is a great producer, but not just a great producer, but a great guy," says Glenn, asked about working with the Colonel. "Tom just has a way with the band. He knows us as individuals. He's very diplomatic and he's got the ability to get what we want but put his own stamp on it as well. And all credit to Tom, he worked with us on some great albums and was responsible for the way, definitely, that the albums sounded. I've got a lot of respect for Tom. He's also a great guy and a great friend and that makes a big difference when you are working with people. You can work with great producers, but if you don't like them it will show in your work. But we get on really well with Tom and I think that's apparent in the sound of the albums and the production."

"But anything we did in Ibiza was difficult," laughs Glenn. "Technically, it was because of the amount of alcohol that was consumed. And we did have to finish one off in America, where we got sane for a little bit. *Point of Entry* was done there. *Screaming* was started there, and *Defenders* was started there, and then we had to go to a sensible country to finish them."

Point of Entry was issued in February of 1981, with different album covers for Europe and North America. Europe got an intriguing and colourful sort of futuristic metal wing over a horizon shot (or is that fire from an aircraft engine?), designed by CBS' Roslav Szaybo, who had done all the band's CBS albums to date. North America got the artsy roll of computer paper in the desert scene, designed by Columbia Records' John Berg, who later rose to a Vice President at the label. The back of the North American issue showed—Hipgnosis-styled—a bunch of white cardboard boxes standing at attention. The cover was stickered with a shot of the band, so metalheads would get the point that this austere scene was indeed the cover of a new Judas Priest album.

"The *Point of Entry* cover was a bit weird," muses Tom. "They had a problem deciding what sort of look they wanted, and it ended up not really being a look. Nice colours though (laughs). It was like a wing of an airplane, which was quite good. But the American cover was a complete disaster. I don't know what on earth that was about. Stupid. Maybe it was something to do with 'Desert Plains' or something. Or as somebody said, dessert pains (laughs)."

Into the music, Priest opened with a song that really told the story of this whole album—even though structures were simple, relaxed, unshowy in the extreme, the writing was fantastic. "Heading out to the Highway" was truly one of those dependable compositions that could conceivably be strummed on a lone acoustic guitar with vocal and still sound good. There's something country and western about it, or at least something wild west. It's a great track, this record's "Breaking the Law," and it's become a lasting Priest anthem.

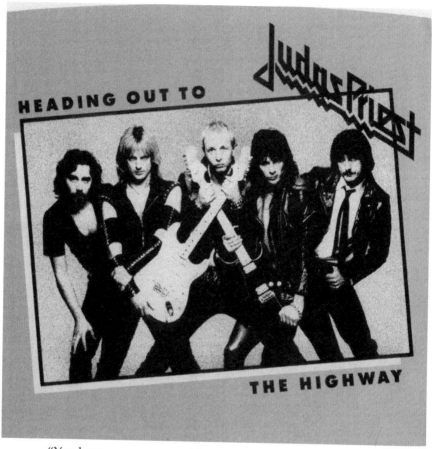

"You know, we never contrive a song," offers Glenn, with respect to "Heading out to the Highway." "We just sit down and write and they come from us. And there's never a reason why we wrote a particular song. We sit down, somebody's got a riff and we kick it around and put a vocal to it, it's all very natural. And that song is still a very perennial live song. But I honestly like all the Priest stuff. I think the album that most people would point out as being the most different is *Point of Entry*. But then again, you've got tracks like 'Hot Rockin',' 'Desert Plains,' 'Solar Angels'..."

The band had written a bunch of songs back in London for the new album, but then decided to scrap the whole lot and start new—it was deemed that the songs were good, but not much different in tone than what was on *British Steel*. Priest were again restless to make a very different album, commendable and creatively bold, given the long-awaited breakthrough success they had with *British Steel*.

Label folks noticed "Heading out to the Highway"'s personable, soulful, wistful quality and issued it as a single two months after the album's release, but the song failed to chart either side of the pond. The video for the song was an endearing clip. Dave looks tidy and new wave-like in his skinny tie and dress shirt under leather jacket. Rob could pass for an old punk. In total, this was really the band at its most charming from a visual standpoint. Marketing hadn't avalanched in on the look. It was thrown together, it was real, the guys were innocent, and they had a bit of a sartorial eye to the future. Interspersed are scenes from a good old fashioned drag race, '50s style (filmed at an old British Royal Air Force strip), Rob in jeans and T-shirt, his moves still a bit feminine and actorly, again, not so studied – Rob later quipped that they had a Marlon Brando thing going. This is a great video, and the song's stirring melodies provide the perfect soundtrack to the action.

The aforementioned "Don't Go" came next, and I remember friends who were fans being shocked at how it was barely there. Still, it grows on you, and little musical events, most notably a type of conversation between the guitars, lift it along as the band progress through to a conclusion much louder and more robust than the way the track began. The video is another charmer, set to a surreal scene typical of the very first videos as video directors stretched their creativity as far as they could without spending too much money. Rob has longish blond hair and a moustache as he exhorts various band members not to leave, not to open that white door and enter a crazy world.

"It's more gruelling than you think," says Ian with respect to making these clips. "You tend to be sitting around for ages doing nothing punctuated by a few minutes of intense activity. On the 'Don't Go' video, I remember Rob throwing up into his space helmet one time (laughs). He does this flying thing in a space suit and he's up on wires and they're spinning him around and all this business and he actually threw up in the helmet (laughs). That was quite an event. But I quite liked 'Don't Go.' I liked working on it as well. It was one of the first times we worked with Julien Temple, who went on to bigger and better things, I believe. That was quite exciting. We were generally on location, so the chances of meeting any movie star would be quite remote. 'Don't Go' was done in London. It's usually locally done where we happened to be."

Next up was "Hot Rockin'," perhaps the album's heaviest track, this one recalling "Breaking the Law" as well, with its all-business, meat-and-potatoes straight-line trajectory. Almost a punk rocker, there's a great dramatic break late in the track, before an inspiring lapse into another verse.

For the video (also directed by Julien Temple), Rob was singing expressively, convincingly, in a car, out for a night on the town, positively raging for a bit of mischief. This footage was interspersed with the band live on a soundstage, increasingly lighting bits of their gear on fire in front of a small crowd of egregiously committed metalheads. Recalls Ian, "Rob set his boots on fire and he couldn't put it out; he was putting this jelly stuff on his palm, I think. And he couldn't get his boots off because they were hot. He was running around there until somebody found a fire extinguisher." Indeed, by the time Rob got his long, tight boots off, his toes were apparently half-burnt from the heat.

"Turning Circles" is the record's second shocker, its opening riff sounding like something off of a Lou Reed album. Fortunately, the song up-ratchets to what is at least a dark pop rocker, reminiscent of something Blue Öyster Cult might have done that same year. "Desert Plains" follows, and this one underscores the album's essence as something slightly morose, laid-back, understated. It's a rocker, one that could have fit on *British Steel*, or strangely *Defenders*, but again, the fireworks are kept in the box, although for ear candy there are vocal harmonies and drum overdubs.

Amusingly, the 2001 reissue of *Point of Entry* includes a crazy-fast live version of the song—this is in actuality, the biggest change in tempo of a song, from studio to live, I've ever heard out of any band. The song is wholly transformed in the process.

Side two of the original vinyl opens with another languished but, on the main, heavy rocker, "Solar Angels" helping define the *British Steel/Point of Entry* era as built around simple structures, plain but competent recording values, excellent expression out of Rob, and sophisticated chord changes leading to a certain pop timelessness. Next was "You Say Yes," which Tipton deems a brave experiment if not a successful one. Again, it's part and parcel of this album's identity. Arrangements are similar throughout the album, and some songs are just happier—this is one of them, its funky, circular riff working well with Rob's flirting lyric. "All the Way " continues in this mainstream mode, sounding like a cross between glam, the Stones and "Living After Midnight." "Troubleshooter"—same thing. This was a Priest pared down and pert, ready to compete perhaps with the world of post-punk new wave.

The album closes with "On the Run," more of a conventional Priest rocker with distinct echoes of *British Steel*'s point-blank rockiness. Still, its shuffling Status Quo strut was a far cry from the note density strafing a "Hell Bent for Leather" or a "Dissident Aggressor."

Commercially, *Point of Entry* would be considered a pronounced falter after *British Steel*'s seemingly effortless vault to gold status. The album peaked at around 425,000 for a while and then finally was awarded gold on November 10, 1989. In its day, it would rise to No.14 in the UK charts, and No.39 in the States, compared to No.4 in Britain and No.34 in the States for its more well-endowed partner *British Steel*. The album went silver in the UK representing sales of 60,000 copies with claimed worldwide sales to date hovering around 1.6M units.

Oddly, the band, in retrospect, talks about the album as very strong but perhaps self-indulgent, inventive, even progressive. It is in fact, none of these things. And Priest were the band of record when it came to being self-indulgent and progressive and pulling it off with almost Queen-like flair. This is what they were like during their golden period in the late '70s. But come *Point of Entry*, no, all you had really was simple and poppy—nicely done mind you, but simple and poppy all the same. If writing music pointedly to make some dosh at the expense of purity and creativity was self-indulgent, well, then Priest was being self-indulgent.

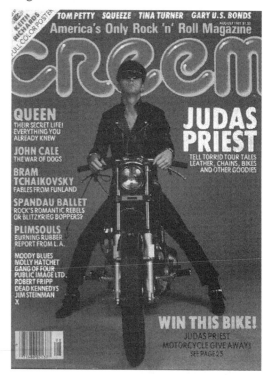

"We still play 'Heading out to the Highway' live," reflects Ian, somewhat contradictorily, looking back at this contentious record. "It's a great live track. We didn't make a conscience effort where we went, 'We'd better try and sell this to the teeny boppers.' There was none of that. It was just that we went in the studio and did what we did. There was no conscious effort to make the album commercial—it just turned out the way that it did."

Between record release and touring, Priest parted ways with their management. Amidst accusations of financial mismanagement, there was a difference of vision. Management wanted Priest to ditch the black leather and studs, the whole heavy metal image, along with the Harley. Priest figured this was central to their identity and decided to manage themselves for a time, under the guise of Secret Management Associates Inc..

The *Point of Entry* tour kicked off in mid-February of '81, with Saxon as support. Perhaps cognizant of their slip, the band played the four heaviest metal songs from the album, and nothing else, although "Troubleshooter" was given a test run. Arguably, "On the Run" is the key heavy metal deletion, but other than that, *Point of Entry*'s dark side was covered, through the proprietorship of "Heading out to the Highway," "Hot Rockin'," "Desert Plains" and "Solar Angels." The opener was in fact the panoramic and languid, though wall-to-wall guitary "Solar Angels," the band hitting the stage after an extended atmospheric intro. The back catalogue semi-hits were piling up, with perhaps "Don't Have to Be Old to Be Wise" being odd man out on a set list starting to solidify for all time. In the US, Priest took out a rocketing Iron Maiden, along with a fading Humble Pie and for the second time, The Joe Perry Project.

The stage set was a step up, with hydraulic platforms, a futuristic star-shaped lighting system and more room to roam—which the band did enthusiastically, aided as well by the use of new wireless guitar systems. A curious red and yellow pattern in front of the amps had Glenn quipping that it looked like a Chinese restaurant. Glenn's black leather jacket and red pants were displayed in all their glory, but Rob looked kind of casual in a denim and leather ensemble. At one show, the lighting system came unhinged on one side and swooped down upon the band, missing the guys but actually taking out a few cymbals in the process.

"Paul Di'Anno apologised personally to me for causing bad air between Maiden and Priest," said K.K., looking back in 2003 at Priest's relationship with the eventual usurpers to the metal throne. "What a great gesture. But he wasn't the main reason for the rivalry. At the time of *British Steel*,

Priest was the bigger band and Maiden was the supporting act. They were saying that they'll blow us off the stage without any problem. Well, I thought their behaviour wasn't very nice. I'd have loved to send them home and take another band with us who would have appreciated the chance. But we were told not to do it as it would have looked like we were frightened by them. So we kept on going. But they were very arrogant. And I remember the main rehearsal before the tour, there were a few guys hanging around in the room who didn't say a word and watched everything we did, every step we made and every move of the stage lights. I wasn't very pleased and asked the guitar tech to tell the guys to leave the place."

"Don't get me wrong," continued Downing, "I'm not 'too good' to play in front of the supporting band, but they could have at least asked if it was okay to attend the rehearsal. We went on tour and they didn't blow us off the stage, of course. I watched quite a lot of the Maiden shows, but the reaction of the audience wasn't very explosive, because the fans were waiting for us. Okay, Maiden became one of the biggest bands of the metal scene, and I'm proud of them. We made a big mistake by focusing more on the US than on Europe after releasing *British Steel*, which means, we lost a lot of attention at home. In the US, we were quite big, and Maiden asked us for a support slot on our US tour. We said yes—

and the same old story happened again. It had a lot to do with rivalry and jealousy. But it's an old story. Like I already said, I'm proud of what Maiden achieved and of what they did for British metal. It might sound stupid, but it's true."

The band was in the States from May '81 through July, followed by November and December dates in Britain. Noted Geoff Barton, reviewing the band's Hammersmith Odeon show of November 22nd, 1981, "It was obvious from the outset that this was going to be one of the bozo metal concerts of our time. Arriving on stage via hydraulic lifts and in a haze of dry ice smoke, the Priest broke into 'Solar Angels,' and instantly took their positions (did you notice those little Isla St. Clair-style 'Stand here' squares on the stage floor?) for the first

choreographed movements. In unison, guitar necks moved to and fro, heads shook up and down, and it was like a Status Quo cartoon animated by Hanna-Barbera on a cheapo repeat-frame basis. Meanwhile vocalist Rob Halford stood at the back, amused, and maybe anxious to dissociate himself from the ridiculous goings-on down at the front."

Next came mainland Europe with Def Leppard and Accept in tow. Curiously, at least early in the campaign, the *British Steel* album cover was being used on tour posters, its distinct image perhaps making a subtle shift from album cover to a descriptor of the upcoming show: Judas Priest—British Steel!

Forever a burr in Priest's saddle, Gull Records returned in '81 with a double album called *Hero, Hero*, which trotted out the old *Rocka Rolla* and *Sad Wings of Destiny* material (already reissued in various territories, and in a number of ways), yet again. Cool little changes were part of the package though, best addition being the early, warmer, more relaxed version of "Diamonds and Rust." Both are good, sure, but this one is positively cushy compared to the thin and frenetic take that showed up on *Sin After Sin*. Also, through a Rodger Bain remix, "Rocka

Rolla" was slightly rearranged, with the harmonica taken out and some soloing lost. "Deep Freeze" was made nastier, finicky things were done to various guitar and vocal parts, and all of those bitty pieces of the *Rocka Rolla* Winter Suite epic were chopped up properly. Finally, Melvyn Grant was called upon to provide the rights to his fantasy warrior painting "Sword of the Gael," already used for a book cover in 1975. It was one of at least three fetching new fantasy-based paintings Gull would use to tart up the venerable Priest material they kept reconfiguring, and, although they looked good and fit the bill for the band's moody, mysterious first two records, one can't—and shouldn't—purge the iconic *Sad Wings* art from one's mind. *Rocka Rolla* is another story, but ultimately, these things should remain as they were...

Picking a *British Steel* track as the b-side speaks volumes about what folks thought about *Point of Entry*.

BREAKING THE LAW
Recorded live February 1981

Glenn in iconic black and red leather. Maple Leaf Gardens, Toronto.

Twin turbo *British Steel* promo displays. © Dave Hogue.

Dave Holland, drummer on all six Judas Priest albums of the 1980s (Sort of. Long story).

Rob in full S&M mode, complete with bullwhip.

Locked in: Glenn and K.K.

Columbia Records promo shot. Left to right; Dave Holland, Glenn Tipton, Rob Halford, K.K. Downing, Ian Hill.

Case study in the design of graphic materials perfect for merchandising.

Get Thee Behind Judas Priest!

Rob reaching for inner strength, Toronto.

The weapons of war.

Rob, Glenn and Ian: four decades of dominance. © Trevor Shaikin.

Chapter 9:
Screaming for Vengeance –
"We could afford to go out and buy a decent car!"

No question, *Point of Entry* knocked Priest down a peg. Fans had it in the back of their minds that even before their heroes got to become ambassadors of metal (a phrase that was thrown around in later years), Priest had stumbled with a weak tea album, leaving the door ajar for lustier romps from the likes of Saxon, Maiden and Def Leppard.

But the band's next album would prove that there was more gas in the tank, that metal still lived and breathed inside this beast from Birmingham. Ibiza, Spain would again be home to the band as they formulated plans to return strong, with two studios in Florida used for mixing purposes (and the fateful recording of "You've Got Another Thing Comin'"). These were BeeJay Recording Studios and Bayshore Recording Studios, both in Coconut Grove. *Screaming for Vengeance* would be recorded over a five-month period, from January until May 1982, the album shipping shortly thereafter, on July 17th. In fact, the band had spent late '81 in Ibiza writing and rehearsing. After they took a break for some UK dates in November, they went into recording mode, only to end up scrapping the handful of songs they had worked up the previous October.

"Oh Lord, you probably heard the stories of Ian destroying half a dozen rental cars, and ending up in the pool outside the studio," chuckles Rob, recalling the sessions. "Nights at the infamous clubs in Ibiza called Pacha and Ku. I don't know how we got that record made. It might show some of the benefits of procrastination. Not that musicians are very timely people anyway. Dear me, forget the weekends. Between Friday nights and Monday morning anything could happen. Me and Glenn driving really seriously drunk—I'm not laughing at this in an approving way—it was just like, man the risks we took, it's just remarkable. There was a party going on in that studio and there were guests coming and going, friends we'd made coming and going. Let's face it, it was the start of the '80s, the infamous decade of debauchery that Priest and a lot of other bands were diving into and enjoying. Out of all that came this masterpiece! It's a miracle really."

Screaming for Vengeance would quickly prove to be a success, hitting gold four months after issue and platinum six months later. Although likely passing double platinum much earlier, October 2001 marked the official designation for the record at that level. It was of little concern that these numbers were not higher than that, indeed, as high as the numbers many other metal bands were about to achieve, for Priest would be getting the same high level of press and attendant photography, their crowds would be huge and adoring, and most importantly, they were about to enjoy a few magic years as the gold standard of metal bands. Slow and steady wins the race—the album would spend 53 weeks on the Billboard charts, achieving a No.17 placement in the US, No.11 back home in Britain. Eventually, worldwide sales would be estimated at five million copies.

No doubt the artwork chosen for *Screaming for Vengeance* helped the band's commercial purposes. *Point of Entry* was a disaster graphically, nice, a bit arty, intriguing for an album cover, but of little use beyond into the world of merchandising. *British Steel* had it all, and frankly, its cartoony feel was a big part of that. Even more cartoony was Doug Johnson's Hellion, essentially becoming a mascot for the band, even if short-lived. The bold, primary-coloured graphics surrounding this mythical, mechanical beast communicated something to the punter, and the fact that the overall design was essentially yellow... well, that was something fresh, cheerful, bright, the new colour at the party—it was is if Priest was trying to say that yellow was the new black.

"Somewhere I've got the original transparency for *Screaming for Vengeance*," says producer Tom Allom. "It's a great cover. *British Steel* is probably the best, for me, the razor blade. That and *Screaming for Vengeance*—God, great covers. That's the first time they used a designer. I can't remember his name, but they used him again for *Defenders*." "The artwork, the big 12" by 12" screaming eagle was another part of the success of that record," adds Rob. "People would walk into the record store and see that display and go, 'Man what is this? I've got to check it out!' I think as a record it's more than just the music."

Halford has remarked that he had the word "vengeance" firmly in mind for the title of the next record. Of course, Halford, as well as the others, would be too polite and also too careful on a publicity tack to suggest the vengeance they desired was toward a) slaggers of their slaggable last album; b) the band themselves for screwing up and making that slaggable album; or c) slaggers of heavy metal itself. Once Rob had seen the cover image concocted by Johnson, he realised "vengeance" fit fine, as well as the word "screaming," given that Johnson's eagle looked like it was screaming as it swooped in for the kill, as the band's early tour mates Budgie might surmise. K.K. was further pleased by the fact that the cover brought forward, and only slightly, elements from the *Sad Wings of Destiny* art used six years earlier.

Diving into the record now, *Screaming for Vengeance* opened with one of the great metal intros of all time. "The Hellion" was 41 seconds of molten metal drama. K.K. has mentioned that the original plan was to turn the track into a song in its own right, which of course never happened. Instantly one notices that Tom Allom's production proves sizzling, far above the humourless knob job afforded *British Steel*, with "The Hellion" proceeding proudly like a flawless sound check, smiles all around, all systems go.

"We'd never done that type of opening before," explained Rob. "And obviously it came from Glenn and Ken at the time. I can't really remember how it came together in the studio—was it one person? Was it collective? I don't know. But we were always experimenting, always trying to do something that we hadn't done previously. We were inspired by what Brian May was doing with a lot of the Queen stuff. Brian was doing those same types of multi-guitar track things. As you get more experienced in a band, you understand the value of setting the scene. We quickly thought, 'We can use this as an intro tape.' And we did. In terms of setup, in terms of getting an audience's attention, it just works magically, even now, when we did it at our last show at Hammersmith—once you start it, the audience just grabs onto it right away."

"Hellion," unlike many intros, actually does end, after which "Electric Eye" bursts forth like a thousand hellions from thunderous skies, the song instantly heavier than anything on *Point of Entry*, again, smiles all around this time on the faces of the faithful that had to endure their band's year of red faces at the hands of countless NWOBHM bands handing them a beating.

Again, Tom Allom had triumphed at the recording desk. No surprise that the guitars sound bold and searing, but drummer Dave Holland is captured adequately as well. Sure, Allom goes for more of a continuous, high frequency bass rumble, rather than having bass emerge from the kick drum. But the cymbals sizzle loudly and often, and the overall effect is one of potent, profound metal unity.

"That was a tricky album for them to make," recalls Allom. "Because we went back to Ibiza and we did a few songs, I think, from memory, about five or six, and the album was stalled, in the new year, by an internal dispute with their management. And their management split into two, and they went with one half, and we didn't actually resume that album until, if I recall correctly, April or thereabouts. And that again got mixed in the States. I was living there by then, and so we mixed that in Bill Szymczyk's studio, in Coconut Grove."

"There were some powerful songs," continues Tom, asked about the complexion of the material versus that of *Point of Entry*. "One particularly stuck in my mind—'Bloodstone,' great riff. I think they were always really guided by the reaction they got from their fans live. By then, they had played some pretty big audiences in America, and they knew what their fans wanted. I think I'm probably right in saying this—they were kind of trying, on *Point of Entry*, to pander to the label. I think when it came to *Screaming for Vengeance*, it's, we're going to give the fans what they want. We're not going to give them what the record company thinks we should be giving them. And there was quite a lot of pressure from CBS in America, I remember, because there were other bands, other quasi-heavy metal bands, heavy rock bands, who were making very radio-friendly music—you know, AOR—and they decided they would resist that temptation and just stick to what they knew their fans loved about them. And that really epitomises *Screaming for Vengeance*. There was no attempt to do anything other than be very heavy. Probably 'You've Got Another Thing Comin'' was the only track that smacked of commercialism, and they just hit upon that riff. I don't know if it was Glenn or Kenny or both of them or whatever, who hit upon that riff, but it was very catchy."

Remarks Rob on *Screaming for Vengeance*'s first full song, forever to be a live classic, "'Electric Eye' is relevant because it talks about an invasion of privacy by spy satellites, but the cool thing is that I revisited that approach and wrote 'Cyberworld' on the *Resurrection* CD from the Halford band, and it just talks about the way that no matter where we go and what we do in the world, we're always under a microscope, and that there is no such thing as 100% privacy in your life." Tipton adds that he admired the way that this was a modern lyric, more sci-fi versus the "dungeon" lyrics of the '70s. Rob's flash words were designed to fit the flash "'80s"-style heavy metal he and K.K. were crafting.

"I love the rhythmic setup on that song," continues Halford. "Emotionally again, it starts roaring right from the opening bars. We're a metal band and if you're that sort of band it's important that you make sure you have that type of attitude and approach within your first two or three tracks. It reinforces who you are and what you're trying to do. The way that 'Electric Eye' kicks off is very much an assertive statement. It's a really good song and it's just got the attitude and the in-your-face drama that Priest has always tried to put forward."

Noted Rob at the time on the record's lyrical approach, "I'm sure people get sick of hearing me scream about demons and death and destruction all the time. There's always that tendency in heavy metal to have that kind of stylised writing, because the words usually don't mean a great deal. On *Screaming for Vengeance*, however, the lyrics are back to being aggressive; even more so than on *British Steel*. What I write is based on our audience. The great percentage of our audience is able to relate to the lyrical content. People simply want to relate, and that is probably the greatest thing Judas Priest have had going for us. They see us pretty much as themselves, maybe hoping that one day they can do what we're doing."

"Electric Eye" was indeed eyed as a second lead single to drop from the talons of this record. Halford remarked that he had reservations about it, figuring something like "(Take These) Chains" was more suited for airplay. But he had also recognised the visual appeal in the song's subject matter, and that it undoubtedly would have been good grist for a video. MTV was one year old and going gangbusters at the

time, and Priest was in there like a dirty shirt, garnering huge airplay with *Screaming*'s first single, "You've Got Another Thing Comin'." In any event, "Electric Eye" never happened as a single or video. Not that it needed it—it is eclipsed perhaps only by "Victim of Changes" or "Breaking the Law" as the fans' most cherished Priest gem of all time.

Reflects Halford, "You know, people have asked, just because of the texture, the attitude and the atmosphere of *Screaming for Vengeance*, were we on some kind of agenda after the way *Point of Entry* was received? Prior to that, of course *British Steel* was a very, very important successful record. I think all you can say in terms of the way the metal flowed kind of goes back and forth; if you are in any band that's had longevity, certain records get more prominence than others. And certain feelings and things happen that you have no control over. The riffs that came together for *Screaming for Vengeance* were obviously destined to happen at that particular time. Not before or since. Every single record

Martin Popoff

that any band releases is like a metal time capsule of what you're doing and where you are at. And how you are writing and how you're feeling at that particular moment. So, that's just the magic of what we do. We've always said if you try to control it, it becomes artificial. So a lot of things that are out of your control come into play. You're just doing the best that you can at that particular time. A lot of it is a game of luck and chance because you have no idea what you're going to come up with when you go into the studio and turn the amps on and start riffing. As it turned out of course, some of the most exciting songs in Priest's back catalogue took place in those sessions."

Two proper songs into the record, "Riding on the Wind" would represent the second track in a row that clocks heavier than anything across the peaceful, easy azure seas lapping up against *Point of Entry*. By this point in the sequence, fans were getting the message that Priest was deliberately and brutishly stomping all over their recent past. Lyrically, Halford is tossing off bolts of energy, combining the imagery of the much more poetic and dramatic "Rapid Fire" with the sci-fi of various lyrics on *Stained Class*. It ain't much, but it races the pulse.

"I love the way 'Electric Eye' and 'Riding on the Wind' bash into each other," note Halford, always cognizant of pacing and flow. "'Riding' starts with that drum passage, that clattering, and then it just really roars off. It's probably a stronger statement in terms of metal than 'Electric Eye' is musically. It just has a wonderful sense of being determined, and having that type of strong and forceful attitude to it. It's about shooting for the stars. It pertains a bit to being on a bike, riding on the wind, that sort of thing. Lyrically I was trying to take the atmosphere of a lightning storm, or a hurricane, and riding on it and grabbing hold of it. It's a glorious statement in terms of metal."

"Bloodstone" completes side one's trilogy of trouncers, three songs heavier than anything on *Point of Entry* and all a match for the most intense of *British Steel* highlights. What this one lacks in full-throttle guitar, it makes up for with darkness and a pronounced surge come chorus time. The "Bloodstone" lyric is, again, spare but somewhat poignant, its central and quite grand element being Rob's labelling of our corrupt planet as a bloodstone.

"I know I keep saying this, but I love the way that song starts," notes Rob. "It's got a really cool riff that Glenn came up with. Each of the tracks on the record start off with either an individual riff or something of a musical melodic passage that kind of sets the scene before the rest of the song kicks in. It's got a great breakdown, this kind of rhythm where—I don't know whether Dave Holland came up with it—it's got that 'k-chonk, k-chonk, k-chonk' thing between the vocal phrases after the second line. Then he kind of snaps with the rhythmic 'k-chonk' and it's a very unusual arrangement. It's a little bit paranoid, because it talks about waking up in the night and being afraid of the game going on around you—I have no idea what that really means looking back!"

Side one then turns on a disconcerting note, Priest working up a song by hired songwriting gun from Syracuse, NY, Bob Halligan Jr., later to work with Rob inside of Halford, along with many others, his Priest song being his first credit of a long and distinguished career. "(Take These) Chains" is essentially a hair metal song, definitely a poppy ballad at times, lyrically a cheap and cheesy love song. The pre-chorus melody is a highlight though, hearkening back to "Breaking the Law" and poignant bits on *Point of Entry*. The solo section is nicely assembled as well. Still, this wasn't a band that needed help writing.

"Bob was a songwriter discovered by Columbia in America," notes Halford. "We ended up doing a few of his songs over the years. The label knew we'd recorded other people's songs before, and I think they must've had discussions saying, 'Well, at least the guys can understand the importance and value of what a song that could work on rock radio could do for them.' They sent the demo over and we immediately warmed to it. Again, I think whatever we've done in terms of a cover, we've had to fully understand that it can be given the Priest signature musically. It's a wonderful song in terms of composure and the riffage in it. For the first time, maybe after what we were doing with *Point of Entry*, we were feeling a bit more comfortable with talking about songs that dealt with relationships. It's not really seen as a metal thing is it? But even metalheads have boyfriends and girlfriends."

"Bob was just an extraordinary, gifted songwriter," Rob told me on a different occasion. "I do recall we were looking for some kind of connection with radio and somebody from the label suggested Bob and we met. We loved the guy and we heard some of the demos that he was presenting and we just jumped into '(Take These) Chains,' with hope that it might give us some access to an area that was something our label was looking for. He's tremendous, just a great writer. I don't think he does that much now. I met him on the Halford tour. I can't remember when, but I wanted to say thank you for what he did for Priest. He also wrote 'Twist' for me (note: from 2000's Halford album, *Resurrection*). When we approached him to do something for the Halford band he said that he hadn't written that kind of music for ages. He'd gone into new age, kind of floaty music. He said, 'The reason I took it on was because I was excited to see what I could still do.' I think it proved he's got the chops still to do those kinds of songs."

"Pain and Pleasure," another dark horse track, is an apt follow-up to "Chains," with both being a bit pedestrian and plodding, working hard to erase all that good will built up by the three stormbringers placed mercilessly in succession to open the album. It's another love-gone-wrong song, not one of Halford's strong suits. "'Pain and Pleasure'… I was drunk when I wrote those lyrics," quips Rob. "We were just playing up to the S&M thing. It was like, 'Look at what Rob's wearing.' It was part of the appeal of the visual of the band. We were just having fun with pain and pleasure. Songs like 'Fever' are kind of edgy in terms of the message. Lyrically it was an interesting record. We go from talking about spy satellites to tying people up! (laughs)."

"But I was out of my fucking tree! When you get drunk, some people get violent, some people get giggly and some people get horny— and I just generally got very horny. That's just how I was in those days. Suddenly it's a complete change of tempo and emotion. It's a very simple song rhythmically, but you're kind of delving into a little bit of S&M with the, 'You give me pain but you bring me pleasure' line. That was the reason why we were attracted to the message in that song; we were fully ensconced in that leather image by that point. I love the slide guitar on that record; that's very much in the blues world—there's a portion of the blues that has that type of thing going for it."

Side two opens with the fourth song on the record heavier than anything on *Point of Entry*, or safely we could say at this point, anything on *British Steel*. *Screaming*'s title track is a return to the technical speed metal mastery found on the song "Hell Bent for Leather" and much of the *Stained Class* album, but from a less naïve and bravely optimistic point of view. Still, without a flash drummer to propel the song, it seems a bit shackled, with no help from Allom's modern, effect-treated approach to drum

sounds. Sure, they are slight, and they pose no problem elsewhere, but on a song this fast, the backbeat feels clunky, panicked rather than stridently fast. Halford's lyric is interesting and well off his usual style, almost into an awkward and amusing Ian Gillan "English as a second language" mode. He seems to be on about individuality, essentially a *British Steel* sentiment, but his message emerges more charming than correct.

Says Ian of "Screaming for Vengeance," "It's funny, because that is one of the tracks that Priest will be known for, although also of course,

'You've Got Another Thing Comin',' because it was all over the radio at the time. But 'Screaming' almost epitomises Judas Priest with the speed and aggression. And that was very, very much worked on. That was planned for, that one. It was the key track on the album."

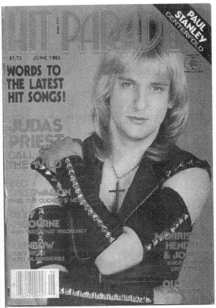

"What I remember about that track," adds Halford, "was that we got the song, we got the components for the instrumentation together, but I went into the studio with literally no idea what I was going to sing, or the lyrics. I was just doing like scratch vocals. I grabbed the mic and just jammed. Then we listened to it and it was garbage, making strange noises and words. But we were so excited by the immediacy of what was happening that we said, 'Let's try to make some sense out of this.' We actually took some of the phonetics and the sounds that I was making and put the words together. 'Tie a blindfold all around your head' and all that—those were kind of subconscious words that were coming out of me as I was doing the track. I think the sense of urgency is in that trying to catch lightning in a bottle moment. It was kind of cool, really. I don't think I've ever done anything since in that kind of manner. Now I just take a long, long, long time to get my vocal chops behind anything. We have so much in the past that we've covered, we just think kind of differently right now. It's a really full-throttle song isn't it? With those extraordinary kind of rhythm breaks between the verses and the bridges. They make you out-of-breath just listening to it rhythmically. So I think it all ties into quite an unusual performance."

"It's not quite thrash, but it's got that attitude about it," continues Rob. "It's really full-on and I get to use a voice that I don't really use on the other tracks. Everything goes into top gear and I think it's a wonderful complement to the way 'Pain and Pleasure' has been slugging along like an 18-wheeler. Then suddenly the thing lifts off again—it's easily the fastest song on the record."

Next comes a song even more similar to something from Kiss than was "Living After Midnight." "You've Got Another Thing Comin'," like that incendiary 1980 track built of dependable "Louie Louie" chords, presents Priest to the masses in dumbed-down form. Unlike "Living After Midnight," this one's not even particularly good. The cosy charm isn't there, nor is the heavy yet energetic verse. This one thunders along threatening to collapse under its weight, shackled by a four-on-the-floor beat, rarely a good idea, namely the idea of snare drum, as is typical, on two and four, but bass drum on one, two, three and four. Plus the premise is weak. The call-and-response vocal/riff structure is straight off a Sammy Hagar solo album, the lyric an unimpressive rehash of past themes, the title, long awkward and boring. As mentioned, there was a well-used video, again Julien Temple called upon to do the business. And there you go: inexplicable to this writer, "You've Got Another Thing Comin'" would become the band's biggest hit ever.

"You always think that with every album!" says Ian, asked whether he had any notion this album would wind up platinum, driven by the band's surprise radio anthem. "We got lucky with it as it contained 'You've Got Another Thing Comin'.' That song was very much an accident. We recorded a lot of the material in the Mediterranean. We went to Orlando, Florida and mixed the album and discovered we were a little short on time. We were mixing down, at Beejay, and we thought that we could do with another three or four minutes. We did our best to get something together—a bit of an album filler. That is very unusual for us because we never take that sort of attitude. It was that song and it was written and recorded within hours. It was an afterthought. It might have been because it was so spontaneous and fresh that American radio picked up on it and the next thing you know it was being played all over the place. It was the song that broke us in a big way in the States."

"Everything that followed really owed itself to that song," continues Hill. "It is spontaneous things like that that are sometimes the best. How did the success change us? I don't know. You have no basis for comparison. You don't know what you would have been like if you had never gone through it. It was great doing something that you loved but it was hard. We didn't earn any money for ten years. We were living from hand to mouth for a long time. It was not until *Screaming for Vengeance* that we could afford to go out and buy a decent car! It was a long hard road. Everything that we earned

went back into the band. This was the days before renting PA's and trucks. We had roadies we were paying. Like I say, most of the income that came in went back into the band."

"I think we were just going full-on like any band attempts to when you become successful," muses Halford, using the record's last track to exemplify the sense of horseshoes within the band at the time. "It's just a wonderful feeling. There's so much energy and excitement surrounding everything that you do. You're constantly inspired by the fans that are growing into your life. You're just going for it full-roar and that's how we were when we returned to Ibiza to make *Screaming for Vengeance*. I will tell you what is cool, if you look at the first few years of 1980, we were literally banging out a record every year, with a world tour. And I don't know how we did that! I just know that we'd come off a world tour, we'd have a couple of weeks to take a breath, then we'd go into the studio, more often than not with practically no songs created, just fragments of ideas. The main point that we enforce is that 'You've Got

Another Thing Comin" was the last track we wrote in those *Screaming for Vengeance* sessions. It wasn't exactly an afterthought; it's just that we needed one more song and that was the one. It just turned out that the last song turned out to be the biggest one for the band, particularly in the States. Just a lot of great memories, full of life and energy and vitality."

"That song has had a second lease of life because it's on one of the Guitar Hero games," notes Rob. "I met a guy recently whose 14-year-old son's favourite song is 'Another Thing Comin',' and he got to it via Guitar Hero. It's a song that's transcended from place to place. It goes from a record onto radio, onto a cassette player, then onto a CD, and then to an MP3 and then to a video game. That's a blessing for musicians really, that your songs reach people through ways that ordinarily you wouldn't imagine."

"Yes, 'You've Got Another Thing Comin'' was very much thrown together in the studio," emphasises Ian. "Also, the record company was screaming at us for a commercial type song—or something commercial for us—that they might be able to get on radio. And it very much took shape within an afternoon really (laughs). Although obviously it took a couple of days to get it put down. We got in there, started kicking a few ideas around, and that's what came out. It was very much a last-minute thing."

"That didn't get written until just about the beginning of the second load of sessions," confirms Tom Allom. "I'll tell you how that was recorded. They got this idea for this song, without any lyrics, without a melody or anything. And they put it down, just guitars, bass and drums, while we were setting up in the studio. And in fact I was just sort of getting drum sounds together, and I just happened to roll the tape, and that was a one-taker (laughs), and we used it. It's the only time they ever played it in the studio, was that once. Even in rehearsal; it was a rehearsal room. And it had such a good feel, we overdubbed one other rhythm guitar part on it, because they were turned down in the studio, so I could get the drums going. And they were just turned down with a lot of overdrive, and we recorded one other rhythm guitar over the top of that. I think the final lyric and melody was about the third attempt of the song, over this backing track. But again, you know, they hadn't really intended to write a single. It just turned out to be what it was. It was a big radio hit in the States, but it didn't make much noise here in the UK. So that was a big radio hit, but there was some of the heaviest stuff they've ever done. The title track was very heavy."

Adds K.K. on the subject of commerciality, "Obviously we started recording in the early '70s. I suppose inevitably when you start to travel the world and go to different countries… I mean, before we actually went to America or Canada, people would say, 'When you hit that continent, it's going to change you. You'll hear things on the radio and you'll be influenced by this.' And whether we were or not, I'm not exactly sure. The only thing I know is that it seems that every few years, things take a little bit of a turn in that direction and you start to create a bit of different rock or metal, as people know. But with *Screaming for Vengeance*, I think that was one album that just came out very, very naturally, as did *British Steel*, from the band, and we didn't have to work at it. And I think it shows. We say if the record seems to have a good flow to it, good continuity, then the band didn't have to work hard to come up with material. Whereas other albums, I think it kind of shows a little bit. Even though they might be good albums, it shows that we had to work at it. And in actual fact, *Screaming for Vengeance* is our biggest selling album."

K.K. often seemed both bemused and intrigued by what had happened with the band in the States, claiming that the nation's love affair with radio is more intense than elsewhere. To that end, he always got a kick out of hearing his song blasting out of a car rolling by, or even more so, in a supermarket, joking about rolling down the aisle with his cart, in possession of this surreal knowledge that that's him on there.

Figures Rob, concerning radio, "Once you've made your record, you can look at it, you can listen to it, you can sit down with your label and all the important people that are part of the equation and go, 'Yes, that track could be big in America.' I keep emphasizing America as far as the radio connection goes—it was and it still is vital. If you want to be in a successful band you need to have some tracks that are accessible to radio. You've got to have that. As it turned out, 'You've Got Another Thing Comin'' was a track we literally buried on the back of the album. And that was the one that was discovered by radio and made into the hit that it was. That side of it in Priest's world is one of excitement and surprise when tracks have been picked up and given airplay. I don't think we ever specifically sat down and said, 'Today we're going to write a Top 40, rock radio hit.' Because we've never been able to do that. That's not part of who we are. It's just that we've been lucky with some of the songs we've made, that they have achieved that attention."

K.K. adds a comment about song credits—outside of the Bob Halligan Jr. song, everything is credited three ways equally, to Tipton, Halford and Downing—yet, still, his reticence about who does what is a continuing frustration for the fans. "I think what happens is, there are some songs, obviously, that I present to Rob and Glenn, and vice versa. But there is democracy there. When Glenn puts his stuff on there, it might not be a great amount, but he puts some stuff on there. And Rob puts some stuff on there, and we just credit all of us. And the same thing can happen the other way, where Glenn might present something that is 70 or 80% finished, but myself and Rob obviously have our input, and that's the way we work. I know what you're saying, really—it would be interesting for people to know who actually kicked off at least the basic essential ingredients, the idea, but that's a close-guarded secret, and maybe forever more it will be. So for me to say, maybe it wouldn't be fair to the others."

Screaming for Vengeance closes on an uncreative note, with, second to last, the mellow and Americanised "Fever," essentially another proto-hair band ballad, spruced up by a bit of guitar-ish nonsense. Reflects Rob, "I love the floaty, ethereal opening sequence. It's got a wonderful tone to it. It's got all these big multi-vocal tracks and this very dreamy landscape musically to it. I know that at the time we wrote it, Glenn and Ken were always being offered these new types of pedal board switches that would change the sound of the guitar. Some of the gear that was sent over at the time made the guitars sound like I'd never heard them before. It's again, a lonesome, plaintive song. You get the image of this kind of... if you have an argument with somebody, sometimes you just like to slam out the house and take a walk at night and I think that's what that song is. It's a contemplation song. It's got this type of emotional relationship setup in it. It's like lost love. It's a plaintive call to fix something that's broken."

"Fever" is followed by "Devil's Child," which is basically another "You've Got Another Thing Comin'," only a little more sprightly, especially live, where, as with "Desert Plains," Priest kick its ass into a higher gear for fear of boring the fans. Of "Devil's Child," Rob figures, "It's a strong statement whereas 'Fever' is a bit plaintive, maybe a bit full of, not self-pity, but that kind of emotion. This is just the opposite. This is the real stuff, when you meet someone and your head blows off. It's a very secure, aggressive statement about meeting somebody that has a twisted side. It's got that wonderful rolling guitar riff on the chorus, that nice, flowing, almost picking groove to it. It's a great way to end the album."

Out touring *Screaming for Vengeance*, the band skipped the obvious droopers, namely "(Take These) Chains" and "Pain and Pleasure," although "Fever" stumbled its way to the stage, albeit for a grand total of two shows. "Electric Eye" and "You've Got Another Thing Comin'" became perennial live essentials and "Devil's Child" enjoyed quite a sustained life upon the stage. The thrashy and technical title track however... K.K. saw "Screaming for Vengeance" as a bit much for unforgiving hockey barn sound systems, with the song having worked its way out of the set-list by 1984.

It was quite a stage the band mounted, Priest's most elaborate set ever, the guys having to wait until the day before their first show to test it out. The tour kicked off in late August 1982, supported by the likes of Krokus, The Rods, Def Leppard, Axe, Coney Hatch, Heaven and a rejuvenated Uriah Heep. A low point might have been Dave Holland getting beat up by a cab driver in Dallas, although the high was undoubtedly playing a sold-out date at Madison Square Garden, October 2nd, 1982. On December 12th, in Memphis, the show was recorded for issue as the Judas Priest *Live* VHS video and laser disc, later reissued with different cover art with two less tracks, with the footage also being used for broadcast on MTV, the band's latest best friend by far. Later, the concert showed up as part of the *Metalogy* box set and then in 2006, as the *Live Vengeance '82* DVD.

Breaking for Christmas, it was decided that the album was doing so well in the States, that the band had better add a second leg, forsaking their planned European and UK jaunt, something that upset the faithful who had been all too familiar with that strategy from the likes of Led Zeppelin, Black Sabbath and Deep Purple... even Sweet, who became a famous career cases study with respect to botching a career.

"First of all," defended Rob at the time, "recording *Screaming for Vengeance* ran far longer than we thought, then took off like a rocket in the States. Also, in terms of production, we had to get this mammoth stage set together, and there was no way to use it in England. So we figured, let's do America, go back to England, then do the next album. But of course, the US tour went for nine months instead of six. And because we haven't been back in this length of time, it's important that we really show them what we're doing now. We'll try to put together a bill with three big acts and have a heavy metal Christmas tour."

Rob went so far as to take up permanent residence in Phoenix, Arizona, which in the '90s became a bit of a bedroom community for many metal stars. Previously, he had been in Walsall, England, not far from where he was raised, his dad's line of work being the steel industry, albeit comfortably well up the line from on the line. Additionally on the family front, Rob's mom had worked at a nursery school; the couple had three children, Rob, his sister Susan (married to Ian Hill), and a much younger brother Nigel.

"It's a pity you have to stay in America for so long before you get your total green pass," mused Rob. "In my head, I feel totally English and always will be, but America has certainly become my second home. I spend more time here than anywhere else in the world. So there's the proof really, of how much I enjoy the place. The general attitude of the fans, the audience, of people in the music business here, I feel, is more professional, or dedicated, more enthusiastic, far more committed. If they get excited over things, they push, they assist you. All those things that happen here simply do not happen anywhere else in the world. And that's all a musician ever wants, as far as I'm concerned."

Madison Square Garden was to be topped by the band's sunny 70-minute set at Apple executive Steve Wozniak's US Festival, on what was called heavy metal day. There were an estimated 300,000 people there that day, the most successful day of the event, with Ozzy, Van Halen, Triumph and Scorpions rocking the metal faithful. It was, as the band has noted, pretty much the perfect exclamation point to the *Screaming for Vengeance* tour, a campaign that found the band playing over 100 shows in the US, solidifying Priest as certainly the top ambassadors of British steel during one of the most competitive ramp-up periods heavy metal as a genre had ever witnessed.

Noted Rob, directly post-event, "We had two days rehearsal before the US show, in which we played about two hours, and then we went out and played to 300,000 people! But the band is so together now, we just blasted through the set. That show was the climax of '83 for the band, considering the tour went through half of '82 as well. What a great way to finish it off before we come back in 1984."

"I think it's the biggest concert we've ever played," reflected Ken, decades later, "the most amount of people. We run into people all over the world, in fact, who were actually at that concert. Whenever they mention it to us, that they were there, they get really excited about it. And I can imagine it would have been. It was just an incredible, incredible concert. And the lineup was really quite phenomenal, I must say. And obviously on the metal day, that we did, it was great. It would be great to see the US Festival II come around at some point, although I don't know if that would ever happen."

Specifically on the topic of the festival's heavy metal day, Glenn says that the festival brought metal "attention" and "a platform." "We'd just finished a tour. We'd done six weeks in Texas, and I forget how many dates we had done, but we were there for five or six months, and we were all homesick and very tired, but we had the chance to play with Zeppelin in California, Oakland Coliseum, and to stay at some very cheap hotels with some 50-50 chance of getting the door kicked in, one of those places. We were all homesick and we had very little money at the time, but we went and played a great show and it gave us a chance to present ourselves to the West Coast of America. I think that's what the US Festival did for these bands. It gave these bands an opportunity to show what they could do. It was a massive event and most of the bands pulled it off. It's great to have an event like that every now and again, to give up-and-coming bands a chance to show what they can do.

Years later, Rob marvels at what took place that scorching summer day. "To actually look at the full show that we played, more than anything it reinforces what we've always said about metal; it's timeless and will live forever. It is literally that flashback, a tremendous flashback to a fantastic time. The numbers have been adjusted to 375,000 people; it's inconceivable. I think it's still a record for the largest attendance for a rock festival. We were in the company of other great talent and hopefully those other bands will look at that footage that we all have and clear the legal hurdles to release it. I think it would be great if there was a full DVD with most of the talent on it. But you walk out on stage—or stroll out like I did—and you just can't get your head around it. It's just too many people! You think Wacken is big, Rock in Rio, but you walk out there and all you have to do is concentrate on doing the best gig that you can and I think Priest pulled it off. When you see the band playing in broad daylight in 120 degree heat, it's just magical to watch. It makes you feel good and makes you feel proud that you're in a band like Priest."

Chapter 10:
Defenders of the Faith –
"The last of the traditional Priest albums"

Over the years, *Defenders of the Faith* has grown to be beloved by Priest fans as more than just a re-examination of the formula used on the record before it. The songs inside are now seen as darker, somewhat heavier in total, more resolute, even more underground. Whatever one's views, Priest continued to thrive well into the '80s because of it, even if at the time it was not as immediately embraced by the mainstream. Indeed this was more about foundation—the old guard was unanimously well pleased, if only for the fact that in no way was *Defenders of the Faith* a relapse.

After the ponderous melodies all over *Point of Entry*, Judas Priest had bound back from twin turbo career highs—both the massive *Screaming for Vengeance* album and subsequent tour cycle had been critical and commercial successes. The album was essentially a flashier, more expansive and yet still somehow more commercially viable version of the *British Steel* experience, and Priest were awarded with platinum sales in the process. Come time for a follow-up, the band looked to maintain the formula, crafting *Defenders of the Faith*, essentially, as *Screaming's* evil twin.

"It was a step forward," reflects Ian Hill. "*Screaming for Vengeance* carried on from what we were doing on *British Steel*, apart from *Point of Entry*, which is arguably the most commercial album we've done. Other than that, it's been a natural progression from the early days, really, culminating with *Defenders*, which is why it's one of my favourite albums because it's the end of an era, before we started a new one."

It is actually Ian's favourite of the whole catalogue. "Yes. Obviously, putting the new one aside, because the new one is always your favourite because you just poured your heart and soul into it for the last couple of years, but of the back catalogue I would have to say *Defenders*, only because it was the last of the traditional Priest albums, know what I mean? Because after that came *Turbo*, which was quite different, not content-wise but sound-wise, with the synth guitars. And from then the band took on a much harder edge with *Ram It Down* and *Painkiller*. It was a harder, more aggressive direction than we'd been known for, culminating with *Jugulator*, which was the end of that sort of line. *Demolition* is the start of the new one with the inclusion of the more subtle passages and some more subtle songs, but *Defenders* is a definite favourite. And double platinum in America now as well" (ed. only *Screaming for Vengeance* is officially certified double platinum, reaching that status in 2001).

"*Defenders* was a really underrated album," adds Glenn Tipton. "Even from our point of view, I tended to think of *Defenders* as just another Priest album. But really, with tracks like 'Love Bites'… it had some great tracks on there. I think it's an album that I underestimated and it turned out to be one of our biggest selling albums."

Asked by Jeb Wright about the pressure of following up *Screaming*, Glenn figured, "We never take any album lightly. We discard a lot of material. The songs have to be good enough to go on an album and if they are not good enough, then we will discard them. *Screaming* was a successful album—we tried to better it with *Defenders of the Faith*. If you look at the songs on the album, 'Freewill Burning,' 'Jawbreaker,' 'Rock Hard Ride Free,' 'The Sentinel,' 'Love Bites,' 'Some Heads Are Gonna

Roll' and 'Heavy Duty'... it is a very, very strong album. In a small way, we were sort of experimenting with *Point of Entry*. If we hadn't done that we would have never come out with songs like 'Solar Angels,' 'Desert Plains' or 'Hot Rockin'.' You have to push the boundaries. When you come out with an album like *Screaming*, it is about doing something a little bit different that is just as good. We like to think that every album Priest has done has been different, but is also unmistakably recognised as Judas Priest. We like to think that we've entered a new territory again and pushed the boundaries further, which helps bands like ourselves to have more room to manoeuvre"

"The tremendous reaction to *Screaming for Vengeance* was propelled by the way radio embraced the song, 'You've Got Another Thing Comin'," added Halford, also speaking with Wright, "which became part of rock 'n' roll history. You get a record that goes platinum pretty quickly, in America at least, and naturally everybody's stoked and excited and you're ready to get to that next level, whatever that might be. There is always an element of uncertainty in rock 'n' roll. You play your heart out and you write and record the best you can, but there is no guarantee what the outcome will be. Having said that, we were completely immersed in this amazing time that we had, particularly in the States, which wound up at the now iconic and infamous US Festival. We shared the stage with our mates on 5/29/83. Ozzy was there, Crüe was there, Triumph was there, Van Halen was there, The Scorpions were there and Priest was there."

"In July we got on a plane to Ibiza, Spain," continues the Metal God. "It is a small bunch of islands off the East coast of Spain. We're all set to go and we get to the studio, and talk about hitting your brakes... there was absolutely nothing left in the studio. There was just the building. It had been gutted. They hadn't been paying the bills and so unbeknownst to us, they'd come in and taken the consoles out. They took the tape machines... everything

that was not secured was taken. We basically went back to square one in the idea of getting off the plane to start making metal. We had to wait two or three weeks before we could fire everything back up again. I look back now at that with kind of bewilderment and amusement, but at the same time, the thing about metal is that whenever these difficulties or adversities are put in your face, metalheads deal with it. We say, 'Bring it on' and we take care of business and that's what we did. Having said that, we just started like we'd done with past Priest albums and we turned the amps on and plugged in the guitars. Slowly but surely, we put together *Defenders of the Faith*."

"All of the songs were great," continues Ian, who is also known to praise the record's variety of speeds and styles. "Very few of them stuck out head and shoulders above the others because they were all so good. As a step forward from *Screaming for Vengeance*, it took that type of metal to about its peak. I don't think we ever topped that in that idiom. And I don't think anybody else has either, really. That was recorded in Ibiza, in the Mediterranean, and it was a holiday island so, as I mentioned earlier, there were multiple distractions—clubs, bars, beaches, boats, the whole thing. We did more messing around than we did recording. And it was just ourselves there; it's really just one studio."

"Similar album, really," recalls producer Tom Allom. "Same sort of approach. But I think we ended up with a bit of a surfeit of material, again. We recorded again in Ibiza and mixed in... well, there wasn't Bayshore Studios by then. The place had been torn down and redeveloped, and all the studio stuff was stored in a warehouse in South

Miami somewhere, and set up in the warehouse office as a control room. They were planning to build a new version of Bayshore Studios and it never got built. But the one in the warehouse was known as Bayshore 1.5 (laughs), in-between two Bayshores, because the new one never happened. So we mix that in this warehouse and it was a nightmare actually, a tiny little room, with near-field JBL speakers of some kind. But it was essentially the same approach to making *Screaming for Vengeance*. Plus we did do some guitar overdubs in a different studio in Miami. Sampling was difficult in those days; it was a lengthy business, but that might be when we started to dabble in that. There wouldn't be any electronics. No, it just would have been triggering, maybe the kick drum, just to reinforce it. But there were no electronics on those drums at all."

As Rob has alluded to, the Ibiza, Spain studio in which the band had recorded both *Point of Entry* and *Screaming for Vengeance* (Ibiza Sound Studios) had "gone out of business" since the band's last rape and pillage of the place, but the band rebuilt the studio from its shell, Dave Holland investing in the venture, staying back from the mixing sessions in the States so that he could work a deal with a pair of prospective business partners.

"When you think about it," explained Rob, to Toby Goldstein of Creem at the time, "here we were, we just had this incredible American success with the platinum album and the big US Festival show, and we went to an island that had a studio with nothing in it! Can you imagine that? Any other band, any other manager... Curbishley must've put a great deal of faith and trust in the fact that we knew what we were doing. There wasn't even recording tape on the island! Although none of us are superstitious in the band, I think we saw there was a bit of magic in that place. With Dave's involvement, I suppose that was the prime factor in making us decide to do it. During the day, I'd go with Dave and we'd paint the walls and put the bedroom furniture back in. It was really bizarre. The first time I went there, Dave warned me, 'You'll really be surprised,' and I said, 'No, I can handle anything; I'm shockproof.' So I went up there, and I nearly fell through the floor! I got there as it was dusk, and there wasn't even any electricity. So for the next few weeks, we put the place back together again. The board came back over from Barcelona, and there were about 20 of us struggling to get this humongous board back into the studio, rolling it on logs… you wouldn't have believed it if you'd seen it. Here we were, the metal gods, sweating our buns off trying to put this studio back together. And then the place was liveable again. That's when we really did sit down and start to write."

In actual fact, the previous version of the studio was an advanced 48-track rig, and it was in the mansion of a German named Fritz, who, according to Ian, had run off owing people a lot of money. The locals got their revenge by raiding the place and taking anything that wasn't bolted down, along with much of what was. The story gets a little incongruous, with Rob remembering that the defaulted payments were on the expensive recording equipment, with the company that supplied it showing up by boat to cart it all back to Spain. Rob then indicates that the initial down payment Priest would make on the equipment turned out to be enough for them to haul all the gear back to the island.

"We had to pay some of the bills off," continues Rob. "Like I say, we actually helped when the trucks showed up at the studio. This is a pretty remote location up a hill, up a dirty track. We actually all got out and helped the guys get the stuff off the trucks and we staggered into the studio with these thousand pound consoles. We were like, 'Wait a minute, weren't we just in front of 300,000 people at the US Festival and now we are truck delivery guys?' Again, like I say, you look back now at those incidents with amusement. It didn't stop us, it didn't jeopardise us. In fact, more determination went into *Defenders* because of that incident more than anything else."

Despite the business shenanigans and manual labour, *Defenders of the Faith* was ably recorded in July and August in Ibiza and then mixed in Miami from September through November of '83 (both Bayshore and DB Studios were used). Tom Allom once again produced, but Mark Dodson made a return engagement as engineer, replacing Louis Austin who had engineered the previous three albums. Dodson would be rewarded for his return by getting hit hard by a taxi at about 60 miles per hour after he and K.K. had just left a nightclub on the island. Miraculously, after bouncing

off the windshield and shattering it, he escaped with minor injuries. As Tom explained, the laborious mixing sessions actually took place in a warehouse, as the studio was between moves. It is here the band decided on the title of the album, *Defenders of the Faith* winning out over *Keep the Faith*, the faith being of course heavy metal, Priest being one of very few major acts that admitted to being a heavy metal band at the time, smartly claiming that lonely space while everybody else was saying they were more like Led Zeppelin, meaning, for everyone (they weren't).

Doug Johnson devised another stylised mascot graphic for the cover art. The colours weren't as distinctive as those on *Screaming for Vengeance*, but the half tank, half monster "Metallian" was more complex and interesting than *Screaming*'s rote-by-comparison eagle, known in its flight log as The Hellion. The band agreed that this was what a defender of the faith would look like, and indeed, the stage show would take its cue from Johnson's biomechanical creation. Warned the back cover, "Rising from darkness where all hell hath no mercy and the screams of vengeance echo on forever, only those who keep the faith shall escape the wrath of the metallian... master of all metal."

As for the title of the record, "We had a lot of ideas floating around," said Rob. "I am assuming that it came out of my head. I think I got it from a British coin. On the currency it will have a picture of the

Queen's head and you have etched into the coin 'Defenders of the Faith,' which means the monarchy are the defenders. I think that is where that came from."

Ads for the record fuelled the fire, claiming "Judas Priest scourge the unbelievers on their hardest album ever," adding "Convert your friends on tour, and on Columbia Records and Cassettes!" and finally in big type, "Get Thee Behind Judas Priest!"

Threats aside, the record opened with "Freewheel Burning" (working title: "Fast and Furious"). This was also the album's advance single, a speed metal highball in the spirit of the previous record's title track or "Ram It Down," the title track from two records forward. Curiously, the early-issued single version of the song, backed with two US Festival live tracks in the UK, featured a quiet fade-in followed by an elegiac and haunting *Sad Wings*-style twin lead wash, before the song shuffles clumsily into corporate metal focus—I say clumsily because frankly, the rhythm bed is abysmal, from production through to performance.

"'Freewheel Burning' and 'Rock Hard Ride Free'... it is all metal, metal, and metal," reflects Rob. "You can never get enough metal, man. That is what I like about *Defenders of the Faith*: it is a very strong sounding record with resilience and determination. We are a heavy fucking metal band and if you don't like it you can fuck off. It is that kind of attitude that I love about Priest. It was a really fun moment to do that fast section. My vague memory is that I wanted to have this kind of semi-automatic delivery. I remember saying to Glenn, this is what I want to do, and he said, then let's do it. That is what I love about Priest. You might have the most ridiculous sounding ideas but we never kill it. We've always said in Priest, try everything. It doesn't matter how absurd it might sound in discussion; you don't know until you try it. You can talk until you're blue in the face about an idea, but until you go through the motions and you hear it coming back through the speakers, you don't know if it is going to work or not."

"Another typical Priest track, fast, aggressive," notes Hill, addressing this mad dragster of a fast track. "We had gone through a phase, our Top of the Pops phase, where you're on the local commercial TV station. I don't know… we just wanted to get away from that and wanted to head into a heavier, contemporary direction, at least superficially. I mean, we've always been that way but people were trying to portray us as something we weren't at one time. That's one of the reasons we thought, well, okay, instead of making a video for the most obviously commercial one, or the ballad or whatever, we'll go ahead and do one with our other dimension (laughs)."

And so they did, churning out a lip-synched live clip set to lasers, interspersed with video arcade hijinks, the lasers getting out of control, Rob looking cool atop his Harley. Glenn's deliberate yet journeying solo is one of his most memorable and wild, and Rob sings his head off. But the track as a whole leaves something to be desired, mainly due to the stodgy drumming and production—for a balls-out rocker, there isn't much energy welling up from the engine room.

But Ian's point is an important one. It says something about the state of metal in 1984 that Priest would use this track as their debut single. Metal had already gone down a storm in the UK for the first few years of the '80s, and by this point there had been a couple years of a second metal revolution happening, this time the centre of attention being the state of California, particularly Los Angeles. Not that this pick for single release turned out to be a great idea; nonetheless, the idea of putting an exclamation point on *Screaming for Vengeance*, which is essentially

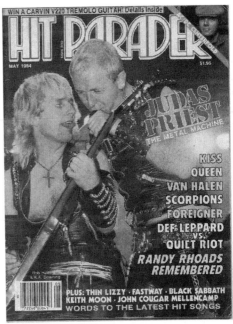

what *Defenders of the Faith* is… there was no way that was going to be a losing proposition given all the success metal bands were having in 1984.

"I guess the initial approach for this album was wanting to come up with ten killer tracks, and at the time not really having a positive theme," said Rob, on the tour trail for the album in 1984. "Just knowing that we wanted the usual series of rhythms, beats across the sections, and metal music from the fast, mad ones like 'Jawbreaker' and 'Freewheel

Burning' to the real slogging ones like 'Heavy Duty' and 'Defenders of the Faith.' Although it's probably taken us longer to write this album than anything else, the songs did seem to come together reasonably easy. It's always a struggle to come up with good follow-up tunes, but I think that we got more of an incentive going for us on the strength of the success in the States. The pressure was there, but it was good pressure."

Asked if the band could or would conjure a single as flagrantly light as Van Halen's "Jump," Rob answered emphatically in the negative. "I'm not saying we wouldn't release a single like 'Night Comes Down;' it's well within our limits. But Van Halen—and I'm sure they'd be the first to admit it—aren't a heavy metal band. They're a pop rock band, and there's nothing wrong with that. I think they're great. But we are heavy metal and there's no way we'd stray from those margins. Otherwise we'd have already done it. We've never really looked at the single chart and said, 'Ooh, we want a hit single.' But we'd be hypocritical to say that we wouldn't like it someday. I'd love to see this band get a Top Ten single in the States."

Notes Tipton on the tenor and tone of the record, "I just remember a video where Rob sat in some sort of racing car. This was us working again with Julien Temple. It's just a great song. We wrote a lot of songs that were designed to be listened to while riding along in a car and 'Freewheel Burning' epitomises that."

"Jawbreaker" was a much more inspired heavy rocker, its strong melody recalling the sturdiness of Priest's writing in the '70s, and even that of Scorpions from a similar time and clime. Lyrically, Rob has said it's about oral sex—pretty bloody obvious actually. The song's highlights include the little staccato guitar breaks, its ripping heavy metal chorus and K.K.'s howling then quite musical guitar solo.

"Rock Hard Ride Free" is an under-rated Priest classic, derided for its pedestrian frame, but unrightly so, given its sturdy construction and complex melodies and mood changes. The song was originally tabled as "Fight for Your Life," much of it the same, save for its completely different chorus, both musically and lyrically, and a somewhat differently meandered instrumental break. This outtake can be heard, incongruously, on the 2001 remaster of *Hell Bent for Leather*. K.K. had joked that the chorus lyric—particularly "Fight for your money"—was obviously a bit ludicrous, noting that anyone could see why they would overhaul the song toward what it became.

"That just means punching the air," remarks Glenn. "You're just doing what the song says: rocking hard and riding free." As it stood proud on *Defenders*, the song took on an overt biker presence, given the title, and given its road song vibe, a palpable case of white line fever riding on the wind after the song's longish 5:34 passes wistfully.

Says Ian of "The Sentinel," arguably the album's masterpiece, "That one's always been an epic, yeah. It's one of my favourite songs as well, and until very recently it's been included in the live set. And I think in fact, we've just only recently dropped it. It's a great, exciting track and it's a bit of a showpiece for Ken as well."

The riff work on "The Sentinel" is exquisite and exacting, Glenn and K.K. demonstrating why they are the kings of twin-axed heavy metal. The chorus is a corker as well, Rob grinding out memorable lines after a curious show tune vocal melody in the brief pre-chorus. The half-speed instrumental break is a treat as well, even if the soloing in this one is both a bit subdued and widdly-widdly. Again, one shakes one's head at the debilitating effect of Allom's awful production. The rhythm section of Dave and Ian sounds declawed, lacking  in power, woefully ungroovy. Nonetheless, Glenn calls this track "one of my all-time favourite songs. I love the breakdown in the middle where it comes down and kicks back in again."

Still, obviously the idea is sacrilege, but whilst driving around in my car playing the Dave Holland/Tom Allom era albums, my mind starts working, fantasizing what it would be like to have the drum tracks erased and Scott Travis massaged in and maybe even have Ian Hill re-do his parts. Leave everything else, but replace the rhythm section parts, which, as they are recorded anew, would take care of the majority of the production travesties. *Turbo* is fine as it is, *Point of Entry* is okay, but *British Steel* and *Screaming for Vengeance* would be nice to hear this way. Top priority would go to *Ram It Down* and *Defenders of the Faith* however, both of which would potentially spring to life given this crazy lab experiment.

Back to reality, side two of the original *Defenders of the Faith* vinyl opens with the perky and efficient "Love Bites." Priest arrange this one rife with pregnant pauses, coming up with a catchy but still thudding heavy metal anthem about vampiric seduction. Says Ian, "We had great fun recording 'Love Bites;' I used a de-tuned eight-string bass on the intro to that." Despite some rudimentary backward effects in the song, there is no  backmasking. In fact Rob joked that Priest considered throwing in a backmask, one that would have said "Drink a lot of milk." Adds Glenn, "That song has a really strong character. I mean, 'In the dead of night, love bites.' It is really heavy and it is a lot heavier live, actually, than it is on the album. It was just slightly different and that is why we liked it."

A faux-live video was also hatched for the song, highlighting the impressive Metallian stage set, and, irritatingly, Holland's cymbal-whacking prowess. "With our videos, we consistently tried to capture the power of the music and put it into a visual format," explains Rob. "Essentially, that comes down to the costumes and the stage set, plus everything else that goes with it. I think we come pretty close to harnessing that power. You can't get more metal than what you see on stage for clip like 'Love Bites.' God only knows how many hundreds of pounds it all weighs. Our stage sets make our videos look a lot stronger. From the early days, we've always put money back into the shows. And obviously, the bigger you get, the bigger the stage show has to be, plus the more money you have to spend. Older videos like 'Breaking the Law' and 'Don't Go' were a little bit like mini movies. Now we find that as we develop sets, like the one we used on the *Defenders of the*

Faith tour, we would much rather exploit the potential behind them rather than going to a location type of situation."

"Eat Me Alive" followed amusingly and logically after "Love Bites," this one being another malevolent and uptempo rocker supporting the premise that Priest wasn't about to go light. The S&M lyric—the song's working title was "Bad Girls Wear Leather"—got Rob in trouble with Tipper Gore and the PMRC. But Rob says, "I just wanted to write a really sexy heavy metal lyric. I was drunk when I wrote that. I was hysterical in a bar in Ibiza and I showed the lyrics to Ken and said, check these out. A lot of the verses we couldn't use, because they were really obscene! We cooled it down a bit." Rob goes on to say that his attitude is, "Get it out in the open and let everybody have a good look at it! Subtlety has never been a trademark of this band."

"I'm afraid so," adds Tipton. "It just happened to be at the time when all of that Parental Guidance was being slammed down everyone's throat. We've never written songs to encourage people to take drugs or be violent. Our fights are these galactical battles, or whatever. We knew we would come under fire for that one a little bit. Our songs can be misconstrued if you look at the titles, but in actual fact, we've never incited

people to do bad things. I think our lyrics have helped a lot of people. There are some bands that do exploit sensationalism and the lyrics do create the wrong impressions. We have to expect it."

The fact that Tipper Gore had stuck the track as No.3 on her notorious "Filthy Fifteen" list of objectionable songs at least worked to give Priest an idea for another song: "Parental Guidance" on the *Turbo* album would be penned as a rebuttal.

"Some Heads Are Gonna Roll" is a moody elephantine rocker somewhat in the spirit of "Rock Hard Ride Free." Unlike the poppier material on *Turbo* or even *Point of Entry*, such writing on *Defenders*, due partially to the mechanistic, turgid mix of the album, came off comparatively leaden and claustrophobic. That, however, made "Some Heads Are Gonna Roll" another strong *Defenders* track—somehow a machine-like vibe fits the song's hypnotic construction. The song came from outside writer Bob Halligan Jr., brought back after penning "(Take

These) Chains" on *Screaming for Vengeance*. Halligan has said the lyric was a warning about future holocausts. Melodically passionate, particularly in the pre-chorus and the break, this one became the album's second single, backed with "Breaking the Law" live in the States and "Green Manalishi" in the UK. It failed to chart in either territory; "Jawbreaker" was issued as a final single, only in America, and it failed to chart as well.

Remarks Glenn, "We played 'Some Heads Are Gonna Roll' a lot live and it is a really heavy song. We're not doing it at the moment. I think you'll find with Priest that some songs, like 'Turbo,' might not come across very heavy, but when you see us play it live—even though it's from another album that we're talking about—it is very, very heavy. I think that is the same with 'Some Heads Are Gonna Roll;' that they are far heavier live than you think they are going to be."

"Night Comes Down" shares the gauzy, bluesy bleakness of "Rock Hard Ride Free" and "Some Heads Are Gonna Roll," but is in fact structured as a sort of power ballad—fortunately, in 1984, these "ballads" had not become formulaic yet, and "Night Comes Down" cogently and effortlessly weaves heavy bits in with the soft reflection.

"The ballad," says Rob wistfully. "It is a passionate song, it has an attitude of sentiment to it but it is still legit, as far as having that kind of metal intensity. It is a nice little breather in the overall assault that surrounds it. It was a pretty intense vocal delivery and I'm not sure I can do it now. I am glad I got it there and then because it is there for eternity now." Recalls Glenn, "There was a concert we did once; it was a big outdoor festival, and the sun was just going down and it was the absolute perfect song to be playing at the time. We peaked into 'Night Comes Down' just as the sun was setting. It was brilliant."

"Heavy Duty," into "Defenders of the Faith," closes the record in plodding, catatonia-inducing "Take on the World"/"United" fashion, this one the closest of the lot to the "We Will Rock You" imprint from stated Priest influence Queen. "Heavy Duty" at least chugs along to a song-worthy enough riff, its 2:25 churn morphing into 1:30 of "Defenders of the Faith," which is essentially a second chorus to "Heavy Duty."

Notes Rob, "I can tell you that the song 'Heavy Duty' came from a washing machine that I owned at the house. As a lyricist, I soak everything up as far as ideas for different song titles, or content, or whatever it might be. As a lyricist, I think you have to have the open mind for any possibility for the idea of a song story. When it comes along you grab it, whether it is a piece of coin or a washing machine, and you use it." Adds Glenn, "That is a typical Priest anthem, where we get the crowd to sing along with it. It really is just a great anthem. We've always tried to include anthems on every album."

As for whether all of the material for this album was brand-spanking new, Rob says, "There were probably some bits and pieces as that is the way with most bands. It's like this giant jigsaw of odds and ends. It is like a big box of Legos and you take a little bit of this and a little bit of that and you build a metal song. I think that is pretty much the way all music is written. You have multiple choices. You have the fast riffs and the slow riffs and the little melodic ideas and the little statements here and there, and you piece together your work. With a metal album it is pretty much that you want to have a certain level of energy consistent with who you are and what you're about. You want to be able to fall back a little bit with some of the more kind of textured songs like, in this case, 'Night Comes Down.' You take your listener on a journey of 40 minutes and some change and you try to capture all of the elements. A little bit on *Defenders of the Faith* came from other places, but a lot of it was written fresh in the studio. If it is usable, then it is good and you take it from any source."

Circus magazine quite liked the record, writing, "Judas Priest was born to be wild. 'Fast and furious, we ride the universe,' howls Rob Halford at the top of this set on 'Freewheel Burning,' a conscious attempt to evoke the heavy metal thunder of the Deep Purple classic, 'Highway Star.' Like *Machine Head*, the watershed album that led off with Purple's road anthem, *Defenders of the Faith* represents a consolidation of energy and technique that enables Judas Priest to arrive at a breakthrough point in its sound. This British quintet has been slashing away for more than a decade, but *Defenders*  leaves the nine previous LPs in the dust. The duelling guitars of Glenn Tipton and K.K. Downing rev things up when Halford isn't flooring his vocals. 'Rock hard with a purpose,' Halford urges in 'Rock Hard Ride Free,' and there's seldom been better lyrical proof of the adage that half the fun is getting there. 'Love Bites' offers the kind of S&M horror story that underscores the leather, chains and dog-collar image the group has always promulgated, while 'The Sentinel' throws in a little post-apocalypse fiction for good measure. If Steppenwolf invented the concept of biker rock with 'Born to Be Wild,' Judas Priest has the last word with *Defenders of the Faith*."

"I guess the fact that we came up with such a good record on *Screaming*, and that was so successful for us, that the pressure was on, really," reflects K.K., 20 years later, on the *Defenders* era. "And I think, even though there is so much good material on there, if you listen— people do actually listen to it as a recorded record—if you listen to it closely, you'll hear us trying to get that extra bit out of it, extra heaviness, an extra bit out of an effect or something, and it probably seems a little bit jumpy in places. You can see us really trying to conjure up new things. But by and large, there's a lot of good material on there."

K.K. and Glenn have also said, in effect, overlapping in agreement, that the album was quite similar to *Screaming*, that it worked with the same basic ingredients but offered better value for the money by covering all the bases. Unfortunately they are right: *Defenders* felt a bit like the work of a band with a checklist, a band boxed in by checking off musical styles, but also boxed in by having to conform in style and tone to their strong-willed previous record. Judas Priest's music was now illustrated when once it was photographed.

Defenders of the Faith would end up going gold immediately but taking four years to reach platinum. Its chart placement in the UK (No.19) and America (No.18) would mark a slight downgrade versus *Screaming* (No.11 and No.17 respectively). But still, this was a band thriving in tandem with its chosen and professed genre at large, heavy metal dominating the charts through young and old bands alike.

As well, *Defenders* was the record for which the band signed on with Bill Curbishley and Trinifold Management. More accurately, this key fortuitous career move occurred back in May '83, smack in the middle of the *Screaming for Vengeance* cycle, Bill working out a new five-year deal for the band, doing the good business that had made him a legend through his association with The Who.

Said Rob, just after the previous year's triumphant US Festival performance, of the Curbishley connection, "It was a thrill when he approached us in the first place, because he'd never managed anyone else other than The Who. He's been watching Priest develop over the years and said, if there was any band that he wanted to get involved with after The Who was finished, it was Judas Priest, an honour in itself, because this guy is a very prestigious person. We're very excited. We've had a couple of deep, meaningful meetings over the past few days, and we've got the next couple of years already planned in terms of what we'll attempt to do."

"This is just the beginning. It might seem as though we've been together for 12 years, which we have, but I'll tell you, you ain't seen nothing yet! I'm sure that having a member of his calibre will enable us to do things and to take entry into certain aspects which we otherwise wouldn't have been able to do. They'll be a general expansion of the band's ability on a worldwide level. We've still got so much work to do in Europe, Japan, Australia, so many places to go to. We've done as much as we could with our previous management company, but Priest is getting bigger and bigger, and we need to be surrounded by the people who are prepared to cope with that situation. Bill's the perfect man. I feel that this is going to be—what's that they said when they stepped off the spacecraft? –one small step for Priest, one giant leap for heavy metal."

Despite the album's success, the numbers for *Defenders of the Faith* were indeed down from those generated from the firecracker response to its predecessor. No monster hit single like 'You've Got Another Thing Comin'' fell out of it, and perhaps hurting more, the album was derided at the time as *Screaming for Vengeance II* or *Screaming for Vengeance Lite*, the former quite true, the latter less so, given the relative lack of party rockers on the present proposal.

On tour, the band played every number from the album save for "Eat Me Alive," although "Rock Hard Ride Free," "Night Comes Down" and "Heavy Duty" wouldn't last past the present tour. In December of '83, the band embarked on a small warm-up tour of the UK, playing smaller venues, mostly theatres, with Quiet Riot as support. In the middle, December 18th, there was one German festival date, Rock Pop '83, where Priest shared the stage with Scorpions, Ozzy Osbourne, Def Leppard, Iron Maiden and Quiet Riot. The European tour proper kicked off in January, with Raven and Ted Nugent supporting.

For their assault on America, Priest ditched the backdrop they had been using in Europe and stretched out with the famous Metallian stage set; Rob would emerge from its mouth every night, and all told, it was quite impressive. Back-up came from Great White, and, into the summer, Kick Axe—this was Kick Axe's third tour for their excellent *Vices* debut, and the Priest slot was instrumental in pushing their album near gold in the US.

Recalls Kick Axe's Victor Langen, "They were top-notch all the way; fine gents. I think Glenn and K.K. liked to go golfing, which I found odd at the time. We didn't know anything about golfing. I guess you have to have a Scottish background (laughs). But yeah, I just remember being in awe of the whole thing, and even meeting them in Calgary, Canada, when we had our official contact with them. They came down and saw us play. It was the very day that *Vices* was released. We were doing a radio broadcast on a radio station in Calgary, CJ92 or something, and these guys came down after they played the Saddledome, and it was Rob Halford personally that came to the dressing room and just said they were giving the toss to Great White, and it was a done deal that we had to open for Priest on the rest of their North American tour. And we thought, holy God, these guys are on heroin. This is just way beyond reality. But he was true to his word. And that was that."

"In Atlanta, Georgia, they summoned us to their dressing room," continues Victor. "The big tour manager guy comes to grab us from our dressing room, at the end of their set, and he says, 'Come with me; Judas Priest wants to speak to you.' And we thought, 'Oh no, we're getting fired' (laughs). And it was to give us shit for hiding from them. Because we were just too scared… I don't know what the word is, not scared, but in awe of it all? We didn't want to press ourselves on them to say hello or anything. But they summoned us to their dressing room in Atlanta and that's where things got much better. They said, 'Look, we like you! Don't be shy. Don't be hiding away. Let's be buddies.' And we did 35 dates with them. I'd like to catch up with them one of these days…"

"We've always put a lot of thought into our production," says Glenn, defending the arguably excessive show Priest had mounted for what was called the Metal Conqueror Tour. "We learned very early on that although the most important thing about Priest is the music, you can still drive the point home harder with a great production. There is more value for the money, and if you are coming to see us in these big arenas, then it is not just these five small dots on the stage. You've got a big, dramatic production. We have always based a lot of importance on that and we've always put a lot of time into that. We sit down with our lighting guy, our set design guy and our sound guy to come up with a great show for the kids. They pay good money for tickets and they deserve a good show. We are all heavily involved."

On June 18th 1984, a gig at Madison Square Garden got out of control, with fans ripping up their foam seats and tossing them toward the stage. One report had Rob sitting on the forks of his motorbike, uttering with a mischievous laugh, "New York, you sick motherfuckers" while a snowstorm of foam covered the stage. K.K. later said that the band's insurers were on the line for more than a half million dollars in compensation to repair the damage. Weeks after the fact, K.K. and Glenn were back at the Garden incognito to watch some tennis, after which an MSG employee came up to them and said, "I just wanted to thank you guys. We really needed some new seats."

The final leg saw the band in Japan for five dates, September 6th through 13th; this would be Priest's first time back since the recording of the landmark *Unleashed in the East* live album from five years earlier.

For the 30th anniversary reissue of the album, a Long Beach Arena live set from the tour was included. "It was a Saturday night, I believe and it was kind of a summer show," remembers Halford. "It was a sold-out event. It was just absolute magic. That night everything was working as you hoped. The crowd was great. It is a classic Priest memory and I am really pleased we were able to have recorded it. When I listen to it now you can sense it. We were playing the music a million miles an hour. I don't know how we were able to play the songs that fast. I know how it happened, as we were just caught up in the energy of the moment and we were pushing it as fast as we could, so the tempo increased dramatically on some of the songs. It didn't create any detrimental effect; in fact, I think it just gave the event more ferocity. It is wonderful that we can marry those two things up with this release. We can marry up the live experience of what the metalheads were going through that night and on that tour, as well as having the studio recordings to kind of make a comparison. *Defenders* is an important record. It brings back memories that I cherish associated around the actual making of the album. The stumbling of going to a studio that was empty and getting through those difficult times and the general outcome of the artwork and the Metallian monster—it's all good stuff."

Good stuff indeed, for the *Defenders* tour, arguably, would represent the culminating concert campaign for the band at the peak of its powers. After the last show in Tokyo, September 13th, 1984, Priest would take a full year's hiatus from the road (save for a 1985 Live Aid performance in Philadelphia) before embarking on the next phase of their bumpy heavy metal ride. It's a career path that soon after takes them sideways, down a few hills, eventually advancing to the quite comfortable crest at which they reside today, lording over a multitude of heavy metal disciples who themselves were raised on the Judas Priest preachings etched into the records created during the band's decade of domination.

Epilogue

As we end our "decade of domination" tale by examining the record Ian Hill calls "the last traditional Priest album," a brief explanation is in order in terms of where the story goes next.

Very much like their younger doppelganger Iron Maiden, Judas Priest would go through all manner of ups and down and interpersonal dramas, but arrive out the other end still playing hockey arenas and making some of the best music of their lives. There have been two records with a different singer, Tim "Ripper" Owens, followed by a celebrated reunion with Rob Halford. There's been a hair metal album, there's been a double concept album, there's been a Rock and Roll Hall of Fame nomination, although we didn't quite get them there. K.K. quit, Rob had a bad back, but he also brought the beard back, although the effect isn't all the way up to the standard of my favourite Rob shot of all time, the legendary "drunken pirate" picture on the back of *Killing Machine*.

Fully nine studio albums have emerged from the mighty Priest in the three decades-plus since *Defenders of the Faith* was issued, with the latest, the action-packed *Firepower*, getting some of the band's best reviews since *Painkiller* recharged a flagging band back in 1990, aided and abetted by Scott Travis and producer Chris Tsangarides, sadly passed January 7th, 2018.

This book is dedicated to Chris, and it is also dedicated to Glenn Tipton, who recently had to relinquish his touring duties with the band as he battles Parkinson's disease, a debilitating illness that figured in my own brother's death, Bradley Dean Popoff, at the age of 49. Myself and my Priest-loving buddies wish Glenn well as he manages this new stage of life. Suffice to say, millions of Judas Priest fans the world over hope and pray that Glenn can contribute to write for the proud institution he commandeered to worldwide success, and that even if he retires fully from the band, he can rest assured that his legacy is forever peerless.

Discography

A few comments for you, I like doing a discography because it doesn't take up a lot of space and it gives the reader a handy dandy spot to check track list, song lengths, release dates etc.... it's like a quick reference or even plot guide, in a few pages. There's a notes section to point out anything else I figured was important enough to make known, such as changes in band personnel and talk of significant variations. The rule of double quotes around songs was set aside for neatness' sake, except in the notes section. For label and catalogue number, I've gone with first British edition, Priest being a British band. For track timings, given that UK issues don't normally provide that, I've gone with first US or Canadian issue, which generally obliges. As all of these records came out during the vinyl era, I've gone with Side 1/Side 2 designations.

Rocka Rolla
(Gull GULP.1005, September 6, 1974)
Produced by Rodger Bain
Side 1:
1. One for the Road (4:40) 2. Rocka Rolla (3:00) 3. Winter (3:00) 4. Deep Freeze (2:00) 5. Winter Retreat (1:30) 6. Cheater (2:55)
Side 2:
1. Never Satisfied (4:50) 2. Run of the Mill (8:30) 3. Dying to Meet You (6:15) 4. Caviar and Meths (2:00)
Notes: inaugural recording lineup is Rob Halford, Glenn Tipton, K.K. Downing, Ian Hill and John Hinch.

Sad Wings of Destiny
(Gull, GULP.1015, March 23, 1976)
Produced by Jeffrey Calvert, Max West, Judas Priest
Side 1:
1. Victim of Changes (7:45) 2. The Ripper (2:50) 3. Dreamer Deceiver (5:56) 4. Deceiver (2:46)
Side 2:
1. Prelude (2:02) 2. Tyrant (4:26) 3. Genocide (5:47) 4. Epitaph (3:16) 5. Island of Domination (4:25)
Notes: Drummer John Hinch is replaced by Alan Moore.

Sin After Sin
(CBS S CBS 82008, April 8, 1977)
Produced by Roger Glover, Judas Priest
Side 1:
1. Sinner (6:42) 2. Diamonds and Rust (3:24) 3. Starbreaker (4:50) 4. Last Rose of Summer (5:39)
Side 2:
1. Let Us Prey/Call for the Priest (6:15) 2. Raw Deal (5:58) 3. Here Come the Tears (4:23) 4. Dissident Aggressor (3:19)
Notes: Drummer Alan Moore is replaced by Simon Phillips, although Phillips is relegated to "special thanks" status. First two tracks on side two originally erroneously listed as "Let Us Prey" (6:15) and "Call for the Priest/Raw Deal" (5:58) causing much confusion over the years—see *Sin After Sin* chapter for full explanation. This was fixed on later reissues.

Stained Class
(CBS S CBS 82430, February 10, 1978)
Produced by Dennis MacKay and Judas Priest
Side 1:
1. Exciter (5:30) 2. White Heat, Red Hot (4:30) 3. Better by You, Better than Me (3:22) 4. Stained Class (5:20) 5. Invader (4:00)
Side 2:
1. Saints in Hell (5:30) 2. Savage (3:26) 3. Beyond the Realms of Death (6:55) 4. Heroes End (5:05)
Notes: Drummer Simon Phillips is replaced by Les Binks.

Killing Machine
(CBS 83135, October 9, 1978)
Produced by James Guthrie, co-produced by Judas Priest
Side 1:
1. Delivering the Goods (4:15) 2. Rock Forever (3:18) 3. Evening Star (3:55) 4. Hell Bent for Leather (2:38)
Side 2:
1. Burning' Up (3:55) 2. Killing Machine (3:00) 3. Running Wild (2:51) 4. Before the Dawn (3:20) 5. Evil Fantasies (4:09)
Notes: Album was re-titled *Hell Bent for Leather* for North American release, adding Fleetwood Mac cover "Green Manalishi (with the Two-Pronged Crown)" (3:21). Release date was February 28, 1979.

Unleashed in the East
(CBS 83852, September 17, 1979)
Produced by Tom Allom, Judas Priest

Side 1:
1. Exciter (5:37) 2. Running Wild (2:55) 3. Sinner (7:22) 4. The Ripper (2:38)
5. The Green Manalishi (with the Two-Pronged Crown) (3:14)
Side 2:
1. Diamonds and Rust (3:39) 2. Victim of Changes (7:14) 3. Genocide (7:18)
4. Tyrant (4:39)
Notes: Live album, subtitled *Live in Japan* and recorded in two venues
in Japan, February 10th and 15th, 1979, although admittedly some
studio doctoring was done.

British Steel
(CBS S CBS 84160, April 14, 1980)
Produced by Tom Allom
Side 1.
1. Rapid Fire (4:07) 2. Metal Gods (3:58) 3. Breaking the Law (2:34) 4.
Grinder (3:56) 5. United (3:31)
Side 2:
1. You Don't Have to Be Old to Be Wise (5:03) 2. Living After Midnight
(3:30) 3. The Rage (4:43) 4. Steeler (4:28)
Notes: Drummer Les Binks is replaced by Dave Holland. North American
issue brings "Breaking the Law" forward to the first track. The rest of the
running order remains.

Point of Entry
(CBS S CBS 84834, February 26, 1981)
Produced by Tom Allom, Judas Priest
Side 1:
1. Heading Out to the Highway (3:45) 2. Don't Go (3:17) 3. Hot Rockin'
(3:13) 4. Turning Circles (3:40) 5. Desert Plains (4:36)
Side 2:
1. Solar Angels (4:02) 2. You Say Yes (3:30) 3. All the Way (3:40) 4.
Troubleshooter (3:17) 5. On the Run (3:42)
Notes: Cover art changed for North American issue.

Screaming for Vengeance
(CBS 85941, July 17, 1982)
Produced by Tom Allom
Side 1:
1. The Hellion (0:41) 2. Electric Eye (3:38) 3. Riding on the Wind (3:06) 4.
Bloodstone (3:49) 5. (Take These) Chains (3:03) 6. Pain and Pleasure (4:14)
Side 2:
1. Screaming for Vengeance (4:43) 2. You've Got Another Thing Comin'
(5:05) 3. Fever (5:18) 4. Devil's Child (4:40)

Defenders of the Faith
(CBS 25713 January 4, 1984)
Produced by Tom Allom
Side 1.
1. Freewheel Burning (4:22) 2. Jawbreaker (3:25) 3. Rock Hard Ride Free
(5:34) 4. The Sentinel (5:24)
Side 2:
1. Love Bites (4:47) 2. Eat Me Alive (3:34) 3. Some Heads Are Gonna Roll
(4:05) 4. Night Comes Down (3:58) 5. Heavy Duty (2:25) 6. Defenders of
the Faith (1:30)

Interviews with the Author

Allom, Tom. 2009.

Atkins, Al, June 1998.

Atkins, Al, February 17, 2006.

Atkins, Al, 2009.

Binks, Les. April 26, 2018.

Bushell, Garry. 2009.

Catley, Bob. April 13, 2007.

Downing, K.K., June 15, 2004.

Downing, K.K., February 11, 1998.

Downing, K.K., July 9, 2009.

Glover, Roger, 1999.

Halford, Rob, 1998.

Halford, Rob, July 30, 2000.

Halford, Rob, February 27, 2001.

Halford, Rob, November 17, 2000.

Halford, Rob, April 13, 2003.

Halford, Rob, Nov. 11, 2005.

Halford, Rob. May 7, 2013.

Harris, Steve. October 13, 1996.

Hill, Ian, February 11, 1998.

Hill, Ian, August 26, 2001.

Hill, Ian, February 1, 2002.

Hill, Ian, December 2, 2003.

Hill, Ian. 2010.

Kay, Neal. 2009.

Langen, Victor. February 23, 2007.

Phillips, Simon, February 17, 1999.

Snider, Dee. August 1, 2006.

Tipton, Glenn, February 1, 2002.

Tipton, Glenn, February 14, 2006.

Tipton, Glenn. June 5, 2009.

Tsangarides, Chris, February 16, 2006.

Tsangarides, Chris, 2009.

Additional Citations

Note: Long story, this list of credits was culled from the credits found in the back of my 2007 book, *Judas Priest: Heavy Metal Painkillers*. I've erred on the side of caution, but what I've done is removed some of those credits from the original list if I thought I had been quoting for use in the timeframe examined outside of the current volume, i.e. after 1984. If I've deleted a credit for an interview from the '90s or 2000s that in fact was cited in the *Defenders* and earlier chapters examined here, I'd be glad to include these citations in future editions.

Advocate, The.
Classic Rock Revisited. Interviews with Rob Halford, Glenn Tipton and Ian Hill by Jeb Wright and Patty Wright.
The Best Of Judas Priest. Insight Series Interview with Original Judas Priest Drummer John Hinch. Transluxe Records, P.O. Box 239, Las Vegas, New Mexico 87701.
Brave Words & Bloody Knuckles and BraveWords.com. Interviews with Judas Priest by Tim Henderson. 1994 to 2015.
Brave Words & Bloody Knuckles. Judas Priest: Second Coming by Carl Begai. No.20, November/December 1997. 354 ½ Yonge St., Suite 38, Toronto, Ontario, Canada M5B 1S5.
Circus. *Sin After Sin* album review by Michael Bloom. 1977. Circus Enterprises Corporation, 115 East 57th St., New York, NY 10022.
Circus. Face to Face with Judas Priest by Philip Bashe. 1982. Circus Enterprises Corporation, 419 Park Avenue South, New York, NY. Circus. *Defenders of the Faith* record review. No.129. April 30, 1984. Circus Enterprises Corporation, 419 Park Avenue South, New York, NY. Circus. Photo Journal: Priestmania The Rage in Japan by Steve Gett. November 30, 1984. Circus Enterprises Corporation, 419 Park Avenue South, New York, NY.
Creem. Judas Priest Eaten Alive! The Gunpoint Confessionals by Toby Goldstein. Vol. 16, No. 2, July 1984. 210 S. Woodward, Birmingham MI 48011.
Dunn, Sam. Interviews with K.K. Downing, Rob Halford and Glenn Tipton. 2009.
Fachblatt Music Magazine. Interview with Rob Halford. September 1976.
Hardradio.com. Interview with K.K. Downing by Bob Nalbandian.
Hit Parader. Judas Priest: The Metal Conquerors by Toby Goldstein. 231, December 1983. Charlton Publications, Charlton Bldg., Derby, CT 06418.
Hit Parader. On the Set with... Judas Priest by Jodi Summers Dorland. 250, July 1985. Charlton Publications, Charlton Bldg., Derby, CT 06418.

Judas Priest Info Pages. Thexquorum.com/mad/MENU.html

Melody Maker. Judas – the high priests of raw rock by Harry Doherty. August 21, 1976.

Melody Maker. Priest ordained by Harry Doherty. June 11, 1977.

New Musical Express, The. Judas Priest/Marquee by Steve Clarke. September 28, 1974.

New Musical Express, The. Judas Priest failed to live up to the presentation by Chas De Whalley. May 29, 1976.

Rock Hard. Interview with K.K. Downing. 2003.

Rolling Stone. *Sad Wings of Destiny* album review by Kris Nicholson. September 23, 1976. 625 Third Street, San Francisco CA, 94107.

Sounds. Unleashed in the Mid-West by Geoff Barton. October 6, 1979.

Sounds. Judas Priest/Iron Maiden, Hammersmith Odeon review by Chris Collingwood. March 22, 1980.

Sounds. Judas Priest Hammersmith Odeon review by Geoff Barton. November 28, 1981.

Photo Credits

Cover photo of Rob Halford, © Martin Popoff; back cover photo of Glenn Tipton, © Rich Galbraith. Additional black and white photography © Martin Popoff and Rich Galbraith. Photography in the two colour sections, © Rich Galbraith, is credited in situ.

Design Credit

The graphic design and layout of this book is by Eduardo Rodriguez, who can be reached at eduardobwbk@gmail.com. Pleasure working with the guy—he's done about 15 for me now.

Special Thanks

John Chronis, a buddy of mine who has helped out with some of my previous books, most pertinently with scan-able memorabilia from his legendary collection. This was his third time copy-editing for me.

About the Author

At approximately 7900 (with over 7000 appearing in his books), Martin has unofficially written more record reviews than anybody in the history of music writing across all genres. Additionally, Martin has penned approximately 75 books on hard rock, heavy metal, classic rock and record collecting. He was Editor In Chief of the now retired Brave Words & Bloody Knuckles, Canada's foremost metal publication for 14 years, and has also contributed to Revolver, Guitar World, Goldmine, Record Collector, bravewords.com, lollipop.com and hardradio.com, with many record label band bios and liner notes to his credit as well. Additionally, Martin has been a regular contractor to Banger Films, having worked for two years as researcher on the award-wining documentary *Rush: Beyond the Lighted Stage*, on the writing and research team for the 11-episode *Metal Evolution* and on the ten-episode *Rock Icons*, both for VH1 Classic. Additionally, Martin is the writer of the original metal genre chart used in *Metal: A Headbanger's Journey* and throughout the *Metal Evolution* episodes. Martin currently resides in Toronto and can be reached through martinp@inforamp.net or www.martinpopoff.com.

Martin Popoff – A Complete Bibliography

Judas Priest: Decade of Domination (2018)

Pink Floyd: Album by Album (2018)

Popoff Archive – 6: American Power Metal (2018)

Popoff Archive – 5: European Power Metal (2018)

The Clash: All the Albums, All the Songs (2018)

Led Zeppelin: All the Albums, All the Songs (2017)

AC/DC: Album by Album (2017)

Tornado of Souls: Thrash's Titanic Clash (2017)

Caught in a Mosh: The Golden Era of Thrash (2017)

Rush: Album by Album (2017)

Beer Drinkers and Hell Raisers: The Rise of Motörhead (2017)

Metal Collector: Gathered Tales from Headbangers (2017)

Hit the Lights: The Birth of Thrash (2017)

Popoff Archive – 4: Classic Rock (2017)

Popoff Archive – 3: Hair Metal (2017)

Popoff Archive – 2: Progressive Rock (2016)

Popoff Archive – 1: Doom Metal (2016)

Rock the Nation: Montrose, Gamma and Ronnie Redefined (2016)

Punk Tees: The Punk Revolution in 125 T-Shirts (2016)

Metal Heart: Aiming High with Accept (2016)

Ramones at 40 (2016)

Time and a Word: The Yes Story (2016)

Kickstart My Heart: A Mötley Crüe Day-by-Day (2015)

This Means War: The Sunset Years of the NWOBHM (2015)

Wheels of Steel: The Explosive Early Years of the NWOBHM (2015)

Swords And Tequila: Riot's Classic First Decade (2015)

Who Invented Heavy Metal? (2015)

Sail Away: Whitesnake's Fantastic Voyage (2015)

Live Magnetic Air: The Unlikely Saga of the Superlative Max Webster (2014)

Steal Away the Night: An Ozzy Osbourne Day-by-Day (2014)

The Big Book of Hair Metal (2014)

Sweating Bullets: The Deth and Rebirth of Megadeth (2014)

Smokin' Valves: A Headbanger's Guide to 900 NWOBHM Records (2014)

The Art of Metal (co-edit with Malcolm Dome; 2013)

2 Minutes to Midnight: An Iron Maiden Day-by-Day (2013)

Metallica: The Complete Illustrated History (2013); update and reissue (2016)

Rush: The Illustrated History (2013); update and reissue (2016)

Ye Olde Metal: 1979 (2013)

Scorpions: Top of the Bill (2013); updated and reissued as Wind of Change: The Scorpions Story (2016)

Epic Ted Nugent (2012)

Fade To Black: Hard Rock Cover Art of the Vinyl Age (2012)

It's Getting Dangerous: Thin Lizzy 81-12 (2012)

We Will Be Strong: Thin Lizzy 76-81 (2012)

Fighting My Way Back: Thin Lizzy 69-76 (2011)

The Deep Purple Royal Family: Chain of Events '80 – '11 (2011)

The Deep Purple Royal Family: Chain of Events Through '79 (2011); reissued as The Deep Purple Family Year by Year (to 1979) (2016)

Black Sabbath FAQ (2011)

The Collector's Guide to Heavy Metal: Volume 4: The '00s (2011; co-authored with David Perri)

Goldmine Standard Catalog of American Records 1948 – 1991, 7th Edition (2010)

Goldmine Record Album Price Guide, 6th Edition (2009)

Goldmine 45 RPM Price Guide, 7th Edition (2009)

A Castle Full of Rascals: Deep Purple '83 – '09 (2009)

Worlds Away: Voivod and the Art of Michel Langevin (2009)

Ye Olde Metal: 1978 (2009)

Gettin' Tighter: Deep Purple '68 – '76 (2008)

All Access: The Art of the Backstage Pass (2008)

Ye Olde Metal: 1977 (2008)

Ye Olde Metal: 1976 (2008)

Judas Priest: Heavy Metal Painkillers (2007)

Ye Olde Metal: 1973 to 1975 (2007)

The Collector's Guide to Heavy Metal: Volume 3: The Nineties (2007)

Ye Olde Metal: 1968 to 1972 (2007)

Run For Cover: The Art of Derek Riggs (2006)

Black Sabbath: Doom Let Loose (2006)

Dio: Light Beyond the Black (2006)

The Collector's Guide to Heavy Metal: Volume 2: The Eighties (2005)

Rainbow: English Castle Magic (2005)

UFO: Shoot Out the Lights (2005)

The New Wave of British Heavy Metal Singles (2005)

Blue Öyster Cult: Secrets Revealed! (2004); update and reissue (2009); updated and reissued as Agents of Fortune: The Blue Oyster Cult Story (2016)

Contents Under Pressure: 30 Years of Rush at Home & Away (2004)

The Top 500 Heavy Metal Albums of All Time (2004)

The Collector's Guide to Heavy Metal: Volume 1: The Seventies (2003)

The Top 500 Heavy Metal Songs of All Time (2003)

Southern Rock Review (2001)

Heavy Metal: 20th Century Rock and Roll (2000)

The Goldmine Price Guide to Heavy Metal Records (2000)

The Collector's Guide to Heavy Metal (1997)

Riff Kills Man! 25 Years of Recorded Hard Rock & Heavy Metal (1993)

See martinpopoff.com for complete details and ordering information.